EDUCATION

in Western Europe

Facts & Figures

EDUCATION
in Western Europe
Facts & Figures

Donald Mackinnon
Dominic Newbould
David Zeldin
with Margaret Hales

Hodder & Stoughton
in association with

The Open University

British Library Cataloguing in Publication Data
A catalogue record for this title is available from the British Library

ISBN 0 340 62100 1

First published 1997

Impression number	10	9	8	7	6	5	4	3	2	1
Year	2002	2001	2000	1999	1998	1997				

Typeset by Wearset, Boldon, Tyne and Wear.
Printed in Great Britain for Hodder & Stoughton Educational, a division of Hodder Headline Plc, 338 Euston Road, London NW1 3BH by Redwood Books, Trowbridge.

CONTENTS

INTRODUCTION

Education in Western Europe: Facts and Figures has been written in the first instance as a set book for the Open University (OU) course EU208, *Exploring Educational Issues*, and as a companion to an earlier book, *Education in the United Kingdom: Facts and Figures*. However, the present book has been designed to stand independently of the course and of its UK companion. We hope it will also be found useful by people studying other education courses, in the OU or elsewhere, and indeed by anyone interested in education, whether as parent, teacher, student or citizen, in the UK or any other country.

The book is in two sections. The first and by far the longer section is a country-by-country description. The second section looks at Western Europe as a whole, with a range of cross-national comparisons.

Secton One covers 15 major countries of Western Europe. In order of the size of their populations, these are: Germany, France, Italy, Spain, Netherlands, Greece, Belgium, Portugal, Sweden, Austria, Switzerland, Denmark, Finland, Norway and Ireland.

Our reasons for including these countries and omitting others are largely practical, and governed above all by the need to keep the book within reasonable dimensions. We have confined it to Western Europe – in the political, not the purely geographical sense – because the education systems, indeed the social structures, of so many of the former communist countries of Eastern Europe are in flux, and reliable, up-to-date information is difficult to find. (The only exception is the former German Democratic Republic, which is included as part of a reunited Germany.) Within Western Europe, we have confined the book to 'major' countries, which we have defined as those that number their populations in millions, not thousands. This is an arbitrary division, but it does leave a satisfactory gap between the smallest country included (Ireland, with a population of 3.6 million) and the largest left out (Cyprus, with 665,000). Turkey is omitted because only 3% of its land area is in Europe, the remaining 97% being in Asia. And the UK is omitted from Section One simply because, as we mentioned above, it already has a 'facts and figures' book devoted to it. However, we do include the UK in the cross-national comparisons of Section Two.

Our major Western European countries, then, overlap considerably with the membership of the European Union (EU), but they do not coincide. We include Norway and Switzerland, which have not (as yet) joined the EU, and exclude Luxembourg, whose population is only 367,000, as well as the UK. For this reason (as well as for reasons of space), we have not included any description of EU institutions or programmes connected with education.

SOURCES

This is not a work of original research. Our purpose is to select the most significant information already in the public domain, bring it together, and express it as clearly and usefully as we can in words and diagrams. Almost all this information comes from published sources, mainly official publications of the various countries covered, but also those of such international bodies as the EU and the Organisation for Economic Co-operation and Development (OECD), as well as published academic research and other reference books more specialised than this one. Occasionally we have supplemented these sources with queries to officials or academic experts in particular countries. Our sources for individual countries are acknowledged at the end of each chapter, and the most frequently used general sources are acknowledged at the end of this Introduction.

However, we do not give exact references to the source of every fact or figure in the book; if we did, then a large proportion of the text would consist of these references. Instead, we follow a few rules of thumb. For our diagrams, and for very precise figures in the text, we usually do give an exact reference, to a specific figure, table or page in a specific publication. For more general facts, or for more approximate figures, we usually refer more generally to the publications listed at the end of chapters, and assume that any interested readers will be able to find their own way around them. And for 'general knowledge' about a country, of the sort that can be obtained from a wide range of standard historical, geographical or reference works, we usually do not give any source.

FACTS

All the chapters below are intended to be *factual*, to tell the reader what the educational world is like, not to give the interpretation or judgements – and certainly not the prejudices – of the authors. Though this is a worthwhile aim, in our view, it is one impossible to fulfil, for a number of reasons.

First, and most obviously, the book is bound to contain errors. Some of these may come from our sources; others, alas, will be all our own work. We hope that our mistakes will be few and trivial, and we deeply regret every one of them; but it is inevitable that, despite our best efforts, a book of this character will have some.

Secondly, a description in just a few pages of the education system of an entire country clearly must be highly selective and simplified, and we make no apology for that. Inevitably, though, the selection and simplification do reflect our judgement of what is most important. Similarly, numbers in the book are often approximate. (Sometimes the 'rounding' of figures means that percentages add up to slightly more or less than 100.) We hope, however, that we have never omitted any information that is really essential for understanding the education systems we describe, or oversimplified any complex structures or processes to the point of misleading our readers.

Thirdly, choosing the categories in which data are presented has also required judgement on our part, and this is not always straightforward, especially if we try to describe different education systems in the same terms. In the entries on individual countries, we have followed a similar pattern, first giving information about the demographic and economic background and the structures of government, especially as these apply to education. In describing the education systems themselves, we have usually divided the entries into separate sections for the following stages – based loosely on the international standard classification for education (ISCED) devised by UNESCO – though we have not adhered slavishly to them where they might misrepresent the way a country's education system is structured.

- preprimary
- primary
- lower secondary
- upper secondary
- tertiary (non-degree, first degree and postgraduate)

Finally, we are only too well aware that we are producing this book at a time of rapid and profound educational change in many countries, and of political change in Europe as a whole. The companion book on the UK mentioned above is now in its fourth edition since its original publication in 1989, as we have attempted to keep it up to date. Inevitably the present book will also become outdated, and the authors and publishers hope to produce new, up-to-date editions as the need arises. We would therefore welcome any comments, criticisms, suggestions for inclusion, information about changes and above all corrections of misunderstandings, oversimplifications or plain mistakes.

TERMINOLOGY AND TRANSLATION

The names of educational institutions, organisations and processes in the various European languages sometimes have no obvious English translation. In translating them here, we have normally used the translations provided by the country in question in its official English-language publications or by EURYDICE (the Education Information Network of the European Union) or OECD. Sometimes we have offered a translation of our own, where we thought an 'official' translation might be misleading to readers in the UK, or where a more literal translation than that offered by the above seemed to make perfect sense. In a few cases, we have not even attempted a translation of any kind – for example for the many versions in many languages of *lyceum* and *gymnasium* – but let the original name stand.

Like the UK, many other European countries regularly use abbreviations and acronyms in place of educational words and phrases in full. We have sometimes done so here, usually where the full word or phrase is very long. A key to any acronyms used is given at the end of a country's entry.

ECONOMIC DATA

The economies of the various countries can be roughly measured and compared with certain standard indicators, which we use both in the individual country entries in Section One and in the cross-national Section Two. The *Gross Domestic Product* (GDP) of each country gives an indication of the size of its economy, and a measure of how rich or poor a country is is given by the *GDP per capita*.

For most countries, we give data about the percentages of the population of working age who are *in employment*. The remainder of the working age population can be described as 'not employed'. The percentage of people who are not employed is different from – and generally much larger than – any of the various measures of the *unemployed*. 'Unemployed' people in official statistics are those who are officially registered as unemployed. But many people who are not employed may not be so registered, for a variety of reasons, and the ease and the advantages of registering as unemployed vary from country to country. Non-employment figures, therefore, allow more straightforward comparisons between countries than those for unemployment, and are generally more stable. They are still not perfectly comparable, though, as there are variations from country to country in the usual ages at which people begin and end their working lives.

In this book, GDP and other data concerning money are expressed, not in the currency of the country concerned, but in a common unit, almost always *US dollars* at their value at the time to which the data refer. Using the currency of a country outside Europe altogether may seem perverse, but this is simply because almost all our sources of cross-national economic figures, above all the publications of the OECD, use the dollar as their standard unit – reflecting its dominance in international trade. Any attempt to translate these dollars into the currency of European nations or to the present time would run into the problem that the relative values of the different European countries change from year to year with respect to the dollar and to one another.

Expenditure is often expressed in *billions* of dollars. By a 'billion', we mean a *thousand million* (and not the older British sense of a million million).

DIAGRAMS

In Section One, the entry for each country has a diagram of its education system. (Spain has two, as its education system is in transition.) In drawing these, we were faced with a choice between making the diagrams clear and straightforward but highly simplified, or more realistic but complicated. We have chosen the former course. The diagrams follow the general style of the simplest we could find, those in the EU's CEDEFOP publications (e.g. European Commission, 1995), though ours are usually even simpler. Our diagrams show only the outlines of the education systems of each country, with detail and internal variation sacrificed for clarity. *They should always be used in conjunction with the text of the entry.*

ACRONYMS AND ABBREVIATIONS

EU   European Union
EURYDICE   Education Information Network of the European Union
GDP   Gross Domestic Product
ISCED   International Standard Classification for Education
OECD   Organisation for Economic Co-operation and Development

BIBLIOGRAPHY

Archer, E. G. and Peck, B. T. (no date) *The Teaching Profession in Europe*, Glasgow: Jordanhill College of Education.

Centre for Educational Research and Innovation (1995) *Education at a Glance: OECD indicators*, Paris: Organisation for Economic Co-operation and Development.

European Commission (1995) *Structures of the Education and Initial Training Systems in the European Union*, Luxembourg: Office for Official Publications of the European Commission.

European Commission (1996) *Key Data on Education in the European Union*, Luxembourg: Office for Official Publications of the European Commission.

Hunter, B. (ed.) (1995) *The Statesman's Year Book, 1995–1996*, London: Macmillan.

Mackinnon, D. and Statham, J. with Hales, M. (revised edition 1996) *Education in the United Kingdom: facts and figures*, London: Hodder and Stoughton.

SECTION 1

WESTERN EUROPE:
COUNTRY BY COUNTRY

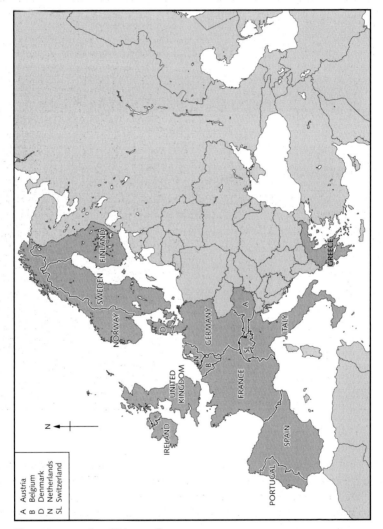

The major countries of Western Europe

BACKGROUND

Austria and its Länder

The modern Republic of Austria dates from 1918, and the dissolution of the Austro–Hungarian Empire after the First World War. In 1938, it was absorbed by Nazi Germany. After the Second World War, it was governed by an administration under the supervision of the victorious Allies until 1955, when it regained full independence.

Austria is a member of the EU, which it joined in 1995.

POPULATION

Population	8.0 million in 1994 (a rise of 0.6% per annum since 1984)
Land area	83,900 sq. km
Population density	94 per sq. km (1992)
Urban/rural balance of population	59%/41%

ECONOMY

GDP	$198.1 billion (1994)
GDP per capita	$24,670 (1994)
In employment	66% of working age population (1991)
	– 92% of men/63% of women aged 25–54
	– 69% of young people (15–24)
Spending on education	5.8% of GDP (1992: public expenditure only)

Austria has 274,000 foreign workers, about half of them from the former Yugoslavia and a fifth from Turkey. Altogether, they form just under 8% of all employed people in Austria. (1992 figures)

RELIGION

The majority of the population are Roman Catholic (78%); 5% are Protestant, 2% are Muslim and 10% are of no religion (1991 Census figures). Church and state are constitutionally separate, but religion is taught in schools.

LANGUAGE AND ETHNICITY

The great majority of the residents of Austria are Austrian citizens (93%) and German speaking (94%). The main minority languages are those of neighbouring countries and regions – Croat, Hungarian, Slovene and Czech. Each is spoken by fewer than 1% of the population as a whole, but in areas with substantial Croat- and Hungarian-speaking communities, these languages are used in some primary schools alongside German for the first three years.

GOVERNMENT

Austria is a federal republic, with three levels of government – federal, state and community. Responsibility for education is divided in a complicated manner between them, and the account here is simplified. (For more detail, see European Commission, 1995, pp. 275–6 and 278.)

The federal government has ultimate responsibility for almost all education at primary, secondary and tertiary levels. This responsibility is divided between three federal ministries, the Ministry of Education and the Arts (primary, secondary and non-university tertiary education), the Ministry of Science and Research (universities and professional colleges) and the Ministry of Economic Affairs (the work experience component of vocational education). The federal government is directly responsible for upper secondary schools and the university sector. In certain other areas (for example, the regulation of the teaching profession in compulsory education), the federal government is responsible for the legislative framework, but its implementation is the responsibility of the states.

The nine states (*Länder*) are responsible for implementing certain federal legislation concerning education. This includes employing teachers for the years of compulsory education (and paying them in the first instance, though for this they are reimbursed by the federal government). In addition, the states are solely responsible for preprimary schools and compulsory vocational schools.

There are 2,350 communities (*Gemeinden*), each with its own council. Their main educational responsibility is for the operational costs of compulsory education, including the construction and maintenance of buildings and the employment of non-teaching staff.

EDUCATION

Education is at present compulsory between the ages of six and 15. It is free in all public schools, compulsory and postcompulsory. Textbooks are supplied free, and become the pupils' property. Pupils may travel free to school by public transport. Higher education is also free for Austrian citizens, and maintenance grants are available on a means-tested basis.

The education system is highly centralised, with the curriculum, assessment procedures and many administrative arrangements specified in detail in law.

Austria has private schools, mostly run by the churches. They may, but need not, teach the official curriculum (see below). Most receive state funds, though to varying degrees. Only private schools run by the Church may have teachers' salaries paid by the state, but other private schools are eligible to have their maintenance costs subsidised.

INSTITUTIONS

The first four years of compulsory schooling are in primary school (*Volksschule*), which is comprehensive. At the age of ten, however, children divide between two types of school:

- the *Hauptschule* – a school that offers only a general lower secondary education for four years, ending at 14;

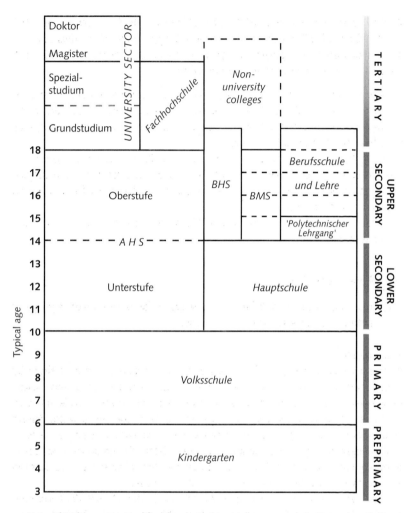

Note: This diagram is simplified for clarity (especially as regards tertiary education) and should be used in conjunction with the text

Austria's education system

- the *AHS* (*Allgemeinbildende Höhere Schule*) – a school that offers an academic lower and upper secondary education for up to eight years. It is divided into two stages, the *Unterstufe*, ending at 14; and the *Oberstufe*, ending at 18.

At the age of 14, there is a division between academic and vocational education, and students follow one of three routes:

- they may stay in or transfer to the AHS for academic upper secondary education;

- they may go to the BMS (*Berufsbildende Mittlere Schule*) or BHS (*Berufsbildende Höhere Schule*) for vocational upper secondary education;
- or they may take a 'polytechnic year' followed by an apprenticeship, which itself involves attendance at a vocational school.

At every stage there is a compulsory curriculum, with the amount of time for each subject specified. Teaching materials and methods are usually left to the discretion of individual teachers, though they can be instructed to change by their head teacher or an inspector.

In the Volksschule, Hauptschule and AHS, pupils are assessed regularly by their teachers, using a combination of course work and tests for each subject. Pupils must normally pass in all the compulsory subjects to be allowed to proceed to the next year.

Tertiary education, from the age of 19, is divided between university and non-university sectors.

Preprimary education

Preprimary education is available in a *Kindergarten* for children from the age of three until compulsory schooling starts at six.

Kindergarten

Most *Kindergärten* are publicly owned and run – three-quarters of them by community councils – but there are private kindergartens too, often established by associations of parents or by churches. There is wide variation in the fees (if any) charged by kindergartens, both public and private. Private kindergartens may be publicly subsidised, but again to widely varying extents.

Kindergartens generally concentrate on children's personal and social development, with emphasis on play rather than formal teaching. The children are usually put into 'family groups' of mixed age and sex.

There are 4,100 kindergartens in Austria, with 18,500 staff (99% women) and 192,700 children. These include 86% of all five-year-olds. (1992–3 figures, Österreichisches Statistisches Zentralamt)

Alternatively, preschool children may be cared for in creches (*Krippen*) or day centres (*Horte*). There are just over 300 creches, with 1,500 staff (99% women) and 6,800 children; and just under 600 day centres, with 2,500 staff (96% women) and 27,100 children. (1992–3 figures, Österreichisches Statistisches Zentralamt)

Primary education

There is just one type of primary school – the Volksschule – attended by all children between the ages of six and ten.

Volksschule

The Volksschule is co-educational. Pupils are divided into classes by age (though where numbers are small, pupils of different ages may be combined in one class). The maximum permitted class size is 30; the average class size in practice is 20. All subjects are normally taught by the same teacher, who remains with a class of children throughout their primary schooling.

When six-year-old children enter school, their maturity is assessed by the head teacher, and those judged insufficiently mature are placed in a one-year 'preprimary class', which has a simplified version of the normal curriculum. Preprimary classes cater for about 10,000 children each year – some 10% of the age-group.

A compulsory curriculum is laid down for all public primary schools, and the number of lessons to be devoted to each subject in each year is specified. The subjects and the percentages of time devoted to each over the four years of Volksschule are shown in Figure 1. (European Commission, 1995)

Assessment at the end of the final year of primary school is particularly important, as it determines admission to secondary education (see below).

There are 3,400 primary schools in Austria, with 30,400 teachers (83% women) and 383,200 pupils. (1992–3 figures, Österreichisches Statistisches Zentralamt)

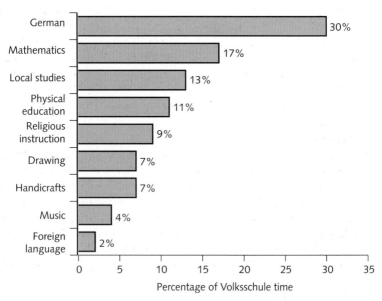

Austria figure 1   Percentage of time spent on each compulsory subject in the Volksschule (Adapted from European Commission, 1995)

Lower secondary education

Children normally begin secondary schooling at the age of ten. As we noted above, there are two main types of lower secondary school. The first type is the Hauptschule. It offers a general lower secondary education for four years, thus normally ending with pupils aged 14, and requiring one more year to complete their compulsory education. The second type is the lower secondary section (Unterstufe) of the AHS, which offers an academic lower secondary education for four years, after which pupils may proceed to the AHS upper secondary section (Oberstufe) or transfer to a different type of school.

To be admitted to any lower secondary school, pupils must have passed their compulsory subjects in the final year of primary school. To be admitted to the AHS Unterstufe, they must either have been awarded high marks in German, reading and mathematics, or pass an entrance test.

Hauptschule
About 70% of children leaving the Volksschule proceed to the Hauptschule. It is co-educational. Pupils are divided into classes by age. Teachers are subject specialists, each specialising in two subjects. Where possible, the same teachers remain with a class of children for their subject throughout their time in the Hauptschule. Mixed-ability teaching is practised except in German, mathematics and foreign language teaching, where each class is divided into three ability bands. Pupils are allocated to these bands after several weeks of their first year, but they may be transferred between bands throughout their school career. Standards in the highest band match those in the AHS.

A compulsory curriculum is laid down, though schools are allowed limited autonomy in the amount of time to be devoted to each subject. The subjects and the percentages of time devoted to each over the four years of Hauptschule are shown in Figure 2. (European Commission, 1995)

There are 1,200 Hauptschulen in Austria, with 33,700 teachers (62% women) and 261,300 pupils. The average class size is 23. (1992–3 figures, Österreichisches Statistisches Zentralamt).

At the end of Hauptschule, pupils receive a certificate (*Hauptschulabschlußzeugnis*), which is the basis for their choice of future education. They are normally aged 14, and require one more year to complete their compulsory education. They follow one of three main routes, according to their levels of attainment and their wishes. About 45% take a 'polytechnic year' (*Polytechnischer Lehrgang*) – which is described below. Another 45% proceed to an upper secondary vocational school (BMS or BHS). About 5% transfer to the upper secondary section (Oberstufe) of the academic secondary school (AHS).

Polytechnischer Lehrgang
The 'polytechnic year' is intended for pupils who will not continue their education after 15, but will proceed to an apprenticeship or directly into

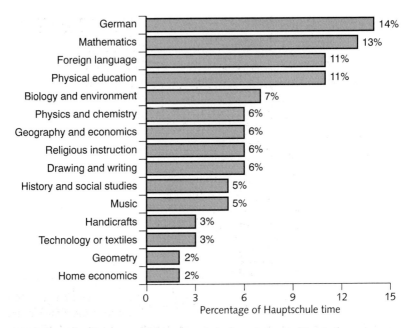

Austria figure 2   Percentage of time spent on each compulsory subject in the
Hauptschule (Adapted from European Commission, 1995)
Note: The foreign language is usually English

employment. It was taken by some 18,200 students in 1992–3 (70% male), who
were taught by 1,700 teachers (51% men). (Österreichisches Statistisches
Zentralamt) It combines general education (in which German, English,
mathematics and the use of computers are compulsory) with information,
observation and work experience in a variety of occupations geared especially
to the local labour market. It may take place in association with a Hauptschule,
or in a separate establishment.

AHS – Unterstufe

About 30% of children leaving the Volksschule are admitted to the lower
secondary section of the AHS. It provides a four-year academic education for
pupils aged 10–14. It is co-educational. Pupils are divided into classes by age,
and there is no internal differentiation by ability or attainment.

A compulsory curriculum is laid down, and the number of hours to be
devoted to each subject in each year is specified. In the first two years, all
pupils study the same subjects. In the third and fourth, there is a division
between three different types of curriculum: the major differences are that the
Gymnasium includes Latin, but the Realgymnasium has instead extra
mathematics and technology and the Wirtschaftskundliches Realgymnasium extra

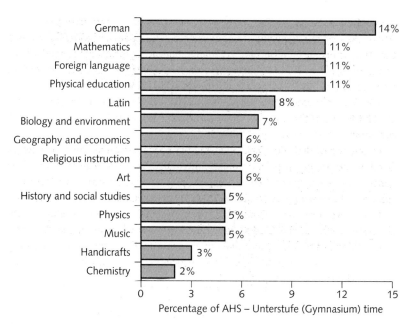

Austria figure 3   Percentage of time spent on each compulsory subject in the AHS –
Unterstufe (Adapted from European Commission, 1995)
Note: The foreign language is usually English

chemistry and technology. The Gymnasium subjects, and the percentages of time devoted to each over the four years of the AHS – Unterstufe, are shown in Figure 3.

(For AHS statistics, see under *AHS – Oberstufe* below.)

At the end of their four years in the Unterstufe, about two-thirds of pupils continue into the Oberstufe of the AHS, and about a third transfer to a vocational upper secondary school.

Upper secondary education

The upper secondary stage is divided between academic education in the upper secondary section (Oberstufe) of the AHS, and vocational education and training, which itself offers three main routes: the intermediate secondary vocational school, the BMS; the upper secondary vocational school, the BHS; or an apprenticeship (*Berufsschule und Lehre*), which often follows a polytechnic year, and combines theoretical education at a vocational school with practical training in a firm. In addition, there are training colleges at upper secondary level for preprimary teachers and non-teaching supervisory staff for schools.

AHS – Oberstufe
About 20% of the age-group are admitted to the upper secondary section of the AHS. It provides a four-year academic education for students aged 14–18, and is designed to lead to university. It is co-educational. Students are divided into classes by age, and there is no internal differentiation by ability or attainment. A compulsory curriculum is laid down, similar to that of the Unterstufe, and the time to be devoted to each subject in each year is specified.

At the end of their final year, students who have passed all their subjects (or failed in no more than one subject) may sit the AHS *Matura* exam. This consists of seven papers (or six papers plus a dissertation) in at least four subjects. Those who pass (called *Maturanten*) are qualified to enter university.

There are just over 300 AHS, with 167,600 students – 60% in the Unterstufe, 40% in the Oberstufe. 52% of them are female. In the AHS as a whole (Unterstufe and Oberstufe), there are 18,600 teachers (55% women). The average class size is 25. (1992–3 figures, Österreichisches Statistisches Zentralamt)

BMS and BHS
The Berufsbildende Mittlere Schule (BMS – intermediate secondary vocational school) and the Berufsbildende Höhere Schule (BHS – upper secondary vocational school) prepare their students for specific occupations. Both require entrants to have successfully completed their schooling up to the age of 14, and to have passed an aptitude test for their chosen occupation. Attendance at both is normally full-time. The curricula for the various subjects or occupations in each are laid down nationally. The major differences between them are as follows:

- BMS courses last from one to four years; BHS courses last five years;
- the BMS concentrates on practical training, whereas the BHS combines practical training with theoretical vocational study and general education;
- successful completion of a three- or four-year BMS course entitles the student to practise a trade or occupation; BHS courses can in addition lead to the BHS Matura examination and qualify students to enter university or other institutions of higher education.

There are about 750 BMS, with 66,300 students, 59% female; and 300 BHS, with 99,200 students, 53% male. (The numbers of students in BMS are declining year by year, and those in BHS rising.) Between them, the BMS and BHS sectors have 18,600 teachers, 52% of them men. (1991–2 figures) They cover a wide range of occupational sectors, including industry, trade and commerce, domestic science, agriculture, nursing, hotel management and tourism, nursery school and sports teaching, fashion and social work.

Located within BHS establishments, but regarded as separate institutions, are the *Kollegs*. These offer two-year courses, mainly for holders of the AHS (academic) Matura who want to obtain a BHS (vocational) Matura as well.

Berufsschule und Lehre (Apprenticeship)

Apprenticeship in Austria is strongly influenced by the German 'dual system', in which the apprentice combines theoretical education at a vocational school (*Berufsschule*) with practical training in a firm (*Lehre*). Apprentices must have completed the nine years of compulsory education. Apprenticeships last up to four years.

At school, in addition to studying theoretical subjects related to their intended occupation, all apprentices study a number of general subjects, including German, English or French, economics, accounting, communication and correspondence.

At work, apprenticeship training must be given by qualified instructors, and follow national syllabuses.

Apprenticeships cover over 200 occupations, including traditional trades (such as plumber, joiner, bricklayer, electrician, mechanic, etc.) but also a wide range of other occupations in office work, sales, catering, tourism and so on. At the end of their apprenticeship, apprentices must pass an examination (*Lehrabschlußprüfung*) set by a board which includes representatives of employers, trade unions and other interested parties in their field.

There are 145,700 apprentices, 65% male. They constitute about half of the population of young people aged 15–18. They attend 230 vocational schools, with 4,700 teachers, 75% male. The average class size is 24. (1991–2 figures, Österreichisches Statistisches Zentralamt)

Special education

Austria has special schools (*Sonderschulen*) for physically and mentally disadvantaged children, whose attendance at mainstream schools is not deemed feasible.

There are 320 special schools, with 18,800 pupils (62% of them boys), and 5,200 teachers (82% of them women). (1992–3 figures, Österreichisches Statistisches Zentralamt)

Tertiary education

Tertiary education is divided into two sectors. The first consists of those that have university status and can award degrees – the universities themselves (*Universitäten*), the art colleges (*Kunsthochschulen*) and the new professional colleges (*Fachhochschulen*). The second (*Sonstiger Nichtuniversitärer Sektor*) includes a range of mostly vocational colleges and academies without university status. In recent years, the numbers of students in the university sector have been increasing, and those in the non-university sector decreasing.

Tuition is free for Austrian citizens (who comprise 90% of university students), and means-tested maintenance grants are available.

Universitäten

Austria has 12 universities – five of them in Vienna. A Matura is normally required for admission (though people not holding it may be admitted under certain circumstances, sometimes on the basis of an entrance examination) and normally sufficient (Austria does not operate a *numerus clausus* system). Some universities (notably the Universities of Vienna, Graz, Innsbruck and Salzburg) cover a wide range of subjects in their teaching and research; others are more specialised (such as the agricultural and the veterinary universities in Vienna, and the mining university in Leoben).

University courses last between four and six years – normally a two-year basic stage (*Grundstudium*) followed by a specialisation stage (*Spezialstudium*). The first degree is the *Magister/Magistra* (Master), except for agro-forestry, engineering and mining, where it is the *Diplom-Ingenieur*.

Magister/Magistra and Diplom-Ingenieur graduates from any institution can normally obtain a doctorate after two years of postgraduate study at a university.

Universities also offer a range of short courses (*Kurzstudium*), of up to three years, which do not lead to a degree.

Universities do not require formal attendance at courses as a condition of enrolment, and do not attempt to supervise students closely. Drop-out rates are high; in many subjects, more students drop out than complete their courses. (OECD, 1992)

The proportions of men and of women graduating from university differ significantly between subject areas. About two-thirds of students of education are women, as are just over half of those in the arts. Women form just under half of students in health and social services, a third of those in business administration, and just over a tenth of those in technology.

In 1991–2, the universities had 194,900 students (56% men) and 11,400 teaching staff (78% men). About a third of the students were in the University of Vienna. (Österreichisches Statistisches Zentralamt)

Kunsthochschulen

The six art colleges (three in Vienna) cover the fields of fine arts, applied arts, music and drama. A Matura is not normally required for admission, but there is an entrance examination. Art colleges have university status, and award the degree of Magister/Magistra after courses lasting between five and eight years (the latter for students of instrumental music).

In 1991–2, the art colleges had 7,000 students (50% of each sex), and 680 teaching staff (75% men). (Österreichisches Statistisches Zentralamt)

Fachhochschulen
From 1994–5, a new category of institution, the Fachhochschule (professional college) has been introduced. They are vocational in orientation, specialising in engineering and economics, and having the right to award degrees. They may be publicly or privately owned, but the private establishments are publicly subsidised. The Matura is normally required for admission. Their courses last at least three years, and they award the degrees of Magister/Magistra and Diplom-Ingenieur, but with the letters 'FH' added.

Non-university colleges
The non-university colleges cover the following main vocational areas.

- teacher training (for the Volksschule and Hauptschule) (6,200 students, 84% women)
- medico-technical services (including laboratory services, physiotherapy, occupational therapy, radiology, orthoptics, audiology, dietetics and nutrition) (2,000 students, 87% women)
- social work (1,100 students, 74% women)
- vocational teacher training (780 students, 58% women)
- religious teacher training (660 students, 83% women)

Adult education

Evening classes for adults are available in adult education departments of the AHS, BHS and BMS. They offer both academic and vocational courses at a variety of levels, in modular form. At the end of their courses, adults can obtain qualifications equivalent to those obtained by the younger full-time students at these types of school.

Funding

Austria spends about 5.8% of its GDP on education. (Public expenditure only: 1992 figures, CERI, 1995)

The funding of education is shared between the federal government, the state governments and the municipalities, in complicated ways.

For almost all primary and lower secondary education, the municipalities are responsible for funding the construction and maintenance of school buildings, and the schools' operating costs, including the employment of non-teaching staff. The states are responsible for employing teaching staff, but their salary costs are repaid in full by the federal government.

The federal government is directly responsible for the funding of upper secondary and tertiary education.

Teaching profession

Kindergarten teachers have traditionally been trained in specialist schools at upper secondary level; now, however, their training is being progressively transferred to new specialist colleges at tertiary (but non-university) level. Admission to these colleges is open to holders of the Matura; others must pass an entrance examination. College courses last two years.

Teachers in the Volksschule and Hauptschule are trained at *Pädagogische Akademien* (teacher training academies), at tertiary (but non-university) level. Admission to these colleges is open to holders of the Matura; others must pass

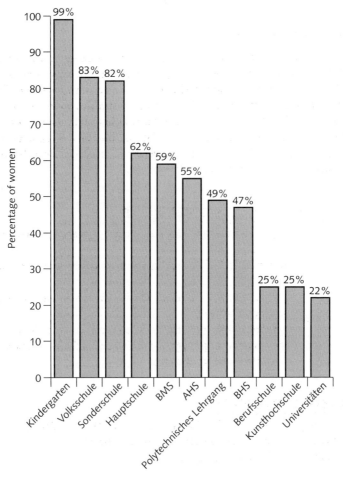

Austria figure 4   Percentage of women in different sectors of the teaching profession, 1992–3 (Adapted from Österreichisches Statistisches Zentralamt, 1993)

an entrance examination. Students are normally trained to teach all the subjects of the curriculum. To qualify as teachers, they must pass an examination at the end of their course – usually after three years.

Teachers in the AHS and those of academic subjects in the BMS and BHS are graduates of university (or art college): their courses last four-and-a-half years, the first two devoted to academic study (usually in two subjects), the rest to training in teaching, including teaching practice. Teachers of vocational subjects in the BMS and BHS have a much wider range of training, at specialist academies or (for such subjects as engineering and law) universities.

The majority of teachers are women, but the relative numbers of women and men differ from sector to sector of education, as Figure 4 illustrates.

Parent/school relationships

Parents are represented on the school committee or school forum of each school (see above). They are also represented (as are teachers) on the *provincial school board* in each state and the *district school boards* within it. These boards are part of the federal, not the state, administration, but their members are chosen to reflect the balance of political parties in the state assembly. They have the right to be consulted on a range of issues, notably the appointment of teachers, including head teachers, to secondary schools – though the actual appointments are made by the state administration.

ACRONYMS AND ABBREVIATIONS

AHS   Allgemeinbildende Höhere Schule (academic secondary school)

BHS   Berufsbildende Höhere Schule (upper secondary vocational school)

BMS   Berufsbildende Mittlere Schule (intermediate secondary vocational school)

FH   Fachhochschule (tertiary vocational college – the letters 'FH' are added to degrees from the Fachhochschulen to distinguish them from university degrees)

ACKNOWLEDGEMENT

We are very grateful to Dr Gehart, Director of the Library of the Österreichisches Statistisches Zentralamt, who supplied us with extensive information about education in Austria.

REFERENCES
●●●●●●●●●●●●●

Austrian Academic Exchange Service (1993) *Information for Foreign Students Intending to Study at an Austrian Institution of Higher Learning*, Edition '94/'95, Vienna: Austrian Academic Exchange Service, University of Vienna.

Bundesministerium für Unterricht und Kunst unter Mitwirkung des Österreichischen Statistischen Zentralamtes (1992) *Österreichisches Schulstatistik*, Vienna: Bundesministerium für Unterricht und Kunst in Zusammenarbeit mit dem Österreichischen Statistischen Zentralamt.

Bundesministerium für Wissenschaft und Forschung (no date) *Study in Austria*, Vienna: Bundesministerium für Wissenschaft und Forschung.

CERI (1995) *Education at a Glance: OECD indicators*, Paris: Organisation for Economic Co-operation and Development.

European Commission (1995) *Structures of the Education and Initial Training Systems in the European Union*, Luxembourg: Office for Official Publications of the European Commission.

OECD (1992) *From Higher Education to Employment: Volume 1: Australia, Austria, Belgium, Germany*, Paris: Organisation for Economic Co-operation and Development.

OECD (1995) *OECD Economic Surveys: 1994–1995: Austria*, Paris: Organisation for Economic Co-operation and Development.

Österreichisches Statistisches Zentralamt (1993) *Das Schulwesen in Österreich: Schuljahr 1991/92*, Vienna: Österreichisches Statistisches Zentralamt.

Österreichisches Statistisches Zentralamt (1993) *Österreichische Hochschulstatistik: Studiennjahr 1991/92*, Vienna: Österreichisches Statistisches Zentralamt.

Österreichisches Statistisches Zentralamt (1993) *Statistisches Jahrbuch für die Republik Österreich: XLIV Jahrgang, Neue Folge 1993*, Vienna: Österreichisches Statistisches Zentralamt.

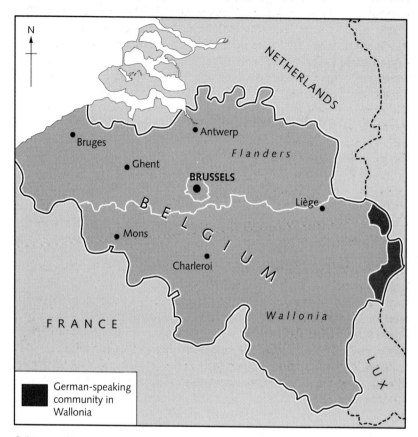

Belgium and its regions

The territory of modern Belgium became part of the Hapsburg Empire in 1477, and for more than three centuries was ruled by either the Spanish or the Austrian branch of the Hapsburg royal house. It was conquered by France in 1795, and on the defeat of Napoleon in 1815, was united with the territory of the modern Netherlands and with the Duchy of Luxembourg as the Kingdom of the Netherlands. This lasted only until 1830, however, when the southern provinces won independence, to become the Kingdom of Belgium.

The Netherlands, Belgium and Luxembourg came together once more in 1948 to form a customs union ('Benelux'), and in 1957 were founder members of the European Economic Community, the forerunner of the EU.

Belgium was originally a unitary state, but between 1970 and 1993 it was progressively transformed into a federation, with a federal government and a dual structure of three territorially-based *regions* — Flanders, Wallonia and Brussels — and three language-based *communities* — Flemish (Dutch speaking), French and German. The relationships between the regions and the communities are described below, in the section on government.

POPULATION

Population	10.1 million in 1994 (a rise of 0.3% per annum from 1984)
	– Flanders 5.8 million
	– Wallonia 3.3 million
	– Brussels 950,000
Land area	30,500 sq. km
	– Flanders 13,500 sq. km
	– Wallonia 16,800 sq. km
Population density	329 per sq. km
	– Flanders 430 per sq. km
	– Wallonia 196 per sq. km
Young people (5–24)	25% of population

About 9% of the population are resident foreigners.

ECONOMY

GDP	$227.9 billion (1994)
GDP per capita	$22,500 (1994)
In employment	57% of working age population (1991)
	– 89% of men/57% of women aged 25–54
	– 31% of young people (15–24)
Spending on education	6.0% of GDP (1992: public expenditure only)

RELIGION

There are no official figures for religious adherence, as the Belgian Census no longer asks about it, but the great majority of the population are Roman Catholic.

Freedom of religion is guaranteed by law, and the state pays a proportion of the income of clergy of every denomination.

Schools run by the communities (see below) are non-denominational, but those run by provinces, communes and private individuals or organisations may be denominational.

LANGUAGE

There is no Belgian language as such. Belgium has three official languages, which are those of its more populous neighbours – Dutch, spoken by 60% of the population mostly in the north of the country; French, spoken by 30%, mostly in the south; and German, spoken by about 1% in the east. The remaining 9% are bilingual in Dutch and French.

The three language-speaking communities form part of the federal government structure of Belgium, and each community has its own community council, with responsibility for cultural matters – including education.

GOVERNMENT

Belgium is a federal constitutional monarchy, with five main levels or types of government, the *federal government, regions, communities, provinces* and *communes.*

Since Belgium became a federal state in 1993, the functions of the central government have been limited to such matters as foreign policy, defence and internal security, justice and social security. It administers the tax system, and allocates funds from taxes to the regions and communities, for purposes including education. Otherwise its educational responsibilities are confined to setting the age-limits for compulsory education (currently 6–15 full-time and 15–18 part-time); defining the minimum requirements for educational qualifications; and administering teachers' pensions.

As we noted above, since 1993 Belgium has had a dual structure of three territorially-based regions (Flanders, Wallonia and Brussels) and three language-based communities (Flemish, French and German). The Flanders region corresponds closely to the Flemish community, and the Wallonia region to the French-speaking community. But the Brussels region (whose population is divided between Dutch and French speakers) does not correspond to a community, and the German-speaking community does not correspond to a region.

Indeed the correspondence of the Flanders region to the Flemish community is so close that they share a single legislative council. With that exception, each region and each community has its own legislative council, which forms a government headed by a chief minister – the regional authority being responsible for territory-based matters, and the community authority for cultural matters, including education and training. The council of the Flanders region and Flemish community has responsibility for both territorial and cultural matters. The possibility has been discussed of a similar unification of the Wallonia regional council and the French community council, but this has not happened.

The three communities run and finance a number of schools directly, but these are a minority, catering for just under 16% of pupils in Belgian schools.

The communities also supervise and subsidise schools run by the provinces, communes and private organisations and individuals.

The 10 provinces and 289 communes both run a number of schools. Those run by provinces are few in number, catering for only 2% of pupils in Belgian schools; those run by communes cater for 21%. These schools are subsidised and supervised by the communities.

EDUCATION

The Flemish, French and German communities have separate education systems, but they are similar to one another. A single description will be given here for Belgium as a whole, though illustrative examples will be drawn from the individual communities. Where appropriate, Flemish terminology will be given first, then French, then German. (For more detailed descriptions of the three separate systems, see European Commission, 1995. For more detailed diagrams of the Flemish and the French systems, see CERI, 1995.)

The Flemish school system has 1,065,000 pupils (57% of all pupils in Belgium), and the French system 798,000 (43%). The German system is much smaller, with under 12,000 pupils (fewer than 1%). (European Commission, 1995)

Education throughout Belgium is compulsory from the age of six until 18; until at least 14 it must be full-time, but thereafter it can be part-time.

INSTITUTIONS

In all three communities, schools are administered in four different ways:

- financed and run directly by the community;
- run by provinces and subsidised by the community;
- run by communes and subsidised by the community;
- as 'free' schools (i.e. private schools, in practice almost all Catholic), subsidised by the community.

To qualify for subsidy from a community, schools must comply with a number of conditions, including using the community language, having a structure approved by the community, following the prescribed curriculum, possessing adequate facilities, using adequate teaching materials and being open to inspection. Community-run schools must be non-denominational, but those run by provinces or communes, as well as free schools, may be denominational.

The percentages of pupils in these schools are shown in Figure 1: a majority (61%) of pupils overall are in private schools. The percentage is higher in the Flemish community (70%) than in the French community (48%); and in secondary schools (66%) than in primary (56%) or preprimary schools (57%).

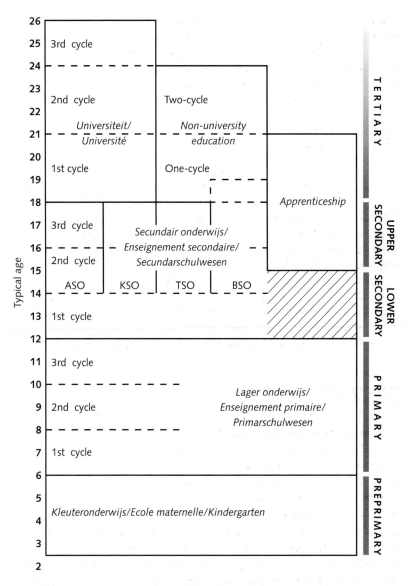

Note: This diagram is highly simplified: it does not show variations between the
Flemish, French and German communities, and it shows only the newer (Type I)
structure of secondary schooling. It should be used in conjunction with the text

Belgium's education system

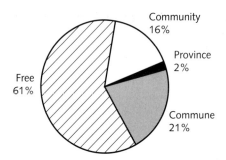

Belgium figure 1   Percentage of pupils (preprimary, primary and secondary) in different categories of school, 1991–2 (Adapted from European Commission, 1995)

Preprimary education

Preprimary education (*Kleuteronderwijs/Ecole maternelle/Kindergarten*) is available, free of charge, for children aged from two-and-a-half until six. It is not compulsory, but is attended by over 90% of eligible children – virtually 100% by the age of five. Most of these children are in private schools (70% of those in the Flemish community, though only 40% of those in the French).

Preprimary schools are normally attached to primary schools, and aim to prepare children for primary education, physically, socially and intellectually. The schools are co-educational. Children are usually placed in classes with other children of the same age, each class with its own teacher, but there are no formal lessons.

In 1991–2, there were 4,000 preprimary schools in Belgium, with 22,500 teachers (full- and part-time) and 398,100 pupils. (European Commission, 1995)

Primary education

Primary education (*Lager onderwijs/Enseignement primaire/Primarschulwesen*) is compulsory, lasts six years – normally from age six to 12 – and is divided into three two-year cycles. In recent years, official policy in all communities has encouraged equal opportunities, and most primary schools are now co-educational and do not differentiate by ability or attainment. Official policy also encourages flexibility in teaching, to allow for the different speeds and styles of learning of individual children; the adaptation of education to meet changes in the outside world; an emphasis on skills rather than factual knowledge; and a move from summative to formative assessment. It is officially acknowledged, however, that many schools have not yet responded to these policies.

There is a prescribed curriculum and timetable in each community. There are some differences between them, but the following example from the French community (European Commission, 1995) is typical of the subjects encompassed, though obviously Dutch or German would replace French in the other communities.

- French
- writing (first cycle)
- mathematics
- history
- geography
- science
- religion or ethics
- physical education
- music
- manual education
- civics
- road safety
- second national or first foreign language (third cycle)

Teaching methods, textbooks and materials are not centrally prescribed. Teaching is usually by class teachers, who take all subjects, but there may be specialist teachers for physical and artistic education, and more generally in the third cycle.

Children are assessed formatively by their teachers throughout the school year. Traditionally they have been assessed summatively at the end of each year, though official policy is now to confine summative assessment to the end of each two-year cycle. The methods of assessment are at teachers' discretion; these may but need not include formal tests. Children whose progress has been unsatisfactory may be required to repeat a year. At the end of their primary schooling, successful pupils (about 80% of all pupils) receive a primary education certificate (*Getuigschrift van het Basisonderwijs/Certificat d'Etudes de Base/Abschlußzeugnis der Grundschule*), which qualifies them for direct entry to secondary education. Those (about 10%) who do not obtain the certificate usually have to spend time in a special preparatory class at secondary school before transferring to secondary education proper.

In 1991–2, there were 4,200 primary schools in Belgium, with 49,100 teachers (full- and part-time) and 711,500 pupils. (European Commission, 1995)

Secondary education

Secondary education (*Secundair onderwijs/Enseignement secondaire/Secundar-schulwesen*), which has recently been reorganised in all three communities, is now divided into three two-year cycles. Students are differentiated at the end of the first cycle but they have opportunities to change routes thereafter.

Secondary schooling lasts six years, from ages 12 to 18. It is free and compulsory, but from 15 it may be part-time. It is divided into three two-year cycles. (An extra year may be organised after the third cycle for students who need another year to obtain a qualification or wish to prepare for university.) Some schools (*Middenscholen/Lycée*) teach only the first or the first and second cycles; others (*Koninklijk Atheneum/Athenée Royal*) teach the second and third cycles or all three cycles. Secondary schools are normally co-educational, especially those run directly by the communities. Teachers are subject specialists.

First cycle
In this cycle, all students follow a common curriculum prescribed by their community. There are some differences between the communities here, but the following example – the first-year curriculum of the Flemish community (European Commission, 1995) – is typical of the subjects encompassed. (French or German would replace Dutch as the first language in the other communities, and Dutch would replace French as the second.)

- Dutch
- French
- English (second year)
- mathematics
- history
- geography
- art
- science
- technical education
- physical education
- religion or ethics

The common curriculum subjects occupy about 85% of students' study time; the remaining 15% is allocated at the discretion of individual schools.

Second cycle
In this cycle, students are differentiated into four tracks. (Their Flemish community titles and acronyms are given here.)

- general education (ASO – *Algemeen Secundair Onderwijs*)
- artistic education (KSO – *Kunstesecundair Onderwijs*)
- technical education (TSO – *Technisch Secundair Onderwijs*)
- vocational education (BSO – *Beroepssecundair Onderwijs*)

Schools can specialise in one or other of ASO, KSO, TSO and BSO, or they can offer several tracks. There is a common core curriculum across all four tracks, which is an abridged version of the common curriculum of the first cycle, plus a set of optional subjects for each track.

Third cycle
In this cycle, the four separate tracks are maintained, as is the structure of

common core plus options; but the common curriculum element is further reduced, and the time spent on options increased.

For students following the vocational track, the core curriculum remains academic, but the options are vocational, as in the following example from the French community. (European Commission, 1995)

- agronomy
- arts
- clothing
- construction
- economics
- hotel work
- industry
- social service
- sciences

Methods of assessment and the award of certificates are determined by the individual schools, though the upper secondary education certificate is externally ratified. This certificate (*Diploma van Secundair Onderwijs/Certificat d'Enseignement Secondaire Supérieure/Abschlußzeugnis des Sekundarunterrichts*) is awarded at the end of the third cycle to students who have successfully completed a general, technical or artistic track. It may also be awarded to students who have successfully completed a vocational track plus an extra (seventh) year.

In 1991–2, there were 1,800 secondary schools in Belgium, with 103,100 teachers (full- and part-time) and 766,200 pupils. (European Commission, 1995)

As an alternative to continuing in a secondary school, young people aged 15–18 (that is, those for whom only part-time education is now compulsory) may attend a training centre – such as those established for apprenticeships (see below) – where they may study a combination of general and vocational subjects, at the discretion of the centre.

Apprenticeship

An alternative to secondary education in school for those aged 15–21 is an apprenticeship. There are different schemes within as well as between the different communities, but all are based on a combination of education and formal training in a training centre with practical experience in a firm.

Special education

Special education is provided for children and young people who have problems with mainstream education. It is regulated by legislation of 1970, which distinguishes eight types of special education, according to the kind and severity of the child's handicap or problem – mild mental handicaps; serious mental handicaps; emotional handicaps; physical handicaps; chronic illnesses; visual handicaps; hearing handicaps; and serious learning difficulties not explicable by mental handicap.

Special education may take place in special schools, or, for those with less severe problems, in mainstream schools under the integrated education system (GON – *Geïntegreerd Onderwijs*). In either case, the aim of special education is to integrate children with handicaps or problems into mainstream education and the wider society. In practice, however, few children return from special to mainstream schools.

About 4% of all pupils are in special education. (Verhoeven and Beuselinck, 1995; Dens and Hoedemakers, 1995)

Tertiary education

Belgium recognises two types of tertiary education: university education (*Universiteit/Université*) and non-university education, which is itself divided into short (one-cycle) and long (two-cycle) courses. The Flemish and French communities provide all types of tertiary education, but the German community only short non-university courses.

Just over half of the 18-year-old population are in tertiary education: approximately 20% in universities, and 23% on one-cycle and 8% on two-cycle non-university courses. (Flemish figures: 1994–5 for university and 1991–2 for non-university education, Verhoeven and Beuselinck, 1996)

Universiteit/Université

Belgium has 17 universities, institutes, free-standing faculties and other establishments with university status. They have 116,300 students in all, 29% in state-run and 71% in private institutions. They range in size from the Catholic University of Louvain, with 43,100 students, to the Protestant Faculty of Theology in Brussels, with 155. (1992–3 figures)

For admission, an upper secondary education certificate is necessary and normally sufficient, though in engineering and applied sciences, numbers are limited and an entrance examination is also required. There are tuition fees in all types of tertiary institution. The universities set the level of their own fees, but for non-university education, these are set by the communities. Means-tested student grants are available from the communities.

There are three cycles of university education. The first, lasting two or three years, leads to the degree of *Kandidaat/Candidat*; the second, normally lasting a further two or three years, leads to the *Licenciaat/Licence*. (In some subjects, such as medicine, veterinary medicine and engineering, the second cycle lasts longer.) The third cycle leads to a doctorate, after a further one, two or more years and the submission of a thesis.

As well as final examinations, students must sit examinations at the end of each year of study; according to their performance, they may be allowed to proceed to the next year, to resit the examinations or to repeat the year. There is a high drop-out rate: just over half of university students abandon their studies without taking a degree, a quarter after just one year. Just under a third of students complete their studies successfully in the specified time. The remaining 18% do complete their studies, but one or more years late. (Flemish figures, OECD, 1992)

In the academic year 1994–5, there were 13,600 first-year students in Flemish universities, with equal numbers of men and women. This constitutes 20% of the population of 18-year-old Flemings – an increase from 13% in 1984–5. (Verhoeven and Beuselinck, 1996)

The distribution of students among different areas of study is illustrated for the Flemish community in Figure 2.

Although there are equal numbers of men and women at university, there are often substantial differences in the numbers of men and of women taking particular subjects. In the Flemish community, for example, women constitute four-fifths of students of pharmacy, three-quarters of those in psychology and education, and two-thirds of those of languages. By contrast, only 40% in economics, 36% in mathematics and 16% in civil engineering are women.

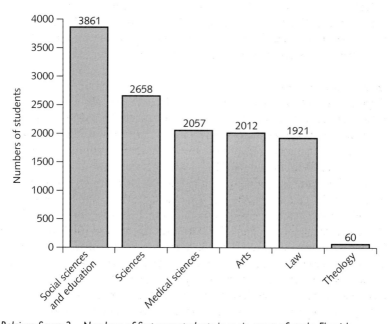

Belgium figure 2   Numbers of first-year students in main areas of study, Flemish universities, 1994–5 (Adapted from Verhoeven and Beuselinck, 1996)
Note: The data have been recategorised here

Non-university education
Courses in non-university colleges of tertiary education may be of one or two cycles. Two-cycle courses are similar in organisation and equivalent in level to those of the first two cycles of university education, and lead to qualifications of equal status. Men outnumber women in two-cycle courses by about two to one, but women outnumber men in one-cycle courses by about three to two.

In the Flemish community, there are 29 non-university colleges (*Hogescholen*), which were formed in 1995 by the merger of 160 smaller and more specialist establishments. In 1992–3 (before the merger), these colleges had about 83,600 students, 70% on one-cycle and 30% on two-cycle courses. (Verhoeven and Beuselinck, 1996)

Both two-cycle and one-cycle courses encompass a range of subjects, mostly vocationally-oriented, of which economic and commercial, educational, paramedical and technical subjects are the most popular. The percentages of women vary greatly from subject to subject. About 80% of students on education and paramedical courses are women, as are 75% of students of translation and interpretation. By contrast, women constitute 30% of the students of architecture, 20% of agriculture, and 17% of industrial engineering. (1989 Flemish figures, OECD, 1992)

Adult education

Opportunities for adult education are increasing, and about 15% of the active adult population now participate. (1990–1 figures) There are different types of adult education, under the aegis of different government ministries and departments. In the Flemish community, for example, the Ministry of Education is responsible for distance education and 'second chance' basic education, and the Ministry of Economy, Labour and Home Affairs for vocational training. The Departments of Health, Welfare and Culture all have responsibilities for adult education in their own specialist areas. (Verhoeven and Beuselinck, 1995)

Funding

Belgium spends about 6% of its GDP on education. (1992 figure: public expenditure only)

The federal government collects taxes, and allocates funds for education to the communities. However, it has little discretion in this allocation. The funds for the Flemish and French communities are allocated largely on the basis of the allocation in 1987 (56% to the Flemish community, 44% to the French), adjusted according to subsequent changes in population. The allocation to the German community is set separately.

Teaching profession

The structure of teacher education is similar in the three communities. (Secondary teachers for the German community are trained in French community institutions, as the German community has none of its own.) Teachers in preprimary, primary or lower secondary education require a specialist qualification for that sector from a higher teacher training institution (*Pedagogische Hogeschole/Institut d'Enseignement Supérieur Pédagogique/Pädagogische Hochschule*). Courses last three years, and combine general education (with subject specialisation for lower secondary teachers), pedagogical education and teaching practice.

Upper secondary teachers require degrees at Kandidaat/Candidat and Licenciaat/Licence levels, and must also complete a part-time teacher training course, either at the same time as their degree courses or afterwards.

After qualifying, a would-be teacher in the state system must serve a period of at least 240 days (though in practice it can be much longer, depending on the availability of appropriate posts) as a temporary teacher, followed by a probationary year and satisfactory reports from their head teacher and a school inspector, before being accorded the status of permanent teacher. In private schools, these procedures need not be followed. Inservice training is available at all levels, and is encouraged but not compulsory.

There are no heads of subject departments in Belgian schools, and so promotion prospects are limited. To be eligible to become a head teacher in the state system or an inspector, a teacher must be at least 35, have at least ten years' teaching experience, and pass a special examination.

Parent/school relationships

With some differences in regulations between the communities, each state-run or state-subsidised school has to have an advisory committee on which parents and other interested parties are represented. For community schools in the French community, and all state-run or subsidised schools in the Flemish, this is a participation council (*Participatieraad/Conseil de Participation*), on which parents are represented alongside teachers and other staff, pupils, unions and members of local authorities. Participation councils have a right to be consulted, and to receive relevant information, on a wide range of teaching and administrative matters.

Education inspectorate

School inspection operates differently in the Flemish and French communities. (At present, the French inspectorate also inspects German community schools, but a German inspectorate is being created.) In the Flemish community, inspectors operate in teams and inspect whole schools rather than individual teachers. In the French (and the German) community, their counterparts inspect the work of individual teachers, and offer support and advice. Inspectors in all three communities concentrate on the community-run schools. They do visit community-subsidised schools also, but there their functions are more limited, and concerned mainly with checking that basic legal requirements are being met.

ACRONYMS AND ABBREVIATIONS

AESI	Diplôme d'Agrégé de l'Enseignement Secondaire Inférieure (the lower secondary school teaching qualification in the French and German communities)
AESIS	Diplôme d'Agrégé de l'Enseignement Secondaire Supérieure (the upper secondary school teaching qualification in the French and German communities)
ASO	Algemeen Secundair Onderwijs (general secondary education in the Flemish community)
BSO	Beroepssecundair Onderwijs (vocational secondary education in the Flemish community)
CEB	Certificat d'Etudes de Base (the primary school certificate in the French community)
CESI	Certificat d'Enseignement Secondaire Inférieure (the lower secondary school certificate in the French community)
CESS	Certificat d'Enseignement Secondaire Supérieure (the upper secondary school certificate in the French community)
CQ	Certificat de Qualification (the technical or vocational secondary school certificate in the French community)
GON	Geïntegreerd Onderwijs (integrated education in the Flemish community)
KSO	Kunstsecundair Onderwijs (artistic secondary education in the Flemish community)
PMS	Psycho-Medisch-Sociale Centra/Centres Psycho-Médico-Sociaux/ Psycho-Medico-Sozial-Zentern (psychological, medical and social guidance centres)
TSO	Technisch Secundair Onderwijs (technical secondary education in the Flemish community)

ACKNOWLEDGEMENTS
We are very grateful to Dr Hilde van den Bulck of the Universities of Leuven and Leicester, and to Tony Anthoni of the Open University, for information and for comments on an earlier draft.

REFERENCES
Archer, E. G. and Peck, B. T. (no date) The Teaching Profession in Europe, Glasgow: Jordanhill College of Education.

CERI (1995) Education at a Glance: OECD indicators, Paris: Organisation for Economic Co-operation and Development.

Dens, A. and Hoedemakers, E. (1995) 'Belgium', in O'Hanlon, C. (ed.) Inclusive Education in Europe, London: David Fulton Publishers.

European Commission (1995) Structures of the Education and Initial Training Systems in the European Union, Luxembourg: Office for Official Publications of the European Commission.

Hunter, B. (ed.) (1995) The Statesman's Year Book, 1995–1996, London: Macmillan.

OECD (1992) From Higher Education to Employment Volume 1: Australia, Austria, Belgium, Germany, Paris: Organisation for Economic Co-operation and Development.

OECD (1995) OECD Economic Surveys: Belgium: 1994–1995, Paris: Organisation for Economic Co-operation and Development.

Verhoeven, T. and Beuselinck, I. (1995) Organisatie en Processen op School, Leuven: Department of Sociology, University of Leuven.

Verhoeven, T. and Beuselinck, I. (1996) Higher Education in Flanders, Leuven: Department of Sociology, University of Leuven.

BACKGROUND

Denmark and its counties

Denmark has been a united and independent monarchy since the 10th century. At various times, its kings have also ruled Sweden (until 1523), Norway (until 1814) and Iceland (until 1943). The Faroe Islands and Greenland remain overseas territories of Denmark, and send representatives to the Danish parliament, but have had home rule since 1948 and 1979 respectively. (In 1984, Greenland chose to leave the European Community.) Throughout the 19th century, Denmark was in conflict first with Prussia and later with united Germany over its southern territories of Holstein and Schleswig, whose populations were partly Danish, partly German speaking. Eventually these territories were lost by Denmark, but northern Schleswig was restored to Denmark after the First World War.

Denmark is a member of the Nordic Council (with Finland, Iceland, Norway and Sweden) and of the EU. A Danish referendum in 1992 initially refused to ratify the Maastricht Treaty for closer union within the EU, but this was reversed in a second referendum in 1993.

POPULATION

Population	5.2 million in 1994 (a rise of 0.2% per annum since 1984)
Land area	43,000 sq. km
Population density	121 per sq. km
Young people (5–24)	25.3% of population
Urban/rural balance	80%/20%

Unlike its Nordic neighbours, Denmark is small and densely populated.

ECONOMY

GDP	$147 billion (1994)
GDP per capita	$28,200 (1994)
In employment	73% of working age population (1991)
	– 83% of men/77% of women aged 25–54
	– 63% of young people (15–24)
Spending on education	7.8% of GDP

RELIGION

About 90% of the population belong to the national church, the *Folkekirke*, which is evangelical Lutheran and state-controlled.

LANGUAGE AND ETHNICITY

The great majority of the population are Danish speaking. The population of the Faroe Islands (about 45,000) are predominantly speakers of Faroese. There are some 30,000 German speakers in northern Schleswig, with German-speaking schools. (There is also a Danish-speaking minority of about 50,000 in southern Schleswig in Germany, with Danish-speaking schools.) Copenhagen has a small Greenlandic community.

GOVERNMENT

Denmark has three levels of government – *central, county* and *municipal*. Each has direct responsibility for a stage of education: the central government for further and higher education; the counties for upper secondary education; and the municipalities for primary and lower secondary education, that is for the years when it is compulsory.

The central government is ultimately responsible for all levels of education, approving or determining the subjects of the primary and secondary school curriculum and controlling examinations – though detailed curriculum planning and teaching methods, especially during the years of compulsory education, are increasingly left to local authorities and individual schools.

The 14 counties (and the municipality of Copenhagen) are responsible for upper secondary schools (*Gymnasia*) and for institutions teaching higher preparatory (*HF*) courses (see below). They control finance and the appointment and dismissal of staff, but the curriculum and examinations are regulated by the central government. In addition, the schools and other institutions have their own boards, with substantial powers.

The 277 municipalities are responsible for compulsory education, at primary and lower secondary level, in the *Folkeskole*. They appoint senior staff to these schools, and approve the curriculum and examinations. They are subject to less direction from central government than are the counties *vis-à-vis* the gymnasium, but there is still detailed specification from the centre as to what subjects must or may be taught, and when. In addition, the schools have their own school boards.

EDUCATION

Education is compulsory between the ages of seven and 16; children may be educated in the municipality run folkeskole, at a private school or at home. The great majority (88%) attend the folkeskole. Their schooling is free, and free transport is also available for children who live more than a certain distance from school.

About 50% of folkeskole leavers continue into vocational upper secondary schools, and 45% into academic upper secondary schools. Only 5% of each age cohort currently finish their education at the end of folkeskole. (Ministry of Education, 1996f)

About 30% of each cohort complete higher education and a further 40% complete vocational education. The remaining 25% begin courses of higher or vocational education but do not complete them. (OECD, 1996)

INSTITUTIONS
Preprimary education

Denmark has several different types of institution for children under seven.

- *Vuggestuer* (day nurseries) – for children aged 0 to 3

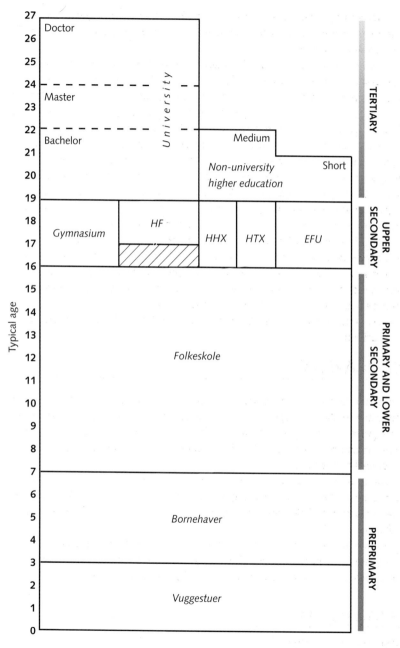

Note: This diagram is simplified for clarity, and should be used in conjunction with the text

Denmark's education system

- *Bornehaver* (kindergartens) – for children aged 3 to 7
- *Integrerede institutioner* (integrated institutions) – for children from preschool age up to 14
- *Bornehaveklasser* (preschool classes in the folkeskole) – for children aged 5 to 7

The first three do not provide formal teaching, but do offer educational activities designed to further the children's personal development. Preschool classes do provide some teaching, in three or four daily lessons, five days a week, to prepare children for school.

The first three are run by municipalities or private organisations, and regulated by the Ministry of Social Affairs. They are subsidised by the state, but parents must pay up to 35% of the costs, according to their income. Preschool classes are also run by municipalities or private organisations, but regulated by the Ministry of Education. Those run by municipalities are free.

Substantial numbers of children attend preprimary institutions, more as the children get older. Around 35% of children under three attend day nurseries, and around 90% of five- and six-year-olds attend preschool classes.

Primary and lower secondary education

State education in Denmark does not differentiate between primary and lower secondary stages, but combines them in the folkeskole, which is attended by 88% of seven- to 16-year-olds.

Almost all the remaining 12% of children aged between seven and 16 attend private schools. The percentage has risen in recent years (in 1985–6 it was 9%) but is now stable. The 415 private schools are very varied, and include denominational schools (Catholic and Protestant), schools based on a particular political or educational philosophy (such as Rudolf Steiner schools and Grundtvigian schools), German schools and schools for immigrants. They are not regarded as schools for a social or academic elite, and confer no status advantages on their pupils. Regardless of the motivation behind their establishment, all private schools are eligible for government recognition and funding, provided that they meet certain conditions: they must be non-profit making and of a minimum size, and their pupils must reach the same standard as those in the municipal schools. It is the responsibility of the parents and not (other than in exceptional circumstances) of the state to appoint an inspector to check that they do so. Private schools may, but need not, enter their pupils for the folkeskole final examination. State grants to private schools vary according to the size of the school, the age of the pupils and the seniority of the teachers, but on average, about 80% of their costs are paid by the state, and 20% by parents as school fees. (Ministry of Education, 1996b, 1996i)

Folkeskole

These schools are run by the municipalities, but within guidelines laid down by the central Ministry of Education concerning their overall educational aims. There are 1,680 of them, with 517,000 pupils and around 50,000 teachers, catering for children from the ages of seven to 16 or 17, in nine forms covering the years of compulsory education, plus an optional tenth form for which about 45% of pupils stay on. (1993–4 figures, Ministry of Education, 1996b)

The maximum class size permitted in the folkeskole is 28, and the average in practice is around 19. The pupil/teacher ratio is 10/1. The folkeskole aims to allow a class to have the same class teacher throughout its school career.

The folkeskole is comprehensive; all classes must cover the whole ability range. However, in English, German and mathematics, teachers are encouraged to differentiate their teaching according to the needs of individual pupils and groups within mixed-ability classes.

The Ministry of Education determines the subjects of the folkeskole curriculum (listed below) and sets attainment targets for them. In addition, it publishes curriculum guidelines for each individual subject. These guidelines are advisory, not mandatory, and schools need not follow them in detail, provided that they reach the targets set. Indeed, the choice of subject content and teaching method is legally required to be made jointly by the teacher and pupils. In practice, however, nearly all schools follow the Ministry's guidelines.

The folkeskole curriculum has three main categories: *compulsory subjects*, *compulsory topics* and *optional subjects*. Schools must offer all the compulsory subjects and topics, and in the first nine forms, pupils must study them all (apart from German/French). From the 8th Form, pupils must choose one from those optional subjects provided by their school. In the 10th Form, pupils choose among the topics compulsory for the school to offer. (Ministry of Education, 1996b) The compulsory subjects subjects in the first nine forms are as follows.

- Danish (all nine forms)
- Christian studies (all nine forms)
- mathematics (all nine forms)
- physical education and sport (all nine forms)
- science (1st to 6th Forms)
- music (1st to 6th Forms)
- art (1st to 5th Forms)
- history (3rd to 8th Forms)
- English (4th to 9th Forms)
- textile design (at least one of the 4th to 7th Forms)
- wood/metalwork (at least one of the 4th to 7th Forms)
- home economics (at least one of the 4th to 7th Forms)
- geography (7th to 8th Forms)
- biology (7th to 8th Forms)

- physics/chemistry (7th to 9th Forms)
- German or French (7th to 9th Forms – German is compulsory for schools to offer, but both German and French are optional for pupils)
- social studies (9th Form)

The compulsory topics cover education about sex, health, drugs, the family and traffic safety, together with educational and vocational guidance. Optional subjects cover the arts, technology, computing and languages.

There is no formal assessment in the first seven forms, but parents must be informed at least twice a year, in writing or more usually by word of mouth, of their children's progress, personal and social as well as academic. From the 8th Form, there must be twice-yearly written reports, and marks are given in the leaving examination subjects.

Pupils reaching the end of the 9th or 10th Form may choose, in consultation with their teachers and parents, to sit the leaving examination, in 11 subjects. About 95% of folkeskole leavers are awarded a leaving certificate; this is necessary but not sufficient for entry to the gymnasium.

Upper secondary education

The upper secondary stage is divided between *general* and *vocational* education and training. It is not compulsory. About 45% of those leaving the folkeskole enter general education and 50% vocational education; the remaining 5% do not continue their studies.

General education

There are two main types of general upper secondary education: *gymnasium* courses, intended for students proceeding directly from the folkeskole, and *Hojere Forberedelseseksamen* (HF) courses, intended mainly for young people and adults who have left the education system and want to return.

Gymnasium

There are about 150 gymnasia throughout Denmark, with around 74,000 students and 9,000 teachers. (1993–4 figures, European Commission) They are co-educational. Their students are normally aged 16–19, entering directly from the folkeskole. They provide a three-year academic course leading to the *studentereksamen*, the upper secondary school leaving examination, which qualifies its holders for entry to higher education.

Entry is selective. To qualify, students must have passed the folkeskole leaving examination, and must be judged *Qualified* or *Perhaps qualified* by the folkeskole they have left. 'Qualified' candidates are automatically admitted to a gymnasium – to the gymnasium of their choice if places are available. 'Perhaps qualified' candidates must sit an entry test set by the gymnasium. In practice, about 45% of pupils leaving the folkeskole go to a gymnasium, but the figure is higher for girls and lower for boys. Just under 60% of the students in the gymnasium are female, just over 40% male.

The gymnasia are almost all run by the counties, but within guidelines laid down by the central Ministry of Education concerning their aims and curricula. Only 6% of gymnasium students are in private schools, which (unlike those at primary/lower secondary level) must follow the same curriculum and enter students for the same examinations as the county schools. (Ministry of Education, 1996i) The county gymnasia do not charge tuition fees, transport is free, and textbooks are provided on loan. Private gymnasia charge tuition fees, but these are small.

The curriculum in the gymnasium is laid down by law. There are two 'lines' – a mathematics line and a language line. The mathematics line is taken by 65% of students (84% of the boys and 50% of the girls), and the language line by 35% (16% of the boys and 50% of the girls).

The Ministry of Education publishes curriculum regulations for each individual subject, and must approve all examination syllabuses. However, the exact details of how a subject is taught – e.g. which textbooks to use – are left for teachers and students to decide.

There is a compulsory core curriculum common to both the mathematics and the language lines. (European Commission, 1995; Ministry of Education, 1996f)

- Danish
- history
- physical education
- biology (first year)
- music (first year)
- geography (second year)
- art (third year)
- religious studies (third year)
- classical studies (third year)

Each line also has its own compulsory subjects. In the mathematics line, these are: mathematics, physics and chemistry, plus English and a second foreign language. In the language line, these are: English, German or French, Latin and a third foreign language, plus science.

In addition, students in their second and third years may choose from a range of optional subjects. There are detailed rules and restrictions as to how they may and may not be combined.

In the first year, all of students' time is spent on the compulsory subjects; in the second year, this falls to about 85%, and in the third year to about 50%.

During their gymnasium course, students are regularly advised about their progress by teachers; however, decisions about whether to proceed to the next year are made by the students and their parents, not the school. In addition, students take a formal set of examinations, the studentereksamen, partly at the end of the second year and partly at the end of the third. The studentereksamen consists of ten separate examinations – about half oral and half written, with the written papers nationally set and externally marked – plus a dissertation, which students are given a week to write. Students who succeed in the studentereksamen are qualified for entry to higher education.

Higher preparatory examination (HF) course
HF (*Hojere Forberedelseseksamen* – higher preparatory examination) courses are offered by some 145 establishments throughout Denmark. They are intended mainly for young people and adults who have left the education system and want to return, and in practice two-thirds of HF students have been away for more than a year. To be admitted to HF courses, students need to have attained a certain number of passes in the folkeskole leaving and advanced leaving examinations.

About 45% of the HF establishments are attached to gymnasia, and generally offer full-time two-year courses. The remaining 55% are mostly attached to adult education centres, and generally offer single-subject courses: adult students may take one subject at a time and spread their work on the complete HF course over a number of years. Like the studentereksamen of the gymnasium, the HF qualifies students for higher education, but in practice most HF students go on to short- or medium-term further education instead.

HF subjects are equivalent in level to those of the gymnasium. The HF course has a common core and a range of options, prescribed by the Ministry of Education, similar but not identical to that of the gymnasium. (See Ministry of Education, 1996f)

At the end of the two years of full-time study (or the part-time equivalent), there is an examination. Most students proceed to short or medium term further education courses, but the examination qualifies for entry to higher education too.

Vocational education and training

About half of those leaving the folkeskole participate in vocational education and training. It is of two main kinds: a more theoretical kind within the secondary school system (*Erhvervsgymnasiale Uddannelser* (EU), with about 117,000 students), and a more practical kind outside it (*Erhvervsfaglige Uddannelser* (EFU), with 51,000). (1992–3 figures, European Commission, 1995)

Within the secondary school system
Secondary school-based vocational education and training (EU) was restructured during the early 1990s. It is itself divided between two types, commercial and technical, in specialist commercial and technical schools. Their courses lead respectively to the HHX (*Hojere Handelseksamen* – higher

commercial examination) and the HTX (*Hojere Teknisk Eksamen* – higher technical examination). HHX and HTX schools are private, and usually run by boards consisting of local employers. Both courses last three years, normally for ages 16–19. Students may enter them immediately after folkeskole, or transfer from vocational training outside the school system (see below). They qualify students for employment, usually in the private sector, or for entry to higher education.

Both the HHX and the HTX courses have a core of obligatory subjects, plus optional subjects with detailed regulations as to how they may be combined. In both courses, students must study Danish, English, and German or French. HHX students must also study commercial subjects, including business economics, commercial law, information technology and sales. HTX students must take mathematics, physics, chemistry and biology, plus one of building, electrical, mechanical or process engineering. Students must pass in every subject: the form of assessment may be a written examination, an oral examination or a project. Both the HHX and the HTX diplomas are qualifications for admission to higher technical education. (Ministry of Education, 1996d)

Outside the secondary school system
A less theoretical and more practical kind of vocational training outside the secondary school system is the EFU. EFU courses last three or four years, and combine instruction by a training school with practical training (and paid employment) in a firm. They are run by the Ministry of Education in association with employers' organisations and trade unions. For admission, students must have completed their compulsory schooling, but need not have gained any leaving certificates. The first year of the course may be taken either in a training school or with a firm; about three-quarters of students choose the former. In the second and third years, all students combine both types of training. About five-sixths of students' study time is occupied by a centrally determined curriculum; the remaining sixth is for general education courses, offered at the discretion of individual schools and chosen by individual students.

At the end of their courses, students take an examination and/or a practical test. Those who succeed are given a certificate qualifying them as a skilled worker in their specialised field.

Special education

Of children of compulsory school age with serious handicaps, about 50% attend special schools (run by the counties), 25% attend separate classes in the folkeskole, and 25% attend mainstream classes in the folkeskole, with special educational assistance. There is a trend away from separate provision and towards integration.

Some education for handicapped young people is also provided in the *ungdomsskoler* (youth schools) (see below under Adult education).

Tertiary education

Tertiary education may be in universities or a variety of other, smaller colleges. All the universities and some of the colleges are owned and funded by the state. Other colleges are private foundations, but they too receive full state funding.

The Ministry of Education decides the numbers of students to be admitted to each course every year, taking into account the needs of the private business sector and likely job prospects. Traditionally, most graduates have taken jobs in the public sector, but the proportion has decreased in recent years (from 71% of all university graduates in 1981 to 54% in 1987). For most courses (medicine being an exception) the demands for places can be met.

Grants and loans may be provided for students to give support for living expenses. The amount depends on the students' financial circumstances (and those of their parents in the case of students under 18), and on whether they are living with their parents. In 1995, 86% of student support was in the form of grants, 18% in the form of loans. (Ministry of Education, 1996j)

Universities
Denmark has five universities that cover a wide range of disciplines. By far the oldest (founded in 1479) and largest (26,000 students) is the University of Copenhagen. The other four are 20th century foundations, with about 35,000 students altogether. In addition there are two specialist universities, the Technical University of Denmark (6,000 students) and the Royal Veterinary and Agricultural University (3,000).

About 80% of students applying for admission to university hold formal entry qualifications; the remainder must take an entrance examination. Those who are qualified form about 48% of their age cohort. They have obtained

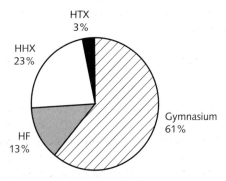

Denmark figure 1   Percentage of students qualified for higher education from different types of course, 1990 (OECD, 1992)

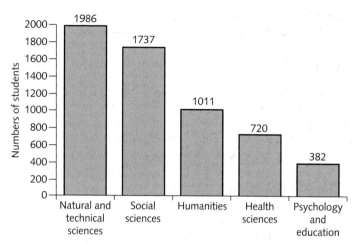

Denmark figure 2   Numbers of students taking university ('long cycle') courses in the main subject areas, 1988 (OECD, 1992)

their qualifications from different types of school or course: the percentages from the main types are shown in Figure 1.

Traditionally, Danish universities offered only long courses (five to six years), but from 1988 they have increasingly offered shorter 'bachelor' courses, lasting three years, and leading to the degrees of BA or BSc. The traditional 'master's degree' (cand. mag., cand. scient., cand. theol. etc.) still takes at least five years.

The number of graduates in the main fields of study in 1988 (that is, when only long courses were available) are shown in Figure 2.

Traditionally, female students have been concentrated in humanities, health sciences and education, with very few in sciences and engineering. This pattern still holds, but to a lesser extent than formerly. For example, the percentage of female students enrolled in technical sciences courses rose from 6% in 1980 to 23% in 1987. (OECD, 1992)

The universities have a high degree of autonomy, being governed by boards consisting of professors, other members of staff and students.

Other colleges

Denmark has about 150 colleges outside the university system, with some 60,000 students. The students are mostly on vocational courses, for occupations such as business administration, engineering, nursing and teaching.

Assessment in tertiary education is normally by examination, and usually requires an element of external examination. Just under two-thirds of students on degree courses or their equivalent gain their degrees – 13,000 students in 1988–9, 62% male, 38% female.

Adult education

Denmark has an extensive system of adult education, in a wide variety of institutions, of which the *folkehøjskoler* (folk high schools) are best known. About a million adults participate in adult education each year. They pay only a small part of the costs of their courses; most of them are paid by local or central government.

Folkehøjskoler

There are about 100 folkehøjskoler: free, residential schools for adults (over 17.5 years old), offering general academic, practical and creative subjects. They offer both short (from one to four weeks) or long (ten-month) courses. No qualifications are required for admission, and there are no examinations. The costs of courses are met by the central government, and participants with low incomes are eligible for grants from the central government or the municipality. Currently a high proportion of students on the long courses are unemployed young people.

For young adults (or older children aged 14 to 18), there are *ungdomsskoller* (youth schools), *efterskoler* (continuation schools) and *production schools*.

Ungdomsskoler

These schools, run by municipalities, offer varied forms of education and training, including preparation for exams, vocational education, special education for handicapped people and leisure activities. They are usually run as leisure-time courses and as a supplement to other forms of education and training. About 200,000 students participate in these.

Efterskoler

Approximately 200 in number, these are private foundations, with central and municipal financial support, which offer a year's boarding education, often emphasising creative and practical subjects and sport. About 15,000 students attend them each year.

Production schools

About 60 in number, these provide job training in the form of practical work and production. Again, they are private foundations, with central and municipal financial support.

In addition to these institutions, there are *continuing training courses* in which employed people may develop and update their skills. About half of the courses are privately run, by the employers themselves or by specialist training companies. The other half are state-run. Some 250,000 employees participate in these each year.

Since 1990, educational institutions under the Ministry of Education, both vocational schools and universities and higher education colleges, offer *open education*, that is part-time courses leading to qualifications, and single-subject courses studied part-time. Admission requirements are normally the same as for full-time courses. Approximately 90,000 people are estimated to participate in open education each year (equivalent to 21,000 full-time students) – 61% in vocational schools and 39% in higher education institutions in 1994. (Ministry of Education, 1996e)

Funding

Public expenditure on education amounts to about 6% of GNP, and 12% of all public expenditure. Of this, roughly half is on the preprimary, primary and lower secondary stages, just under a quarter is on the upper secondary stage and just over a quarter on tertiary education. (Ministry of Education)

Education at all levels is either funded or subsidised by the central government. Establishments run by the counties are fully funded, with funds directly allocated by the government. Establishments run by the municipalities are also fully funded, but not directly; 'block grants' for all purposes are allocated to the municipal authorities, and it is they who decide how to allocate these among schools and other functions for which they are responsible.

Higher education is funded directly by the central government: expenditure on teaching depends on student numbers, and other expenditure is assessed for each individual institution. Universities may also earn money by mounting special courses and offering consultancy services.

Teaching profession

Traditionally, teachers were classed as civil servants, but this is no longer so for teachers appointed after 1992.

Since 1992, teachers for all the types of preschool education follow the same three-and-a-half year course at a teacher training college, of which one-third is practical.

Training of teachers for the folkeskole takes place at 18 teacher training colleges of university level (*seminarier*) throughout Denmark. The colleges are controlled by the Ministry of Education, which sets standards for their qualifications by appointing external examiners. The course lasts four years, and leads to a teacher's certificate that is held by the Ministry to be equivalent in academic standard to a bachelor's degree in the UK or the United States. It follows a curriculum prescribed by the Ministry of Education.

Formally, the teacher's certificate qualifies a teacher to teach any subject at any level in the folkeskole, but in practice teachers at secondary level normally teach only their main subjects.

About two-thirds of the students at teacher training colleges are women, one-third men. About 75% of the students at teacher training colleges complete the course (though only 65% of students do so in the officially stipulated time of study).

Gymnasia and HF teachers are subject specialists – usually in two subjects. They must have a university master's degree in their subject or subjects, and their teacher training is then mostly 'on the job' during their first year of employment.

Teachers of vocational education must first be skilled practitioners of the relevant occupation. Their teacher training then has two elements: attendance for a year at the national college for vocational teacher training (SEL – *Statens Erhvervspaedagogiske Laereruddannelse*); and 'on the job' training at a school, under the guidance of a tutor, to be completed within two years.

Inservice training is available for teachers at all levels, and since 1993 has been compulsory for teachers in the folkeskole.

Parent/school relationships

Legislation of the early 1990s has increased the influence of parents on their children's schools. Every folkeskole, gymnasium and HF course – public or private – must have a board, on which parents are strongly represented alongside staff and pupils. The board determines the institution's policies (within the framework laid down by national and local government), controls its budget and supervises its activities. Every preschool institution must have a parents' committee, which covers a similar range of issues but in an advisory capacity.

Education inspectorate

Denmark has no national inspectorate; supervision of schools is the responsibility of the relevant local authority and of each school's own board. There are, however, nationally appointed *advisers* for each subject of the school curriculum – usually one for every county.

ACRONYMS AND ABBREVIATIONS

EFU   Erhvervsfaglige Uddannelser (three- or four-year course of basic vocational training outside the school system)

EIFU   Erhvervsintroducerende Kurser for Unge (short – 12 to 14 weeks – introductory vocational courses for young people)

EGU   Erhvervsgrunduddannelser (two-year individually tailored training courses, run by municipalities, and almost entirely practical)

EU	Erhvervsgymnasiale Uddannelser (vocational education and training within the secondary school system, consisting of HHX and HTX courses)
HF	Hojere Forberedelseseksamen (higher preparatory examination)
HHX	Hojere Handelseksamen (higher commercial examination)
HTX	Hojere Teknisk Eksamen (higher technical examination)
SEL	Statens Erhvervspaedagogiske Laereruddannelse (State Institute for the Training of Vocational Teachers)

ACKNOWLEDGEMENT
We are grateful to the Danish Ministry of Education for supplying us with extensive information about education in Denmark.

REFERENCES
Baunsbak-Jensen, A. (no date) *Fact Sheet/Denmark: Danes flock to adult-education classes*, Copenhagen: Ministry of Foreign Affairs Cultural Relations Department.

European Commission (1995) *Structures of the Education and Initial Training Systems in the European Union*, Luxembourg: Office for Official Publications of the European Commission.

Hogsbro, K., Jochumsen, H. and Ravn, B. (1991) *Beyond Limits: development of the school as a local cultural centre in Denmark*, Copenhagen: Danish Research and Development Centre for Adult Education.

Ministry of Education (1992) *Education in Denmark: a brief outline*, Copenhagen: Ministry of Education International Relations Division.

Ministry of Education (1994) *Education and Training for all Young People*, Copenhagen: Ministry of Education.

Ministry of Education (1996a) *The Training of Teachers for the Danish Folkeskole (Factsheet No. 1)*, Copenhagen: Ministry of Education.

Ministry of Education (1996b) *The Folkeskole (Factsheet No. 2)*, Copenhagen: Ministry of Education.

Ministry of Education (1996c) *Vocational Education and Training (Factsheet No. 3)*, Copenhagen: Ministry of Education.

Ministry of Education (1996d) *Vocational Upper Secondary Education (Factsheet No. 4)*, Copenhagen: Ministry of Education.

Ministry of Education (1996e) *Open Education (Vocationally Oriented Adult Education) (Factsheet No. 5)*, Copenhagen: Ministry of Education.

Ministry of Education (1996f) *General Upper Secondary Education (Factsheet No. 6)*, Copenhagen: Ministry of Education.

Ministry of Education (1996g) *Higher Education (Factsheet No. 7)*, Copenhagen: Ministry of Education.

Ministry of Education (1996h) *The Basic Social and Health Training Programmes (Factsheet No. 8)*, Copenhagen: Ministry of Education.

Ministry of Education (1996i) *Private Schools in Denmark (Factsheet No. 9)*, Copenhagen: Ministry of Education.

Ministry of Education (1996j) *The State Education Grant and Loan Scheme (Factsheet No. 10)*, Copenhagen: Ministry of Education.

Ministry of Education (no date) *Educational Statistics*, Copenhagen: Ministry of Education.

OECD (1992) *From Higher Education to Employment Volume 2: Canada, Denmark, Spain, United States*, Paris: Organisation for Economic Co-operation and Development.

OECD (1996) *OECD Economic Surveys: Denmark: 1995–1996*, Paris: Organisation for Economic Co-operation and Development.

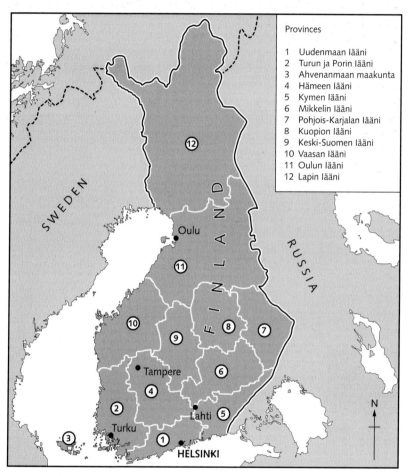

Provinces

1 Uudenmaan lääni
2 Turun ja Porin lääni
3 Ahvenanmaan maakunta
4 Hämeen lääni
5 Kymen lääni
6 Mikkelin lääni
7 Pohjois-Karjalan lääni
8 Kuopion lääni
9 Keski-Suomen lääni
10 Vaasan lääni
11 Oulun lääni
12 Lapin lääni

Finland and its provinces

Finland belonged to the Kingdom of Sweden from the 12th century until the 18th and early 19th centuries, when it was ceded piecemeal to Russia. It gained its independence after the Russian Revolution of 1917. After the Second World War, when it had fought first alongside Germany against the Soviet Union, and later with the Soviet Union against Germany, it was forced to yield Petsamo and Eastern Karelia to the Soviet Union. Thereby it lost 12% of its land area, and 10% of its population were displaced to other parts of Finland.

Finland is a member of the Nordic Council (with Denmark, Iceland, Norway and Sweden). It joined the EU in 1995.

POPULATION

Population	5.1 million in 1994 (up 0.4% per annum from 1984)
Land area	338,000 sq. km (of which nearly 10% are lakes)
Population density	15 per sq. km (of land area)
Urban/rural balance of population	62%/38% (1992)

Like its Nordic neighbours, Finland is large but sparsely populated, with its population concentrated in the south of the country.

ECONOMY

GDP	$97 billion (1994)
GDP per capita	$19,100
In employment	66% of working age population in 1991
	– 85% of men/81% of women aged 25–54
	46% of young people (15–24)
Part-time employment	7.2% of employees
Spending on education	7.3% of GDP (1992)

RELIGION

About 87% of the population belong to the state church, the Lutheran National Church. One per cent belong to the Eastern Orthodox Church, and 10% do not belong to any religious association. (The total number of Jews, Muslims, Roman Catholics and members of other Christian denominations combined amounts to less than 1% of the population.)

LANGUAGE AND ETHNICITY

Finnish and Swedish are both official languages, but Finnish is the language of over 93% of the population, and Swedish of only 6%. All Swedish-speaking children or adults can attend institutions of education where Swedish is the language of instruction. Just under 6% of Finnish pupils do so.

In addition, Saame is the main language of about 2,000 people in Lapland.

GOVERNMENT

Finland has three levels of government – *national, provincial* and *municipal* (or *communal*). Traditionally, the government of education and other matters was highly centralised, but in recent years the national government has gradually been handing over more and more power to the provincial and municipal governments. There is a national Ministry of Education, but it is concerned only with general policy. Detailed policy on schools and vocational education, including the curriculum and evaluation, is devised by a National Board of Education, which includes educational professionals and representatives of employers, trade unions and local authorities.

The educational (and other) responsibilities of the 12 provinces are now few, and those that remain are being transferred to regional councils, consisting of representatives of the municipalities.

There are some 440 municipalities, about four-fifths rural and one-fifth urban. They are the basic unit of local government, and have responsibility for a wide and increasing range of services and activities, including education. They levy their own taxes, independently of national taxes. The municipalities have usually received from the national government between a third and half of the establishment costs, and between half and nine-tenths of the operating costs of their educational institutions (depending on the economic potential of the municipalities in question). Most of the rest has been paid for by the municipalities. However the situation is changing rapidly.

EDUCATION

Education is compulsory between the ages of seven and 16 – except for those children whose parents choose to educate them at home – and children attend the *peruskoulu* (comprehensive school) throughout that period. Education after 16 is divided between general education, in the *lukio* (senior secondary school) and university; and vocational education, in the *ammattioppilaitos* (vocational and professional education institution). About 78% of the population in the early 1990s stayed on in education until the age of 18. Traditionally, the lukio and the ammattioppilaitos have been separate and distinct, but government policy aims to bring about closer co-operation between them, so as to offer young people leaving the peruskoulu a wider range of choice, including the chance to combine courses from both types of institution.

Tertiary education is also divided between general education, at university, and vocational education, recently re-organised in a new type of institution, the *ammattikorkeakoulu* (polytechnic).

Public education is free. In addition, pupils in the peruskoulu are entitled to free daily meals and to free transport if they live far away from the nearest school. This does not apply after the compulsory stage, but pupils in the lukio, ammattioppilaitos and university may also receive financial provision from the state.

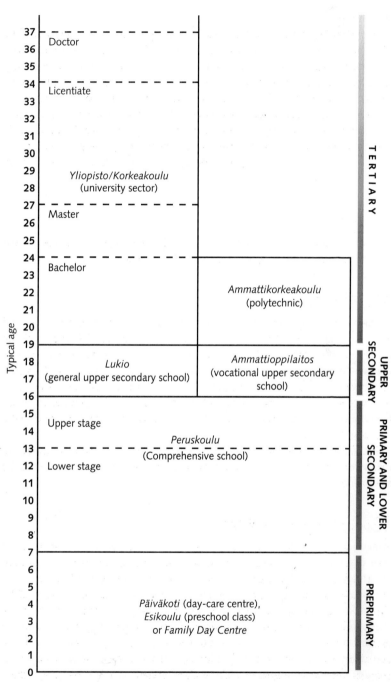

Private sector
Private institutions cater for 6% of students in upper secondary education, 7% of children in preprimary education and 10% of students in vocational and professional education, but for fewer than 1% of pupils in the compulsory years, and no university students. Education provided by private educational foundations is financed by the government on the same basis as education provided by the municipalities (see above). These private foundations are often concerned with providing education through foreign languages – for example Russian or French. Private education does not normally enjoy a higher social status. The schools with highest prestige are state schools with a good academic reputation.

INSTITUTIONS
Finland has about 5,700 schools in all, with 850,000 pupils and students, and 69,000 teachers. (1992–3 figures, European Commission, 1995)

Preprimary education

Finland has no system of preprimary schools, but preprimary care and education are provided for some 180,000 children, about 40% of all children under seven. Of these, 60% attend a day-care centre (*päiväkoti*), and the rest are cared for in private homes by trained childminders. About 80% altogether attend full-time (up to ten hours per day), the remainder part-time (five hours or less). A much smaller number of children (2% of the population under seven) attend a preschool class (*esikoulu*) in a peruskoulu that has obtained a special licence.

Preschool curriculum guidelines are issued by the National Board of Education. Preschool teachers are trained in three-year courses (at university since 1995).

Primary and lower secondary education

Since the early 1970s, one type of school, the peruskoulu (comprehensive school), covers the ten years of compulsory education, normally from seven to 16. There is no legal division between primary and lower secondary education, but in practice, the peruskoulu is divided into two stages around the age of 13, the lower comprising Grades 1–6 and the upper Grades 7–9. (In some municipalities lower-stage and upper-stage schools are organised as separate establishments. In others, the peruskoulu – or its upper stage – may be combined with upper secondary education.) At the lower stage, all or most subjects are usually taught by a single class teacher; at the upper stage, there are usually specialist-subject teachers.

Peruskoulu

There are 4,700 comprehensive schools in Finland, with 590,000 pupils and 44,000 teachers – about 60% of whom are women (1992 figures). The schools are spread evenly throughout the country, with every municipality having at least one. Because Finland's population is small (in relation to its area) and unevenly distributed, they vary greatly in size. In 1990, the smallest peruskoulu had two pupils, and the largest 1,004; the average size was 120 pupils. (Statistics Finland, 1993; European Commission, 1995)

Guidelines concerning the subjects to be taught in the peruskoulu, and the time to be allocated to them, are laid down by the National Board of Education, but since the mid-1980s, the municipalities have some autonomy in implementing them. The guidelines for the lower stage (7–13-year-olds) are shown in Figure 1. Those for the upper stage (14–16-year-olds) are similar, but some extra subjects are added (such as biology and geography), and students may spend up to a fifth of their time on elective subjects.

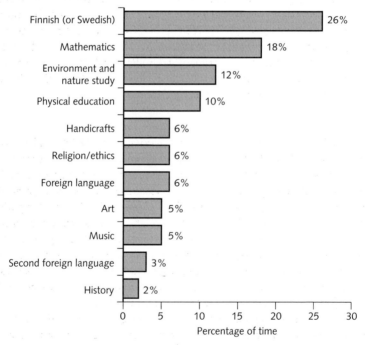

Finland figure 1   *Percentage of time laid down by national guidelines for peruskoulu subjects, Grades 1–6 (European Commission, 1995)*
Notes: (i) This figure shows the distribution of the stipulated minimum teaching hours among the subjects; (ii) Finnish is studied as the mother tongue by 94% of pupils. Swedish is studied by 6%, almost all in Swedish-medium schools; (iii) English is chosen as the foreign language by 92% of pupils

At the end of compulsory education, pupils obtain a leaving certificate showing their level of attainment. There is no formal examination; grades are given by teachers on the basis of tests and class work. Those leaving the peruskoulu may apply for admission to any upper secondary school. How easy it is to gain entry to the institution of their choice varies according to the institution and according to where they live: entry to popular institutions in populous parts of the country may be difficult.

As well as the nine compulsory classes of the peruskoulu, there is a voluntary tenth class, where pupils can continue their education (and improve their chances of entry to a lukio).

Upper secondary education

The upper secondary stage is divided between general education, in the lukio (senior secondary school), and vocational education, in the ammattioppilaitos (vocational and professional education institution). A number of experimental projects are under way or planned for the remaining years of the 20th century, with the aim of bridging the gulf between general and vocational education, and enabling students to combine courses from both sectors and obtain appropriate qualifications. Currently, about 94% of those leaving the peruskoulu continue their education, 54% in a lukio, 40% in an ammattioppilaitos. (European Commission, 1995)

Lukio
There are just over 460 senior secondary schools, with 99,000 students and 6,400 teachers – 60% of whom are women. (1992–3 figures) The schools are spread evenly throughout the country, with every second municipality having at least one. The average size in 1990 was 190 students. This is a three-year stage, normally covering the age-range 16–19 (Classes 10–12), after the period of compulsory education. Entry is selective, but not based on a formal examination. Teachers' judgements play an important part, both by teachers in the peruskoulu of the students' career there, and by teachers in the lukio of the students' ability and promise. A higher percentage of girls than of boys attend the lukio (in 1990, 57% of the females and 39% of the males aged 16, 17 and 18). (Statistics Finland, 1993; European Commission, 1995)

Guidelines concerning the subjects to be taught in the lukio, and the minimum time to be allocated to them, are laid down by the National Board of Education, but the municipalities and individual schools have some autonomy in implementing them. About two-thirds of study time is to be devoted to compulsory subjects; the remaining third is divided (at the student's discretion) between more advanced work in some of the compulsory subjects and a range of 'applied studies'. The guidelines' division of time among the compulsory subjects is shown in Figure 2.

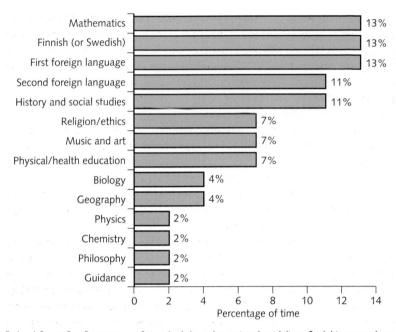

Finland figure 2   Percentage of time laid down by national guidelines for lukio compulsory subjects (European Commission, 1995)
Note: *There are two options for the compulsory mathematics course, of which the less extensive is shown here. The more advanced occupies almost twice as much time, but the extra time is taken from the optional subjects, not the other compulsory subjects*

Since 1994, schools may abandon the traditional division of pupils into age-cohorts ('forms' or 'year-groups'). Instead, individual students may take their courses in any combination and order permitted by the school, provided that they meet the minima specified in the national guidelines.

Schooling at the lukio concludes with a matriculation examination, set nationally, which provides the students' qualification for entry to higher education. Almost all lukio leavers pass this examination, and failure is generally regarded as a catastrophe. However, students who fail can retake the examination. Of those who matriculate, about one-third go to university, and two-thirds to some form of vocational training. (European Commission, 1995)

Ammattioppilaitos
Until the 1990s, the ammattioppilaitos (vocational school) spanned the upper secondary and tertiary stages of education. In the early 1990s, however, vocational education was re-organised, first on an experimental basis, then from 1995 on a national basis. The ammattioppilaitos is now confined to the

upper secondary level, with a new network of ammattikorkeakoulu (polytechnics) being established alongside the university sector and taking over most of the vocational and professional education at tertiary level (see below). During the rest of the 20th century there are to be further experimental projects, aimed at devising ways of bridging the gulf between vocational and general education, and enabling students to take courses and obtain qualifications representing both sectors.

Vocational schools often specialise in one occupational area, such as industry, commerce, maritime studies, agriculture, forestry, catering, health and social work.

Courses typically last two or three years, after which students can obtain an ammattioppilaitos leaving certificate. As well as allowing leavers to practise their occupation at an appropriate level, this certificate qualifies them for tertiary education in the same field of study in a polytechnic.

About 40% of those leaving peruskoulu enter ammattioppilaitos. Entrance was most difficult for health, social work and forestry; and easiest for the clothing, metalworking and mechanical engineering industries. A higher percentage of boys than of girls attend the ammattioppilaitos (in 1990, 40% of the males and 25% of the females aged 16, 17 and 18), though there are differences between the sexes in their choice of fields of study: male students predominate in engineering, and in industrial, agricultural, forestry and fisheries courses; female students predominate in health and commercial courses. (Statistics Finland, 1993)

Apprenticeship

Finland has an apprenticeship scheme, but it is very small, with apprentices numbering under 4% of the numbers of students in the ammattioppilaitos. Apprenticeships last from one to four years, and the apprentices' time is divided between on-the-job training with an employer and vocational education in a school or college. On-the-job training occupies most of the time, sometimes as much as 90%.

Special education

Finland has special schools only in certain areas of the country. Special classes, with specialist teachers, are usually provided in the peruskoulu for those who cannot cope with ordinary instruction.

Tertiary and postgraduate education

University
Finland has 22 institutions of university status. Ten are multi-faculty universities (yliopisto), and 12 are specialist establishments (korkeakoulu) as follows:

- four technical universities
- three schools of economics and business administration
- three academies of the arts (fine art, music and theatre)
- one veterinary college
- one National Defence College

All of them offer undergraduate and postgraduate teaching up to doctoral level. All are required to conduct research.

The institutions set their own entrance numbers and criteria, though within government guidelines. To qualify for admission, students must normally have matriculated from a lukio. But matriculation does not guarantee a university place, as limits are set on the number of students in every subject, and there are usually departmental entrance examinations. Overall, about one-third of applicants are successful, but success varies greatly from subject to subject: for example, from about 4% for applicants to study theatre to over 50% for dentistry and theology.

The degree system in Finnish universities was reformed in the 1980s, with the abolition for many subjects of the 'candidate' (or 'bachelor') degree as it existed and still exists in many other countries. In many cases, first degrees are now the equivalent of 'master' level elsewhere, and take around five to six years' full-time study. The median age of 1989 graduates was 27. However, bachelor-level degrees could always be taken in some subjects, and in the mid-1990s are being re-introduced in almost all others.

Postgraduate degrees are at present awarded at 'licentiate' and 'doctor' level, but the licentiate is likely to disappear. The median age of those taking licentiate degrees in 1989 was 34, and of those taking doctorates 37.

In the early 1990s, about 10,000 degrees were awarded annually, 90% master, 10% licentiate or doctoral. Overall, about 55% of degrees were awarded to women, but the percentage of women varies greatly from level to level, and subject to subject. Women were awarded about 35% of the postgraduate degrees. The numbers of graduates in the main fields of study, with percentages of male graduates, are illustrated in Figure 3.

All universities are owned and funded by the state. For their students, there are usually no tuition fees (only a nominal fee payable to student unions). Students are also eligible for financial assistance from the state, and around 60% receive such assistance. In the past, students normally depended on loans, but this is becoming less common.

Some 70% of students complete their degree. It is relatively easy for students to remain in the system after examination failure: this is part of the explanation of the great length of undergraduate studies. Another factor is relatively high unemployment among graduates, leading many students to postpone leaving university, and to use the extra time there in acquiring credits over and above those required for their degrees, in the hope of strengthening their position in the labour market. (OECD, 1996)

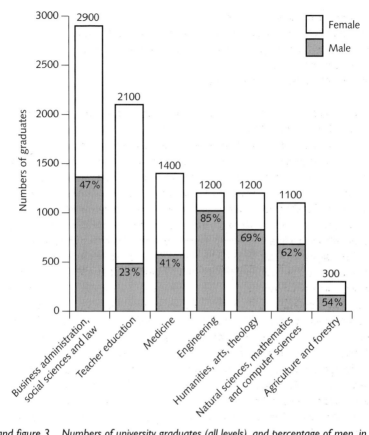

*Finland figure 3   Numbers of university graduates (all levels), and percentage of men, in
the principal subjects, 1989 (Statistics Finland, 1993)*

Polytechnic
As mentioned above, tertiary vocational education is being re-organised, with a
new system of ammattikorkeakoulu (polytechnics) being created alongside the
university system. By 1992–3, 22 experimental polytechnics had been
established, based on 85 existing institutions, and distributed throughout
Finland. Of these, 12 are maintained by local authorities, eight by central
government, and two are privately owned. They vary in size from 50 to 700
students, with an average size of 300. The experiment is intended to produce
models for permanent polytechnics, with new programmes leading to higher
vocational qualifications that will be comparable in standard to academic
degrees at university, but more practically and professionally oriented.
(Ministry of Education, 1993)

To qualify for entry, applicants must either have passed their matriculation
examinations (which qualify them to study any subject at a polytechnic) or hold

a leaving certificate from the ammattioppilaitos (which qualifies them only for entry to the same field of study).

During the experimental phase, around 7,000 students are being admitted to polytechnics each year. The 48 training programmes currently concentrate on commerce, tourism and catering, and technology. Individual polytechnics are responsible for developing their own syllabuses, but these must be approved by the Ministry of Education. Practical training in the workplace is compulsory in all programmes, and will typically occupy about 10% of students' time.

Adult education

Finland has an extensive system of adult education. In 1990, 44% of the adult population (41% of the men and 47% of the women) participated in adult education of some kind. For more than two-thirds of them, this was in order to advance their career. Adult education may take place within or outside the formal education system: in 1990, one-third of participants in adult education took courses within formal education, and two-thirds outside.

Within the formal education system
In school and the ammattioppilaitos, in many cases, and in all universities, there are courses for adults alongside those for younger pupils and students, adapting their teaching as appropriate, for example by offering evening courses, or 'summer university' courses.

In addition, there are institutions specialising in liberal adult education, the adult education centre, the kansanopisto (folk high school) and the study circle centre.

Adult education centre – These offer courses in arts and crafts, and general and practical subjects. They also arrange courses for adults in schools, etc. There are 278 such centres, 90% owned by local authorities, 10% private, with 600,000 students. (1989 figures)

Kansanopisto – These are mostly for boarders, and concentrate on culture, leisure and topical matters. There are 93 such schools, with about 6,000 students on their basic courses (plus over 60,000 on occasional courses). (1989 figures)

Study circle centre – These are maintained by various educational organisations for study groups, courses and lectures. About 350,000 people took part in study groups or courses in 1989.

The costs of liberal adult education are borne in part by the state (50–80%), local government and students' fees. The costs of vocational education are shared by the state, local government and, where appropriate, employers. Full-time adult students may be entitled to substantial financial assistance.

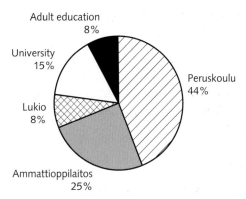

Finland figure 4   Public expenditure on education, 1989 (Statistics Finland, 1991)

Outside the formal education system
Many adult education courses outside the formal education system are run by employers or trade unions, not necessarily as inservice training. In 1989, over 900,000 employees (44% of all employees) attended such a course, for an average of six days. The more highly educated an employee already was, the more adult education he or she received.

Funding

About 90% of the costs of education are met by government – three-quarters of this from local and one quarter from national government. The allocation of funds to different sectors of education is illustrated in Figure 4.

About 60% of this expenditure is accounted for by wages and salaries.

Teaching profession

Finland has a total of some 69,000 teachers – just over half of all employees in the education system. During the 1980s, the numbers of teachers increased by 15%, while the numbers of pupils and students increased by 2.5%. Overall, 56% of teachers are women, but the percentage varies from sector to sector: about 60% of teachers in the peruskoulu and lukio are women, as are half of those in the ammattioppilaitas and a third of those in university.

Parent/school relationships

In the past, most schools had boards of their own, composed of parents and teachers; this is now rare. (Every municipality has a school board, whose members are party-political appointees.) But the number of parent associations has risen rapidly in the past few years, as has the number of 'home–school associations', voluntary organisations which involve parents in the work of the schools and also in such out-of-school activities as school trips and visits.

Education inspectorate

There are now few school inspectors; schools are now supervised by the municipal boards. As in other matters, this represents a move away from the centralised system of the past, and towards giving more responsibility to schools themselves.

ACKNOWLEDGEMENTS

We are very grateful to Ms Pirkko Hautamäki of the Finnish Institute, London, and to Dr Robert Bell of the Open University, for information and for comments on an earlier draft of this chapter.

REFERENCES

Centre for International Mobility (no date) *Study in Finland: international programmes in Finnish higher education 1993–1994*, Helsinki: Centre for International Mobility.

European Commission (1995) *Structures of the Education and Initial Training Systems in the European Union*, Luxembourg: Office for Official publications of the European Commission.

Herranen, M. (ed.) (1993) *An Introduction to Higher Education in Finland*, Helsinki: Centre for International Mobility.

Ministry of Education (1993) *Finnish Polytechnics: an experimental reform*, Helsinki: Ministry of Education Division of Educational and Research Policy.

OECD (1996) *OECD Economic Surveys: 1995–1996: Finland*, Paris: Organisation for Economic Co-operation and Development (especially Chapter IV 'Education and training').

Statistics Finland (1991) *Education in Finland 1991*, Helsinki: Statistics Finland.

Statistics Finland (1993) *Statistical Yearbook of Finland 1993*, Helsinki: Statistics Finland.

BACKGROUND

France and its mainland académies

The emergence of France (and of Germany) as a separate state began in 843, when the grandsons of Charlemagne divided between themselves the empire he had created – Charles taking those lands where Romance languages were spoken, and Louis those where Teutonic languages predominated. However, the authority of the monarchy over France as a whole was securely established only in the 17th century. In 1789, the monarchy was swept away by the revolution, and a republic established – itself soon swept away by Napoleon. After his final defeat in 1815, France underwent decades of constitutional upheaval before being finally established as a republic in 1870.

POLULATION
•••••••••••••••

Population	58.0 million in 1994 (a rise of 0.5% per annum since 1984)
Land area	544,000 sq. km
Population density	105 per sq. km
Young people (5–24)	28% of population in 1992

In area, France is the largest country in Western Europe. In population, only Germany is significantly larger (with 81.4 million). The UK (58.4 million) and Italy (57.2 million) are very similar in population to France.

ECONOMY
•••••••••••

GDP	$1,300 billion (1994)
GDP per capita	$23,000 (1994)
In employment	60% of working age population (1991)
	– 90% of men and 66% of women aged 25–54
	31% of young people (15–24)
Part-time employment	12.7% of employees (1992)

RELIGION
•••••••••

France has no official religion, but the majority of the population (42 million) are members of the Roman Catholic Church. In addition, there are just under two million Muslims and just under one million Protestants.

LANGUAGE
•••••••••

The official language, and the language of the vast majority, is French. However several regional and border-area languages are also spoken and sometimes offered as options in schools. These include Breton, Corsican, Castilian (Spanish), Basque, Catalan, Flemish and German.

GOVERNMENT
••••••••••••

France has four significant levels of government. As well as the national government, there are 22 *régions*, 96 *départements*, and some 36,000 *communes*. The control of education in France has traditionally been centralised, though from the early 1980s, significant powers have increasingly been transferred from the national government to the lower levels. Roughly speaking, the régions have responsibilities for upper secondary education and vocational training, the départements for lower secondary education, and the communes for primary and preprimary education.

Overall responsibility for education and training lies mainly with three national ministries, the Ministry for National Education (responsible for schools), the Ministry for Higher Education and Research and the Ministry of Labour, Employment and Vocational Training. In addition, some other ministries have more specialised responsibilities (such as the Ministry of Agriculture and Fisheries for agricultural education and training, and the Ministry of Defence for military academies). The national government decides educational policy, defines curricula, assessment and qualifications, and lays down rules for the management of educational establishments. It determines the qualifications and training of teachers, and supervises their appointment and professional conduct.

The implementation of educational policy is shared between the national government and the three levels of local government. To represent the national government at local level, the country is divided into 27 administrative districts (*académies*), each covering several (usually four or five) départements. Each académie is headed by a *recteur*, appointed by and representing the Minister, who is assisted by an inspectorate and advisory councils. The recteur is represented at the département level by an académie inspector, who has responsibilities for administration, finance, examinations and teachers. The reforms of 1982 gave the recteurs more autonomy from the Ministry; but the Ministry retains control of the curriculum, qualifications, the recruitment and training of teachers and general educational aims, so as to maintain quality and consistency throughout the country.

The 22 régions date from the 1960s. They each have an elected council, with responsibility for a range of services. These include constructing, maintaining and paying the running costs of upper secondary schools (apart from staff salaries, which are paid by the national government), and the provision of certain types of vocational training.

The 96 départements date from the 1789 Revolution. They each have a locally elected council, but they are also administrative units of the national government. The départements are responsible for constructing, maintaining and paying the running costs of lower secondary schools (apart from staff salaries, which are paid by the national government), and the provision of school transport.

The 36,000 communes are responsible for establishing and running preprimary and primary education, though the appointment (and payment) of teachers is a national government responsibility, and requires the approval of its representatives.

EDUCATION

Education in France is founded on the ideals of the 1789 Revolution, which were incorporated into the educational reforms of 1881 and 1882. This

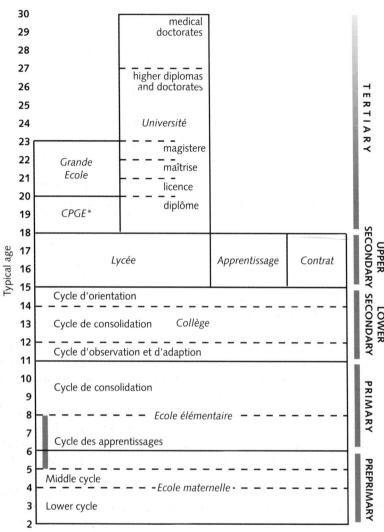

* Although CPGE (classes préparatoires aux Grandes Ecoles) are officially classified as tertiary education, they are usually housed in Lycées

Note: This diagram is highly simplified for clarity, and should be used in conjunction with the text

France's education system

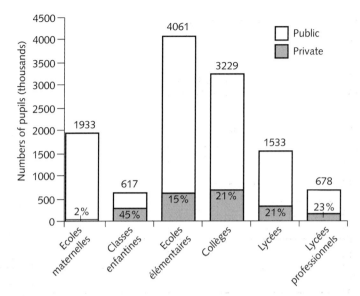

France figure 1   Numbers of pupils in different types of school, with percentage in
private schools, 1992–3 (European Commission, 1995)

legislation, introduced by Jules Ferry, made schooling compulsory and affirmed
the principle of secularity. Compulsory education is now from six to 16, but
almost all French four- and five-year-olds attend schools, as do an increasing
number of two- and three-year-olds.

The French state does not have a monopoly of schooling; about one-sixth of
France's 11.6 million children attend one of 10,000 private schools (though the
figure is much higher in a few regions). There is considerable variation
between stages and types of education in the proportions of public and private
schooling, as Figure 1 illustrates.

The private sector has declined in size since the 1960s. In general, private
schools are socially selective in practice, especially during the compulsory years
of schooling, though there are many exceptions. Overall, private schools do
not achieve examination results as high as those of state schools, though again
there are many exceptions. (Teese, 1989)

Both state and private educational establishments are subject to national
legislation, and to the decrees and regulations of the Ministry of National
Education and its agencies. The obligatory national curriculum applies to both
the state and the private sectors. Private schools may add religious studies to
the curriculum, whereas they are technically banned in state schools.

The private institutions are sponsored mainly by Catholic religious orders
and bodies, but also by other professional organisations and individuals. In
most cases, they receive financial support from the state.

The Framework Education Act of 1989, rather than reform the structure, initiated a continuous and gradual modernisation of the system. It identified the educational stages (*cycles pédagogiques*) of children's schooling and introduced the setting of educational targets for each stage (and no longer for each school year). The aim was to enhance educational continuity and to improve the matching of the teaching to each individual pupil's development. The expectation is that teaching flexibility will increase and fewer French children will 'redouble' or repeat a year.

In addition, the 1989 Act requires the state to provide nursery places for three-year-olds on request, and for two-year-olds in 'underprivileged' areas.

INSTITUTIONS

Preprimary education

Preprimary education (*enseignement préélémentaire*) is optional for two- to five-year-olds, but virtually all French three-, four- and five-year-olds take part, as well as 35% of two-year-olds. There are two main types of preprimary education – nursery schools (*écoles maternelles*) with 1.9 million pupils, almost all of them in state establishments; and infant classes in primary schools (*classes enfantines*), with 617,000 pupils, just over half in state establishments. They are taught by some 91,000 teachers – a pupil/teacher ratio of just over 27/1, in both the state and the private sector. (1992–3 figures, European Commission) State schools are free; private schools charge fees of varying amounts. The state schools are run by the communes – in areas of low population, several communes often combine to provide one – but under the direction of the Ministry of National Education, which sets out the general aims, defines the curriculum, covers the costs of the salaries of the staff and is responsible for teacher training.

Teaching is divided into three cycles ('lower', 'middle' and 'upper') – basically according to the children's age, but with flexibility to cater for different rates of development. The teaching is intended to prepare children for primary school; like primary schools, preprimary schools have a 26-hour teaching week. Children whose progress is judged inadequate by their teachers may be kept longer in preprimary education instead of proceeding at the age of six to primary school.

Primary education

Primary education (*enseignement élémentaire*) is compulsory, free and comprehensive for 6–11-year-olds. About 4.1 million children attend in all – 85% in publicly run and 15% in private schools. The state schools have about 188,000 teachers, giving a pupil/teacher ratio of 18/1. (1992–3 figures,

European Commission) The state schools are run by the communes, but still under the detailed direction of the Ministry of National Education, which sets out the general aims, defines the curriculum, covers the salary costs of the staff and is responsible for teacher training.

Responsibility for the day-to-day running of the school rests with the school council. It consists of the elected parent representatives, and the teachers' council (comprising all the teachers in the school), a representative of the local authority and the département education inspector. It is chaired by the head teacher (*directeur*). The school council's terms of reference are wide: for example, it is consulted on the teaching of slow learners, parent–teacher relations, hygiene, canteens, school transport, extracurricular and after-school activities, and the care of pupils out of school.

Primary schooling lasts for five years, and is divided into two 'cycles'.

- *cycle des apprentissages*
  The first two years in primary school (together with the last year in preprimary school) form the 'basic learning cycle' (ages 5/6–8).
- *cycle de consolidation*
  The last three years in primary school form the 'consolidation cycle' (ages 9–11).

The subjects studied during the five years are divided into three groups. Individual schools may vary the proportions of time devoted to each group, but within maximum and minimum limits as shown approximately below (there is some variation between the basic and the consolidation cycles) and adding up to a total of 26 hours per week.

- French, history, geography and civics (at least 30% but not more than 50%)
- mathematics, science and technology (at least 20% but not more than 40%)
- physical education and sport, art and crafts, and music (at least 20% but not more than 30%)

In 1989 the teaching of foreign languages was introduced, occupying three hours a week.

Lower secondary education

Lower secondary education takes place in the *collège*. It is compulsory, free and comprehensive, and normally for 11–15-year-olds. About 3.2 million children attend in all – 80% in publicly run and 20% in private collèges. (1992–3 figures, European Commission) The state collèges are funded largely by the départements. Since 1985, individual collèges have a measure of financial and educational autonomy, but still under the detailed direction of the Ministry of National Education, which sets out the general aims, defines the curriculum and covers the salary costs of the staff. The Ministry is also responsible for teacher training.

Responsibility for the running of a collège rests with its administrative council (conseil d'administration). It consists of representatives of the local authority, staff, parents and pupils. The head teacher (principal) in consultation with the staff draws up a school plan for meeting the objectives and organising the curriculum laid down by the government; this plan must be approved by the administrative council.

Education in the collège lasts for four years (numbered sixième, cinquième, quatrième, and troisième in reverse order to the UK convention), and since 1995–6 is divided into three cycles.

- cycle d'observation et d'adaptation
  The 'observation and adaptation' cycle occupies the first (sixième) collège year, and completes the transition from primary to secondary education.
- cycle de consolidation
  The 'consolidation cycle' lasts two years (cinquième and quatrième).
- cycle d'orientation
  The 'orientation cycle' occupies the final (troisième) collège year.

After the observation and adaptation cycle, pupils move to either general education or technological education classes. Both types of class study general subjects, but the 'general' classes in a more abstract and academic way, and the 'technological' classes in a more practical way. Both study technological subjects (principally mechanics, electronics and computing, and business management) but the 'technological' classes devote about five times as much of the timetable to them.

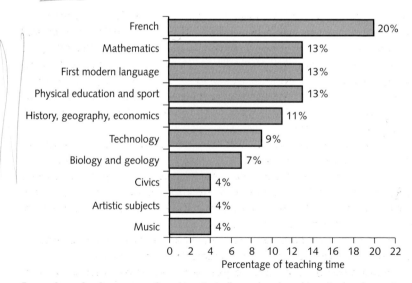

France figure 2   Percentage of teaching time allocated to the subjects in the observation cycle curriculum of the collège

The details of the compulsory curriculum are changed by the government from time to time, but usually in relatively minor ways. The subjects of the 1993 curriculum for the – undifferentiated – observation cycle are shown in Figure 2, with approximate percentages of the timetable devoted to each.

In the later cycles, physics and chemistry are added as compulsory subjects for both the general and the technological classes; and pupils select one or two optional languages.

A collège may also provide extra tuition in music or art.

The progress of individual students is monitored by the teachers' council (composed of all the teachers of a particular grade) and the class council (chaired by the head teacher or his/her representative, and including the class teachers, two parents' and two pupils' delegates, and possibly also a counsellor, medical officer, social worker and nurse). Parents are informed of their children's progress in a report at the end of each term, and also in a *carnet*, a notebook for correspondence and exchange of comments between parents and teachers.

At the end of the troisième in the collège, pupils may be awarded a national certificate, the *diplôme national du brevet*, mainly according to their marks in a final examination. At the same time, the class council decides – after consultation with pupils and their parents – what educational route pupils should take after collège (though the pupils and their parents have a right to appeal against the decision).

Upper secondary education

Upper secondary education, normally from the age of 15, takes place in the lycée. Admission is not automatic: students who have not attained the required standard at the end of the collège troisième year remain in the collège to complete their compulsory education. For those who are admitted to the lycée, attendance is normally not compulsory after the first year. For those who remain, the first three years of study (ages 15–18) prepare them for the upper secondary examinations, leading to a *Baccalauréat*, technician's certificate or vocational certificate.

The Baccalauréat qualifies students to enter a university, but those wishing instead to attend one of the *Grandes Ecoles* (see below) must also sit a competitive entrance examination. Many lycées offer post-Baccalauréat 'preparatory classes', lasting one to three years, for those intending to take these examinations. (Some Grandes Ecoles themselves also offer preparatory classes for their entrance examinations.)

For students who have obtained a technician's certificate, further courses are also available in the 'higher technical sections' of many lycées.

There are two types of lycée, the 'general and technological education lycée' (*lycée d'enseignement général et technologique*), usually known simply as 'the lycée'; and the 'vocational lycée' (LP – *lycée professionnel*). About 1.6 million students attend general and technological education lycées, and about 520,000 attend vocational lycées – just under 80% in publicly run and 20% in private establishments for both types of lycée. (1992–3 figures, European Commission) The state lycées are funded largely by the regions. Since 1985, individual lycées have a measure of financial and educational autonomy, but still under the detailed direction of the Ministry of National Education, which sets out the general aims, defines the curriculum and covers the salary costs of the staff. The Ministry is also responsible for teacher training.

Responsibility for running a lycée rests with its administrative council (conseil d'administration). It consists of representatives of the local authority, staff, parents and students. The head teacher (proviseur) in consultation with the staff draws up a school plan for meeting the objectives and organising the curriculum laid down by the government; this plan must be approved by the administrative council.

Lycée d'enseignement général et technologique
The general and technological education lycées admit students who have completed four years in collège, and prepare them in three years (the seconde, première, and terminale classes) for the Baccalauréat (BAC), which may be the general Baccalauréat (Baccalauréat d'enseignement général); the technological Baccalauréat (BTn – Baccalauréat technologique); or the technician's certificate (BT – brevet de technicien). Some lycées offer courses for both types of Baccalauréat, others for only one.

In 1992 the curriculum of the lycées was reformed (renovation pédagogique du lycée). Now in their first (seconde) year in the lycée, students prepare to choose the type of Baccalauréat they want to take. Everyone must study eight compulsory subjects (occupying about 27 hours per week in total) and two optional subjects (about 3–5 hours per week). (Students intending to take the technology Baccaulauréat must choose at least one technology option.) The compulsory subjects are shown in Figure 3, with approximate percentages of the timetable devoted to each.

In four of these subjects (French, mathematics, history/geography and the foreign language), one 45-minute period per week must be devoted to group work catering for students of differing ability and interests.

The optional subjects include languages, economic and social studies, artistic studies, management, technology and sport.

Students wishing to take the technology Baccalauréat must choose at least one technology option.

The progress of individual students in the lycée is monitored in a manner similar to that in the collège (see above). Before the 1989 Framework Education Act took effect, between 10% and 15% of students were recommended to repeat the first or second year, and about 20% to repeat the third year. (Teese, 1989) The Act is intended to reduce these figures.

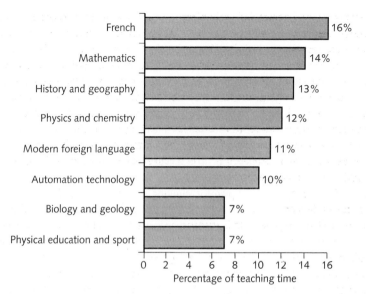

France figure 3   Percentage of the timetable allocated to the subjects of the compulsory curriculum in the first year of the lycée

For those taking the various Baccalauréat routes, the 1992 reformed syllabus simplified the curriculum for the final two years. Now students may choose between seven main lines (instead of over 20 options previously on offer). For the general Baccalauréat, there are three lines:

- literary (L);
- economic and social sciences (ES);
- sciences (S).

And for the technological Baccalauréat, there are four main lines:

- laboratory science and technology (STL);
- industrial science and technology (STI);
- tertiary science and technology (STT);
- social-medical sciences (SMS).

(In addition, there are at present specialised technological Baccalauréats for applied arts, music, dance and the hotel trade, but these are under review.)

Each option usually has within it a number of compulsory and optional components. Students not only study these specialist options but also continue with their general education, studying other subjects at a less advanced level.

The Baccalauréat examination is set nationally, and has both compulsory and optional papers based on the curricula for the third (terminale) year of the lycée. Those who pass are qualified to enter university or to apply to enter a preparatory class for the competitive examinations for the Grandes Ecoles (see below). Those who fail but obtain marks of at least 40% are awarded a leaving certificate (*certificat de fin d'études secondaires*), but this does not qualify them for admission to higher education.

Those taking the technician's certificate route in their second and third years combine courses in their specialist area with compulsory general studies. For both the general and the specialist courses, curricula are set nationally. Those who obtain a technician's certificate may proceed directly to employment, continue their studies in the higher technical section (STS – *section technique supérieur*) of a lycée for a higher technician's certificate (BTS – *brevet de technicien supérieur*); or in a university institute of technology (IUT – *institut universitaire de technologie*).

Lycée professionnel
The vocational lycées admit students who have completed four, three or even two years in collège (provided that they are at least 14 years old), and provide vocational training in different specialities – mainly in skilled manual trades, such as carpentry and butchery – leading to one of three qualifications: the vocational aptitude certificate (CAP – *certificat d'aptitude professionnelle*); the vocational studies certificate (BEP – *brevet d'études professionelles*); and the vocational Baccalauréat (*Baccalauréat professionnel*).

CAP and BEP courses are similar in structure and length, but the BEP involves more advanced study. (Some students who have obtained the CAP continue their studies to obtain a BEP.) They normally require two years of study, combining general education, vocational education and on-the-job training. Those who obtain their certificates may proceed directly to employment, continue their studies for a vocational Baccalauréat, or change routes and take a re-orientation class (*première d'adaptation*) to prepare for a technology Baccalauréat. The general education component of CAP and BEP courses continues many of the collège subjects, but with a vocational emphasis. In addition to their inherent value, they are especially important for students intending to proceed to a Baccalauréat.

The vocational Baccalauréat normally requires four years of study (or two years after CAP or BEP). It was introduced in 1985, partly in response to the development of electronic and other new technologies, and the concomitant spread of the ownership and use of personal computers and sophisticated audio and video equipment. Their manufacture and maintenance were held to require technicians with more advanced training than the two-year CAP or BEP could give. Unlike the general and technology Baccalauréats, the vocational Baccalauréat was intended primarily to qualify for direct entry to employment, and most of those who obtain it do go straight into jobs.

Vocational Baccalauréat courses involve 30 hours study per week, from half to a third devoted to vocational studies and the remainder to general studies.

Classes préparatoires aux Grandes Ecoles
Students who pass the Baccalauréat may proceed to a preparatory class (CPGE or *'prépa'*) to prepare for the competitive examinations for admission to one of the *Grandes Ecoles*, elite higher education colleges specialising in professional training. These preparatory classes are normally held in the lycées, but exceptionally may be housed in the Grandes Ecoles themselves. The Baccalauréat does not give automatic entry into a CPGE; admission to the preparatory classes is itself selective and competitive.

Initial vocational training

In France, the 'initial vocational training' of young people in the form of apprenticeship (*apprentissage*) has traditionally been organisationally and financially separate from the 'continuing vocational training' of adults (see below under Adult education and continuing training). During the 1980s and early 1990s, however, a number of other types of initial vocational training were introduced, based on training contracts (*contrats*) between employer and trainee, to bring 'initial' and 'continuing' training closer together. About half a million young people (aged 16–25) are now engaged in initial vocational training, just under half of them in apprenticeships, just over half in the newer, contractual types of training – together making up just under a quarter of the numbers of students (aged 16–19) in upper secondary schools.

Apprentissage
Apprenticeships combine theoretical training in an apprentice training centre (CFA – *centre de formation d'apprentis*) supervised by the Ministry of Education with practical training with an employer recognised by the département. For the latter, the apprentice is an employee, and is paid a wage.

Apprenticeships last up to three years, and allow apprentices to work towards the same qualifications as students in the vocational lycée. In 1993–4, 75% of apprentices were working towards a CAP, 9% towards the more advanced BEP and 4% towards a vocational Baccalauréat. (European Commission, 1995)

Contrats
There are three main types of training contract. (European Commission, 1995)

- 'Orientation' contracts (*contrats d'orientation*) are aimed at young people with limited education and no qualifications. They spend a short period – no more than six months – with a firm and gain basic employment experience, vocational guidance and possibly some specific skills. These accounted for a fifth of training contracts in 1990.
- 'Qualification' contracts (*contrats de qualification*) are aimed at young people who have some appropriate vocational education or training but have not

obtained a qualification from it. The trainees are paid employees, for a period of up to two years. The employer is responsible for ensuring that appropriate training is available; it must occupy at least a quarter of a trainee's time. These accounted for just over two-fifths of training contracts in 1990.

● 'Adaptation' contracts (*contrats d'adaptation*) are aimed specifically at unemployed young people, and are intended to enable them to train or retrain for a specific type of job. The trainees are paid employees; there is no statutory limit to the period of employment. The employer is responsible for ensuring that at least 200 hours appropriate training is available. These accounted for just under two-fifths of training contracts in 1990.

Special education

A child identified as having learning difficulties is assessed by a district commission for special education. After consultation with the child's parents, the commission prepares a report (*évaluation*), specifying the child's problems and needs, and making recommendations for his or her educational provision. A number of options are available for such children. These include:

● 'special education sections' (SES – *sections d'éducation spéciale*) for children and adolescents with psychological, emotional, or behavioural problems in school and for slow learners, though these are being converted into 'adapted general and vocational education sections' (SEGPA – *sections d'éducation d'enseignement général et professionnel adapté*). The aim is to provide a more effective training in a skill leading to a qualification and employment;

● 'classes for school integration' (CLIS – *classes d'intégration scolaire*), introduced from 1991 for children with physical disabilities, including deafness and blindness, and intended to enable them to become integrated into mainstream education;

● ordinary classes in mainstream schools. In principle, parents have a right to insist on this, regardless of the recommendations in the evaluation. (In practice, however, almost all parents accept the recommendations.)

Lower secondary pupils who have not achieved the level required to move into the quatrième are taught in small prevocational classes (CPN – *classes préprofessionnelles de niveau*) where they are given special help, particularly in French and mathematics. Others move into preparatory apprenticeship classes (CPA – *classes préparatoires à l'apprentissage*). These arrangements are currently under review.

Tertiary education

Tertiary education takes place in several different types of institution, of which the most important are the following.

- lycées, where courses after the Baccalauréat (notably the CPGE) or after the brevet de technicien (notably the STS) are defined as tertiary (see above)
- universities (universités) and university institutes of technology (instituts universitaires de technologie). Admission to universities is open to anyone with a Baccalauréat (with the exception of courses in medicine and related fields). Universities do not enjoy the highest prestige among tertiary institutions in France; this is reserved for the Grandes Ecoles
- Grandes Ecoles, for the training of engineers, administrators, industrialists, business people and other professionals. Admission to a Grande Ecole is selective: a Baccalauréat is necessary but not sufficient. After obtaining their Baccalauréat, candidates for admission must normally follow a one- or two-year preparatory course, and then enter a competitive examination
- specialist colleges (écoles spécialisées), which may be run by central or local government, offering a wide variety of mostly short courses in a wide range of subject areas
- distance education (enseignement à distance), which is available nationally or from a number of local institutions

Tertiary education in France is thus pluralistic and diversified, and there are often several quite different routes to qualifying for the same profession.

Universities

France has 77 universities and university institutes. They are all either under the control of or under contract to the Ministry of Higher Education and Research, which has a monopoly of the conferment of university degrees and diplomas, but they are accorded a high degree of autonomy in their teaching and research. Anyone holding a Baccalauréat is entitled to enter university (apart from courses in medicine and related fields, such as dentistry and pharmacy, which are selective). Applicants without a Baccalauréat may also be admitted at the discretion of a university on the basis of their experience or ability. Certain universities themselves offer a one-year preparatory course for an alternative entry qualification, the access diploma for university studies (DAEU – diplôme d'accès aux études universitaires).

University education is not free, but fees are set by the Ministry of Higher Education and Research, and are intended to be modest. Grants and interest-free loans are available for students, some according to national criteria, and others according to criteria set by individual universities.

Universities offer short courses (usually two but occasionally up to four years) and *long courses* (from two to twelve years). Thus some 'short' courses can actually be longer than some 'long' ones.

Short courses – Most of these courses are intended to prepare students for employment at managerial level in the industrial or service sectors of the economy. The main qualifications available are the university diploma in technology (DUT – *diplôme universitaire de technologie*) and the diploma in scientific and technical university studies (DEUST – *diplôme d'études universitaires scientifiques et techniques*).

Long courses – 'Long' courses at university are organised in three successive *cycles*. Each cycle prepares the student for the next cycle, but also offers its own qualifications for those who do not wish or are not permitted to pursue their studies any further. Admission to the next cycle is not automatic, though access to parallel training is sometimes available instead.

- *1er cycle*
  The first cycle is a two-year course leading to a university diploma in general studies (DEUG – *diplôme d'études universitaires générales*) or scientific and technical studies (DEUST – *diplôme d'études universitaires scientifiques et techniques*). It is multidisciplinary, and most literary, scientific, or technological subjects may be studied.
- *2ème cycle*
  The second cycle is usually a one-, two- or three-year course leading to a degree or *licence* (after one year), *maîtrise* (after two) or *magistère ingénieur* (after three).
- *3ème cycle*
  The third cycle is specialised, and entry is highly selective. There are two main routes. One is a one-year course of professional education, involving time spent with a company: it leads to a diploma in higher specialised studies (DESS – *diplôme d'études supérieures spécialisées*). The other is a one-year course of research, and training in research, leading immediately to a diploma in advanced studies (DEA – *diplôme d'études approfondies*) but allowing the student to proceed to a three- or four-year programme of doctoral studies (longer for medical specialisms). A doctorate qualifies the holder to teach and conduct research in a university.

Grandes Ecoles
Grandes Ecoles are mainly for the training of engineers, administrators, industrialists, business people and other professionals. They enjoy very high prestige. Places in them are limited and entry is highly selective. By contrast with university entry, success in the Baccalauréat is necessary but not sufficient. Candidates must normally take a competitive examination, for which there are one- or two-year preparatory courses, the CPGE (classes

préparatoires aux Grandes Ecoles), in lycées or occasionally in Grandes Ecoles themselves. (Entry to these preparatory courses is itself competitive.) There are several different specialist institutions and types of institution, some public but most independent, with their own teaching and research staff. Those in the public sector include the four *Ecoles Normales Supérieures* (ENS), which prepare students for fundamental scientific research, for advanced philosophy and cultural studies, or for teaching in lycées, universities or Grandes Ecoles; the 20 *Grandes Ecoles Scientifiques* which provide training in both fundamental and applied sciences; and the nine *Instituts d'études politiques*, which prepare students and civil servants for state competitive examinations, and in particular for the *Ecole Nationale d'Administration* (ENA), which is responsible directly to the Prime Minister, and trains civil servants who are expected to be promoted to senior positions.

In addition, there are private but state-recognised Grandes Ecoles, mostly concerned with business management.

Ecoles specialisées
These may be run by the central or local government, and offer mainly short courses in a wide range of subjects, including art, music, ballet, drama, photography, cinema, television, nursing, midwifery, social work, communications, computing, tourism and so on. These courses are offered at different levels, and specialist diplomas (*diplôme d'écoles specialisées*) are available.

Distance education
The National Centre for Distance Learning (CNED – *Centre national d'enseignement à distance*) and a number of universities (often equipped with television facilities) provide courses at all levels – primary and secondary as well as tertiary education. These courses are available to the public in general, young people, adults, or unregistered students, who cannot attend school, an education centre, or a university (be it for health, distance, work, personal or family reasons). The distance learning courses prepare for most examinations including certain civil service competitions.

Adult education and continuing training

In France, the 'continuing vocational training' of adults remains largely separate from 'initial vocational training' of young people. The responsibilities for continuing education and training are shared between the national government, the régions and employers. In 1991, some 1.2% of France's GDP was spent on continuing training (compared with 6.4% on education, including initial training). Of this, 49% came from the national government, 42% from employers, 5% from the régions and the remaining 4% from individuals and other sources. (CEDEFOP, 1994)

Teaching profession

There are three basic categories of teacher in French state schools, each with its own career structure and progression.

- professeurs des écoles
  'School teachers' must have successfully followed the first cycle of university education or its equivalent, studied in a university institute of teacher training (IUFM – institut universitaire de formation des maîtres) for at least one and sometimes two years and succeeded in a competitive examination. They are qualified to teach in preprimary and primary schools.

- professeurs certifiés
  'Certified teachers' must normally have obtained a licence in the second cycle university education, studied in an IUFM and succeeded in the competitive examination for the basic qualification for secondary school teaching, the CAPES (certificat d'aptitude au professorat de l'enseignement secondaire) in their specialist subject, or its equivalent in technical, vocational or physical education. They are qualified to teach their subject in secondary schools.

- professeurs agrégés
  These teachers must normally have obtained a maîtrise in the second cycle of university, studied at an IUFM, and succeeded in the concours d'agrégation, the competitive examination for the highest teaching qualification, in their specialist subject. They are qualified to teach this subject in secondary schools.

Teachers in private schools are not formally required to have followed these routes or obtained these qualifications, but in practice many private schools do look for similar academic experience and qualifications in recruiting teachers – especially those schools receiving government subsidies.

Funding

France spends about 6.2% of its GDP on education – 5.8% from public and 0.4% from private funds. Its distribution among the different sectors is illustrated in Figure 4. The percentage of total educational spending allocated to preprimary education is high in comparison with other countries.

Financial responsibility for public education is shared between the national government and the different levels of local government. The communes have responsibilities for the preprimary and primary stages, the départements for lower secondary schools, and the régions for upper secondary education, vocational training and universities. But for every level of education, the national government remains responsible for some funding, above all for the payment of teachers' salaries.

The government also subsidises private educational institutions that have agreed to follow state curricula and accept state inspection; these subsidies

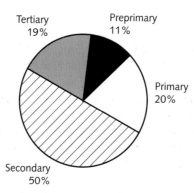

France figure 4   Percentage of total educational spending allocated to the different sectors, 1992 (CERI, 1995)

include the payment of teachers' salaries. Private establishments may also charge fees, whereas public education below tertiary level is free.

Parent/school relationships

Parents as a group are represented on the administrative councils of schools at all levels. Parents of individual children have extensive rights to be informed about their children's progress, and consulted about decisions concerning their educational career. They have rights of appeal against decisions with which they disagree.

Education inspectorate

There are inspectorates at national, regional and departmental level. The general inspectorates (at national level) are concerned with evaluating the entire education system – the curriculum, teaching methods, teacher recruitment and training, the allocation and use of funds, and so on – and informing and advising the Minister for National Education. The local authority inspectors are responsible for the inspection and appraisal of individual schools and teachers – those at regional level for the secondary sector, and those at departmental level for the primary sector.

ACRONYMS AND ABBREVIATIONS

BAC   Baccalauréat (the principal qualification at the end of three years' upper secondary education, qualifying holders to enter university or to compete for entrance to a Grande Ecole. It may be a BAC général, a BAC technologique or a BAC professionnel – a general, technological or vocational Baccalauréat)

BEP	brevet d'études professionelles (vocational studies certificate from the vocational lycée; more advanced than the CAP, but less so than the BAC professionnel)
BT	brevet de technicien (technician's certificate from the general and technological education lycée)
BTn	Baccalauréat technologique
BTS	brevet de technicien supérieur (higher technician's certificate from the general and technological education lycée)
CAP	certificat d'aptitude professionelle (vocational aptitude certificate from the vocational lycée, less advanced than the BEP)
CAPES	certificat d'aptitude au professorat de l'enseignement secondaire (the basic qualification for secondary school teaching)
CFA	centre de formation d'apprentis (apprentice training centre)
CLIS	classes d'intégration scolaire
CNED	Centre national d'enseignement à distance (National Centre for Distance Learning)
CPA	classes préparatoires à l'apprentissage (preparatory apprenticeship classes for children with special educational needs)
CPGE	classes préparatoires aux Grandes Ecoles (preparatory classes, usually in a lycée, to prepare holders of the Baccalauréat for the competitive examinations for admission to one of the Grandes Ecoles; also known as 'prépa')
CPN	classes préprofessionnelles de niveau (prevocational classes for children with special educational needs)
DAEU	diplôme d'accès aux études universitaires (access diploma for university studies – an alternative entry qualification for those who do not have a Baccalauréat)
DEA	diplôme d'études approfondies (diploma in advanced studies, obtained after a one-year course of research, and training in research, in the third university cycle, and qualifying the holder to begin doctoral studies)
DESS	diplôme d'études supérieures spécialisées (diploma in higher specialised studies, obtained after one year of the third university cycle)
DEUG	diplôme d'études universitaires générales (diploma in general university studies, obtained at the end of the first cycle)
DEUST	diplôme d'études universitaires scientifiques et techniques (diploma in scientific and technical university studies, obtained at the end of the first cycle)
DRT	diplôme de recherche technologique (diploma in technological

	research, awarded at the end of a third-cycle course in university or equivalent college)
DUT	diplôme universitaire de technologie (university diploma in technology, usually obtained in a university institute of technology)
ENA	Ecole Nationale d'Administration (the National School of Administration, which prepares students already in the civil service for senior positions)
ENS	Ecole Normale Supérieure (a type of Grande Ecole preparing students for fundamental scientific research, for advanced philosophy and cultural studies, or for teaching in the Grandes Ecoles, universities or lycées)
ESCAE	écoles supérieures de commerce et d'administration des entreprises (a type of private Grande Ecole preparing students for commerce and business administration)
ESSEC	école supérieure des sciences économiques et commerciales (a private Grande Ecole for economic and commercial studies)
HEC	écoles des hautes études commerciales (a type of private Grande Ecole for commercial studies)
IEP	instituts d'études politiques (institutes of political studies)
INSA	instituts nationaux des sciences appliquées (national institutes of applied sciences)
IUFM	institut universitaire de formation des maîtres (university institute of teaching training)
IUT	institut universitaire de technologie (university institute of technology)
LP	lycée professionnel (vocational lycée)
prépa	See CPGE above.
SEGPA	sections d'éducation d'enseignement général et professionnel adapté ('adapted general and vocational education sections', whose aim is to provide training in a skill leading to a qualification and employment for children with special educational needs; they are replacing the SES)
SES	sections d'éducation spéciale (special education sections for slow learners and pupils with psychological, emotional, or behavioural problems; these are being converted into SEGPA)
STS	section technique supérieure (higher technical section of a lycée)
sup de Co	écoles supérieures de commerce (a type of private Grande Ecole for commercial studies)

ACKNOWLEDGEMENTS

We are grateful to Dr Patricia Manning and Professor Bob Moon of The Open University for their comments on an earlier draft of this chapter.

REFERENCES

Armstrong, F. (1995) 'Appellation Contrôlée: mixing and sorting in the French education system', in Potts, P., Armstrong, F. and Masterton, M. (eds) (1995) *Equality and Diversity in Education: national and international contexts*, London: Routledge.

CEDEFOP (1989) *Vocational Education in France: structural problems and present efforts towards reform*, Berlin: European Centre for the Development of Vocational Training.

CEDEFOP (1994) *Vocational Education and Training in France*, Luxembourg: Office for Official Publications of the European Commission.

CERI (1995) *Education at a Glance: OECD indicators*, Paris: Organisation for Economic Co-operation and Development.

CNOUS (1993) *I'm Going to France*, Paris: Centre National des Oeuvres Universitaires et Scolaires (a guide for foreign students).

Corbett, A. and Moon, B. (eds) (1996) *Education Reform in France: change in the Mitterrand years 1981–1995*, London: Routledge.

European Commission (1995) *Structures of the Education and Initial Training Systems in the European Union*, Luxembourg: Office for Official Publications of the European Commission.

French Embassy (1990) *Primary and Secondary Education in France*, London: Press and Information Service.

Ministry of National Education and Culture (1992) *General Organization of Higher Education in France*, Paris: Ministry of National Education and Culture.

OECD (1995) *OECD Economic Surveys: France 1994–1995*, Paris: Organisation for Economic Co-operation and Development.

OECD (1995) *Secondary Education in France: a decade of change*, Paris: Organisation for Economic Co-operation and Development.

Teese, R. (1989) 'France: Catholic schools, class security, and the public sector', in Walford, G. (ed.) (1989) *Private Schools in Ten Countries: policy and practice*, London: Routledge.

BACKGROUND

Germany and its Länder

The emergence of Germany (and of France) as a separate country began in 843, when the grandsons of Charlemagne divided between themselves the empire he had created – Louis taking those lands where Teutonic languages predominated, and Charles those where Romance languages were spoken. However, Germany became a unified nation-state only in 1871.

In 1945, after the Second World War, the occupying armies divided Germany into two parts, on the one hand the American, British, and French military zones, and on the other that of the USSR. The Western Alliance allowed the development of the Federal Republic of Germany ('West

Germany'), and the USSR defended the establishment of the German Democratic Republic ('East Germany'). In October 1990, the two Germanys were re-united. The five East German states (*Länder*) were joined with the 11 Länder of West Germany, and are in the process of adapting to the West German model, in education as in other matters.

POPULATION

Population	81.4 million in 1994 (an increase of 0.5% per annum since 1984 – (West and East Germany combined)
Land area	357,000 sq. km
Population density	228 per sq. km
Young people (5–24)	23.5% of population in 1992

Since re-unification, Germany has by far the largest population of any Western European country – about 80% living in the former West Germany, 20% in the former East Germany.

ECONOMY

GDP	$1,800 billion (1994)
GDP per capita	$27,800 (1994)
In employment	66% of the working age population (1991)
	– 92% of males/70% of females aged 25–54
	– 72% of young people, aged 15–24

Germany has a substantial number of foreign workers and their dependants – over 1.2 million in 1989 in the former West Germany. Of these the largest single nationality was Turkish (45%), a further 24% were from the former Yugoslavia, and the remaining 31% were mostly from the southern EU countries, Italy, Greece, Spain and Portugal. Most of them were long-term residents of Germany: two- thirds had lived there for at least eight years, and a quarter for at least 20 years. (Münch, 1995)

RELIGION

There are almost equal numbers of Protestants (29 million) and Roman Catholics (28 million). The numbers of Jews are now very small, some 37,000. (1991 figures)

LANGUAGE

The official language is German (with a small Danish-speaking minority in Schleswig-Holstein). It is a language rich in dialects and the speech of most

Germans reveals where they come from. German is also the mother tongue of some 100 million people – over 20 million outside Germany. German is the first language spoken in Austria, most of Switzerland, Liechtenstein and small sections of Belgium along the German border. German minorities in Poland, Romania, the former Soviet Union, and Argentina have also preserved the language to some extent. Roughly one-tenth of all the books published in the world are in German. Most translations worldwide are from English and French, with German in third place, but German is the language into which translations are most often made.

GOVERNMENT

Germany is a federation of 16 states (*Länder*), ranging in size from North Rhine-Westphalia with a population of 17.5 million to Bremen with 680,000. The Basic Law, passed in 1949, enshrines the principles which govern Germany as a republic and as a democracy, and defines the relationship between the federal and state governments. It was intended as a temporary frame for a new democratic system, with the weaknesses of the Weimar democracy and the inhuman excesses of the Nazi dictatorship in mind, but with minor changes, it remains in force.

There are three main levels of government, *federal*, *state* and *local government* (itself with two main levels, the *district* and the *commune*), each with its own responsibilities for education.

In the field of education the constitutional powers of the federal legislature and government are specific and limited. For example, the federal authorities are empowered to legislate on general principles for education. They may regulate educational grants, promote scientific and academic research, regulate in-company vocational training, and not least, regulate the payment, benefits and pensions of civil servants, and therefore the working conditions of teachers, who are civil servants in Germany.

There are also established procedures for the federal and Länder governments to tackle the so-called 'joint tasks' stipulated in legislation and emerging in everyday activities. For example, in 1954 and 1964 agreements were reached in the then West Germany that helped standardise the school and university structures: the duration of compulsory education, the dates for the school year, the description of the various educational institutions and their organisation, the transfers between schools, and the marking schemes for school reports and teacher training examinations.

The Basic Law gives the prime responsibility for education to the individual Länder. The German education system is decentralised, and there is no uniform model for an individual state to follow, even if it so wished. Most educational legislation, and all the administration of schools, higher education, adult and continuing education, are the responsibility of individual states.

However, states can and do co-operate with one another, and even set up nationwide bodies independent of the federal government to facilitate co-operation and harmonisation, notably the standing conference of the State Ministers of Education and Cultural Affairs (KMK – *Kulturministerkonferenz*). But the system remains diverse, and appears complex because of differences in local provision, the variety of educational institutions, and the very large number of examinations and types of certificate.

The states are responsible for municipal legislation, but although there is some variety in administrative systems, they are fairly similar throughout the republic in their basic pattern, with districts (*urban* and *rural*) subdivided into communes. In all, there are about 540 districts (80% rural, 20% urban) and over 16,000 communes.

The state, district and communal authorities share the administrative responsibilities for education between them. The precise allocation of these responsibilities varies from place to place, but as a general rule, the older the pupils or students concerned, the higher the level of government likely to be responsible for them.

EDUCATION

Despite variation from state to state, certain common features of German education can be identified.

Schooling is compulsory in all states from the age of six, and remains compulsory in most states full-time until 15 and part-time until 18. The German system provides a general education in a common primary school for all children, and in one of four types of lower secondary school, which children and their parents usually choose. After that, usually at 15, they move into a different educational institution in the upper secondary sector. This may be a *Gymnasium*, specialising in academic education; or a full time vocational school or technical college; or the so-called 'dual system' combining training in a company with school attendance. Alternatively, they may proceed directly into employment, but this is rarer.

As a rule, universities and schools are public institutions; the former are state, the latter may be state or local government establishments. There are also numerous private schools and universities under church, commercial, or independent control. In the 1990s, there were around 3,000 private schools offering general or vocational education with around 500,000 pupils. These private schools are authorised by the states, and in some states receive financial assistance.

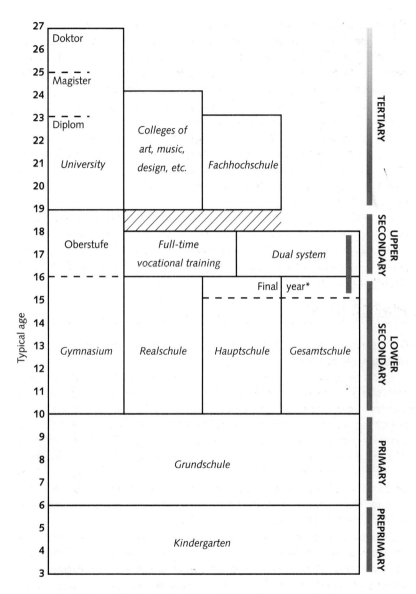

* Pupils (especially those in the Hauptschule or the comparable stream
  of the Gesamtschule) may spend their final year of compulsory
  education as a *Berufsgrundbildungsjahr*, the first year of training in
  the dual system

Note: This diagram is highly simplified for clarity, and should be used in
  conjunction with the text

Germany's education system

INSTITUTIONS
Preprimary education

Children aged three to six may attend a *Kindergarten*. These are run by voluntary associations (about 70%) and by some local authorities (about 30%). The focus is on child-care and socialisation, but an important aim is individual development and preparation for compulsory schooling. Fees are charged; in some states they are means-tested. About two-thirds of three- to six-year-olds attend: over 40% of three-year-olds, 70% of four-year-olds, 80% of five-year-olds, and just under 70% of six-year-olds (the remainder having started school). (European Commission, 1995)

Some Länder provide voluntary preschool classes (*Vorklassen/Vorschulklassen*) for five-year-old children whose parents want them to receive special preparation for school. (In other Länder, these terms have a different meaning; see below.)

Children of school age, six and upwards, who are not deemed ready for school may be required to attend special preparatory classes connected with a primary school. These have different names in different states, including school kindergartens (*Schulkindergärten*) and preschool classes (*Vorklassen/Vorschulklassen*). Between 5% and 6% of all six-year-olds attend these classes.

Primary education

Education in primary schools (*Grundschulen*) is comprehensive and free, and lasts for four years in most states. Children usually spend four years in primary education, and attend between 20 and 30 hours a week, but this varies from state to state and according to the children's age. There are about 17,900 primary schools, with 3.5 million pupils and 170,000 teachers. (1993 figures, European Commission, 1995)

The primary curriculum in each state is decided by the state government, but typically includes the following, whether as separate subjects or as part of interdisciplinary work.

- reading, writing and arithmetic
- German
- mathematics
- religious instruction
- art
- music
- physical education
- *Sachunterrichts* (literally 'factual lessons': an introduction to social studies, history, geography, biology, physics and chemistry – subjects to be studied more thoroughly in secondary school)
- English or French (in some states only, from the third year and not assessed)

Throughout primary schooling, pupils are assessed partly on the basis of class work and partly by written tests. In the first two years, their performance is recorded in report form; thereafter it has traditionally been recorded for each subject as a mark on a six-point scale, from *sehr gut* (very good) to *ungenügend* (very poor), but an increasing number of schools now use reports for these years too.

Regardless of performance, every child is promoted from the first to the second year, but thereafter children may be kept down if their performance is inadequate. There is no formal examination at the end of the primary years. There is guided choice based on teachers' reports and opinions. These help determine the type of lower secondary school chosen, but parents may select their children's schools contrary to the advice given them.

Lower and upper secondary education: academic

In most of Germany, children move at the age of ten into one of four types of secondary school – *Hauptschule, Realschule, Gesamtschule* and *Gymnasium* – though there are variations in terminology and practice from state to state. (We shall not translate these names. Literal translations – 'main school', 'general school', etc. – are not helpful; and the standard English-language versions offered in official publications and some dictionaries – usually in terms of British 'grammar', 'secondary modern' and 'comprehensive' or American 'junior high' and 'high' schools – can be misleading.)

The Hauptschule, Realschule and Gesamtschule provide schooling at lower secondary level, the Gymnasium at both lower and upper secondary levels. Studies in the Hauptschule are less demanding than in the Realschule, and in the Realschule in turn less demanding than in the Gymnasium. The Hauptschule normally completes its students' schooling. Students in the Realschule and the Gymnasium normally continue their education to upper secondary level. The Gesamtschule in effect combines Hauptschule, Realschule and Gymnasium in one establishment, sometimes as three separate streams, sometimes with a limited degree of mixed-ability teaching.

The distribution of students among these different types of school is illustrated in Figure 1.

Hauptschule
In most states, compulsory education in the Hauptschule lasts from the 5th to the 9th Year (ages 10 to 15), with an optional 10th Year. The Hauptschule qualification (the *Hauptschulabschluß*) can be awarded at different levels for those who have and those who have not taken this extra year. Education in the Hauptschule usually leads to vocational study and practical training in the 'dual system' (see below).

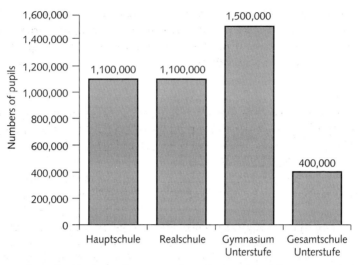

Germany figure 1   Numbers of lower secondary school pupils in different types of school, 1993 (European Commission, 1995)

The compulsory curriculum varies from state to state, but typically includes the following.

- German
- a foreign language (usually English)
- mathematics
- physics
- chemistry
- biology
- geography
- history
- social studies
- *Arbeitslehre* (basic economics and technology)
- religion
- music
- art
- physical education

Mathematics and the foreign language (and sometimes other subjects) are taught at different levels to students of different ability.

There are about 6,200 Hauptschulen, with 1.1 million students and 76,000 teachers. They account for about a quarter of all students at lower secondary level. (1993 figures; European Commission, 1995) However, this figure represents a significant fall in the Hauptschule population, both proportionately and in absolute terms. In 1980, there were 1.9 million Hauptschule students, who represented 40% of the lower secondary school population. The Hauptschule is becoming less and less popular with parents, who prefer their children to take courses leading to the Abitur (see below) than to the Hauptschulabschluß. (Phillips, 1995)

Realschule

Education in the Realschule normally lasts from the 5th to the 9th Year (ages 10 to 16), though again this varies from state to state. The more advanced levels of study, compared with the Hauptschulen, allow entry to training courses for a professional qualification.

The compulsory curriculum in the first two years is similar to that in the Hauptschule, but from the 3rd year, students must study some of the subjects in more depth or add new subjects, for example a foreign language (usually French).

There are about 3,500 Realschulen, with 1.1 million students and 65,000 teachers. Like the Hauptschulen, they account for about a quarter of all students at lower secondary level. (1993 figures; European Commission, 1995) Unlike the Hauptschule, the Realschule has maintained its share of the lower secondary population since 1980. (Phillips, 1995)

Gymnasium

The Gymnasien provide a general education, normally leading to the Abitur, the final certificate, in nine years (ages 10 to 19), though other arrangements exist for students who have attended longer primary courses, or transferred from Hauptschule or Realschule. (The federal government has for many years been trying to reduce the period of study leading to the Abitur by one year, but the Länder have not as yet agreed: see Phillips, 1995.) The Abitur in some Gymnasien provides entrance to any course of university study; other Gymnasien issue certificates that restrict admission to a subject or subject group.

The lower secondary (Unterstufe) and upper secondary (Oberstufe) levels of the Gymnasium are separate, and admission to the upper level is not automatic. In the Unterstufe (Years 5 to 10, ages 10 to 16), the compulsory curriculum includes the following.

- German
- at least two foreign languages
- mathematics
- physics
- chemistry
- biology
- geography
- history
- social studies

- music
- art
- sport
- religion (in most but not all Länder)

In the upper level, there is much more choice of courses for students, though there are still important constraints. There are three subject areas.

- language, literature, arts
- social sciences
- mathematics, science, technology

Each of these subject areas must be represented among the subjects taken by every student up to the Abitur examinations.

Courses in the Gymnasium are of two levels, *basic* and *advanced*. The Abitur is taken in four subjects, two of which must be at advanced level, and consists of written and oral examinations. Successful candidates are awarded the *Allgemeine Hochschulreife* ('general readiness for higher education') certificate, which grants the holder the right to enter any course in any institution of higher education.

At lower secondary level, there are over 3,000 Gymnasien with 92,000 teachers and 1.5 million students – just over a third of all students at lower secondary level (an increase since 1980, when it was just under a third). At upper secondary level, there are some 3,300 teachers and 586,000 students – about a fifth of all students at upper secondary level. (European Commission, 1995; Phillips, 1995)

Gesamtschule

The Gesamtschulen combine the educational programmes, qualifications and certificates of the other types of lower secondary education. They are of two kinds. The *Integrierte Gesamtschulen* (integrated Gesamtschulen) do not differentiate between the various types of education in the lower secondary sector, but place all students in year groups, and teach them in mixed-ability classes. The *Kooperative Gesamtschulen* (co-operative Gesamtschulen) provide the three distinct types of schooling (that is, 'Hauptschule', 'Realschule' and 'Gymnasium' types) on the same site, with their curricula planned together to make it easier for students to transfer from one type to another than with entirely separate schools.

At lower secondary level, there are about 800 integrated Gesamtschulen, with 31,000 teachers and 400,000 students. At upper secondary level, there are 35,000 Gesamtschule students. These constitute just under a tenth of all students at each level. (1993 figures) It is the smallest lower secondary sector, but it is growing in size: in 1980, it accounted for only 4% of lower secondary students. (European Commission, 1995; Phillips, 1995)

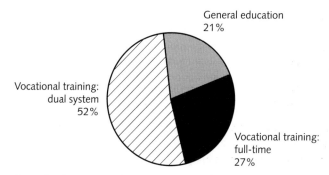

Germany figure 2   Percentage of upper secondary students in general education and vocational training, 1993 (European Commission, 1995)

Upper secondary education: vocational

Only a fifth of Germany's 3.1 million upper secondary students attend the academic schools described above. The remainder are either in full-time vocational education or in the so-called 'dual system' – combining education in schools or colleges with on-the-job training with an employer. The percentages of students in the different types of education and training are illustrated in Figure 2.

Just over half of all vocational trainees are in industry and commerce, and a third in crafts; most of the rest are in training for liberal professions (9%), the civil service (4%) or agriculture (2%). About 43% of all vocational trainees in 1990 were female – an increase from 38% in 1980 and 35% in 1970.

The arrangements described below are characteristic of the former West Germany, but are currently being introduced in the five Länder of the former East Germany too. East Germany did not have a dual system, and most vocational training (about 80%) was conducted in training-schools that formed part of large, nationalised enterprises. Many of these enterprises have disappeared in the economic restructuring that followed unification, and those that survive have often closed down their training schools as an economy measure in their new competitive circumstances. (Münch, 1995)

The dual system

Training in the dual system is available to anyone who has completed nine years of full-time compulsory education, regardless of the types of school they have attended, or whether they have gained any qualifications. Typically it lasts three years (ages 15 to 18), during which students spend three days per week with a company and two days in a vocational school (Berufsschule), though an alternative arrangement is for the students' first year to be spent in full-time study in a school – an arrangement known as the Berufsgrundbildungsjahr, or basic vocational education year.

Training with a company – This component of the dual system is governed by training regulations laid down by agreement between the federal and state authorities after consultation with employers' organisations and trade unions. These specify in detail what is to be taught for each of about 370 skilled occupations in industry, commerce, agriculture, crafts and the public sector, and define the mutual rights and responsibilities of the training firms and the trainees, who sign a training contract (*Ausbildungsvertrag*) in which they agree to abide by these. Training is provided free by the employer, who also pays the trainee a wage set by the regulations. (Funding is not provided by governments at any level, apart from support for socially disadvantaged trainees.)

Berufsschule – The Berufsschule provides students in the dual system with general education as well as the more theoretical component of their occupational training. The curriculum is defined in detail by agreement between the federal and state authorities after consultation with employers' organisations and trade unions. General education occupies about a third of students' time, and includes the following compulsory subjects, regardless of students' occupational specialisation.

● German
● economic and social studies
● religion
● sport

Foreign languages are also taught, though not as part of general education but as part of occupational training in certain fields.

   Not all students in the Berufsschule are participants in the dual system. It can also be used by students who do not have a training contract with an employer to complete their compulsory schooling with part-time vocational education, if they have already completed nine years of full-time education. In addition to contributing to the vocational qualifications of the dual system (see below) the Berufsschule offers its own leaving certificate, which is treated as equivalent to a leaving certificate from the Hauptschule or Realschule.

   The most popular training occupations for men are motor mechanic (64,300 trainees), industrial mechanic (57,000) and electrician (45,000). In each of these, between 97% and 99% of trainees are male. The most popular training occupations for women are clerical (184,000, 68% female), hairdressing (50,000, 94% female) and doctor's assistant (42,000, virtually 100% female). (Münch, 1995)

   Training in the dual system is assessed by a final examination, with written and oral or practical components. The assessment is conducted by representatives of the relevant trades and occupations and of the teachers in the Berufsschule. Those who pass are recognised as competent practitioners of their occupation, and given appropriate certification that entitles them to practise it, or to continue their training to a more advanced level in the *Fachschule* (see below).

Numbers participating in the dual system are declining as numbers in higher education increase: there were about 1.7 million apprentices in the dual system in 1993, compared with 2.2 million in the former West Germany alone in 1980. (Phillips, 1995)

Full-time vocational training
There are about 770,000 students in full-time upper secondary vocational education (1993 figures), in a variety of schools and colleges, including the following.

Berufsfachschule – 'Skilled worker vocational schools' account for 9% of all students in upper secondary education. (1993 figures) They are varied in character, offering training in a very wide range of occupational fields, at a number of different levels. Some require a Realschule leaving certificate for admission, and train students in one or two years for such occupations as technical assistant. Others require only a Hauptschule leaving certificate and offer more basic occupational training, or the opportunity to study for the *Mittlerer Schulabschluß* ('intermediate school-leaving examination'), a vocational qualification equivalent in level to the Realschule certificate. For more demanding occupations, the Berufsfachschulen also offer a one-year course equivalent to the first year of training in the dual system, to which students can then transfer. They also prepare students wishing to continue their vocational education to tertiary level for the *Fachhochschulreife* (the 'readiness for higher technical education' certificate).

Fachschule – The 'vocational school' accounts for 5% of all students in upper secondary education. (1993 figures) Though it is in the secondary school sector, it caters for students who already have basic vocational training and some practical experience in their field, and trains them in one-, two- or three-year courses for responsibilities of middle-management level in such varied fields as engineering, social work, business management and nursing. It also prepares students wishing to continue their vocational education to tertiary level for the Fachhochschulreife.

Berufliches Gymnasium – The 'career-oriented Gymnasium' (also called *Fachgymnasium* in some states) accounts for 3% of all students in full-time upper secondary vocational education (1993 figures). It exists only at upper secondary level, and entrants require a Realschule leaving certificate of the same level as would allow admission to the general education Gymnasium (or its equivalent). The Berufliches Gymnasium is also equivalent to the general

Gymnasium in standards and curriculum, except that in addition to general subjects it has several occupational subjects, such as business studies and various branches of engineering, one of which can be taken as one of the two advanced level subjects required for the Abitur (see above). Successful candidates are usually awarded the same qualification as in the general Gymnasium, the Allgemeine Hochschulreife, granting the holder the right to enter any course in any institution of higher education. In addition, Berufliches Gymnasium students may quite separately take an examination qualifying them in the occupation they have studied.

Fachoberschule – The 'vocational upper school' accounts for 2% of all students in full-time upper secondary vocational education. (1993 figures) It offers mainly two-year courses preparing students holding the Realschule leaving certificate for the Fachhochschulreife, which gives access to vocational education at tertiary level.

Special education

At every level from preprimary to lower secondary, *Sonderschulen* (special or remedial schools) provide education for pupils deemed unable to cope in regular schools because of physical or mental handicap, with curricula and teaching to match the mainstream equivalent where possible, but adapted where necessary to the special needs of the pupils. There are ten different types of Sonderschule, catering for different ages and needs. Very few pupils (about 3%) transfer from Sonderschulen to mainstream schools.

Tertiary education

About a third of each age-group now enters tertiary education (compared with a fifth in 1980) – some 70% of them in universities and comparable academic institutions, and 30% in *Fachhochschulen* ('higher vocational schools'). Entry to all these is allowed for anyone holding the Allgemeine Hochschulreife, and to the Fachhochschulen (and a limited range of university courses) for anyone holding the corresponding *Fachhochschulreife*. Between 1960 and 1990, the numbers of university students increased more than five-fold. Overcrowding and overstretching of resources are widely acknowledged as problems, as are the relatively advanced ages at which students typically complete their education – 28 years for the average university graduate, and just under 32 for doctoral graduates (10% of those leaving university in the former West Germany). In 1993, the federal government proposed expanding the Fachhochschulen, transferring courses, students and resources to them from the universities, and improving employment opportunities in the public sector for Fachhochschulen graduates; but there has yet been little agreement on the implementation of these proposals. (Phillips, 1995)

About 41% of university students in 1990 were female (compared with 28% in 1960). In higher education institutions specialising in technical subjects, however, the percentage of women is 29%. The most popular areas of study for women are teacher training (72% of new entrants in 1988), and languages and arts (65%); the least popular are engineering (10%) and mathematics and science (33%). (Münch, 1995; OECD, 1992)

Germany has over 300 institutions of higher education of various kinds, with some 1.8 million students. The nature of all (public and private) institutions of higher education is defined in the relevant Higher Education Acts of the different Länder. In general, their aim is to foster and develop the sciences and the arts through research, study and teaching, and prepare students for scientific and artistic careers.

The main types of institution (with 1992–3 figures) are as follows.

Universitäten

There are 85 universities, with 1.2 million students. Entry is open to anyone holding the Allgemeine Hochschulreife. A course of study formally lasts four or five years, but in practice many students take one or two years longer. Teaching is by lecture and seminar, with oral and written work (and where appropriate laboratory work) by the students. Assessment is usually by a written examination; course work plays little part. They award degrees at three levels – Diplom, Magister and Doktor. Academic degrees are awarded on the basis of an examination by the institution itself (Hochschulprüfung). Degrees that count as professional qualifications (for example in medicine, law and teaching) are awarded on the basis of a state examination (Staatsexamen).

Fachhochschulen

There are 125 'higher vocational schools', with 370,000 students. Entry is open to anyone holding the Allgemeine Hochschulreife or Fachhochschulreife, and demand for places is high. The Fachhochschulen offer professional courses in engineering, economics, social work, and other applied subjects. These courses are only partly similar to those on offer in the universities and other higher education institutions, being shorter, more practice-oriented and usually characterised by longer periods of integrated practical work. Courses are usually offered at 'diploma' level, which is not considered an acceptable entry for a research degree. The Fachhochschulen do not offer doctorates. The vast majority of the staff have a doctorate and industrial experience. They are civil servants in tenured posts and carry the title of Professor. Contact with industry occurs through students on placements and consultancy by the staff. No fundamental research is carried out in the Fachhochschulen, and even applied research is limited.

Pädagogische Hochschulen
There are 11 'colleges of education', with 25,000 students. Until the 1970s, they were separate institutions, but now (in all but two states) they are part of a university. The colleges' main function is training teachers for primary and certain lower secondary schools. (Other teachers are trained in universities or specialist institutions, such as colleges of art and music.) College courses last for three or four years, after which students take the *Erste Staatsprüfung* – the 'first state examination'. (The second state examination takes place after the students have had preparatory teaching experience.)

In addition, there are 43 colleges devoted to the various arts, with 29,000 students; and 19 colleges of theology, with 3,000 students.

Adult education

In Germany adult education, more usually referred as continuing education, is a complex component of the education system. It is defined by the Federal Länder Commission of Educational Planning as 'the continuation or the resumption of organised learning after the completion of a first phase of education and after embarking on working life'.

Continuing education is varied because of its market character, the plurality of suppliers and the subsidiary role of the state. The providers of continuing education are not only very varied but in competition with each other. The local adult education centres (*Volkshochschulen*) provide continuing general and vocational education. There are some 850 such centres and 3,500 sub-centres. The Länder contribute funds, and the centres are administered by local authorities or registered associations. In 1989, nearly 400,000 courses were attended by 5.5 million people; some 15,000 sat examinations in various subjects such as languages, mathematics, science and technology.

The other main providers include state-run specialised institutes (continuing vocational training), state establishments of higher education (academic/scientific continuing education), the chambers of commerce and industry and a large number of private providers, some commercial, others non-profit making. A number of co-ordinating organisations are also involved, such as the Association of Chambers of Agriculture, the Central Organisation of German Crafts, the Rationalisation Board of German Industry, the German Trade Union Federation, and the separate Adult Education Working Groups of the Protestant Churches and of the Catholic Church.

Continuing education is thus extremely complicated. It is widely acknowledged that what is on offer is not widely known, the alternatives are not clearly understood by most potential users, and the national efforts to establish a system of continuing education with certificates comparable to those for younger pupils and students have so far not succeeded.

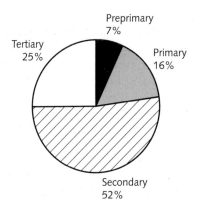

Germany figure 3   Distribution of educational spending among the different sectors, 1992 (Former West Germany only, CERI, 1995)

Funding

The Länder of the former West Germany, taken together, spend 4.9% of their GDP on education (CERI, 1995). Its distribution among the different sectors of education is illustrated in Figure 3.

Individuals have a legal right to financial assistance for training if funds are not available from other sources, but since 1983, only those secondary school students who live away from home are eligible for assistance for their training; they receive a non-repayable grant. Students in higher education receive repayable loans. In 1990 the total average monthly number of recipients in the former West Germany was 371,000, three-quarters of whom lived away from home.

The teaching profession

Teacher training, like much else in German education, varies from state to state, but with broad similarities in the most important respects.

School teachers at all levels must complete two phases of training. The first phase is predominantly academic (though it includes some teaching practice), and takes place at a university or equivalent institution, such as an art or music college. This phase lasts between three and five years: in general, the older the pupils to be taught, the longer the course. Students study both educational theory and their specialist teaching-subjects. At the end of this phase, students take the 'first state examination' (*Erste Staatsprüfung*). Those who pass are admitted to the second phase, which is predominantly practical, with emphasis on actual experience and its analysis. This phase lasts up to two years, and culminates in the 'second state examination' (*Zweite Staatsprüfung*). Those who pass are qualified teachers.

The work of Kindergarten educational staff is defined not as teaching but as *Sozialpädagogik* (educational social work). These staff are trained in Fachschulen (see above), upper secondary level vocational schools. Courses last three years, two in the school itself, and one of supervised practical experience.

Teachers in the former West Germany are civil servants; those in the former East Germany are to acquire civil servant status too.

ACKNOWLEDGEMENTS

We are grateful to the Federal Ministry of Education and Science for supplying us with information about education in Germany, and to Ekkehard Thumm of the Open University for his comments.

REFERENCES

CERI (1995) *Education at a Glance: OECD indicators*, Paris: Organisation for Economic Co-operation and Development.

European Commission (1995) *Structures of the Education and Initial Training Systems in the European Union*, Luxembourg: Office for Official Publications of the European Commission.

Federal Ministry of Education and Science (1991) *Basic and Structural Data: education statistics of the Federal Republic of Germany, 1991/1992 Edition*, Bonn: Federal Ministry of Education and Science.

Federal Ministry of Education and Science (1993) *Numerical Barometer: some educational statistics 1993/94*, Bonn: Federal Ministry of Education and Science.

Münch, J. (1993) *Systems and Procedures of Certification of Qualifications in the Federal Republic of Germany*, Berlin: CEDEFOP.

Münch, J. (1995) *Vocational Education and Training in the Federal Republic of Germany*, Luxembourg: Office for Official Publications of the European Commission.

OECD (1992) *From Higher Education to Employment Volume 1: Australia, Austria, Belgium, Germany*, Paris: Organisation for Economic Co-operation and Development.

OECD (1994) *Vocational Training in Germany: modernisation and responsiveness*, Paris: Organisation for Economic Co-operation and Development.

OECD (1996) *OECD Economic Surveys 1995–1996: Germany*, Paris: Organisation for Economic Co-operation and Development.

Phillips, D. (1995) 'Educational developments in the new Germany', *Compare*, Vol. 25, No. 1, 35–47.

Phillips, D. (1992) 'Transitions and traditions: educational developments in the new Germany in their historical context', *Aspects of Education*, No. 47, pp. 111–27.

BACKGROUND

Greece and its prefectures

(Note: Greek terminology has been transliterated here into roman script.)

After four centuries of Turkish rule, Greece gained its independence during the 1820s, and was recognised as a kingdom by the major European powers in 1830. In 1967, a group of army officers ('the colonels') seized power, declaring Greece a republic in 1973. In 1974, the military government collapsed in the wake of a successful invasion of Cyprus by Turkey, but Greece's republican status was confirmed in a referendum, and a new constitution was introduced in 1975.

Greece has been a full member of the EC/EU since 1981, having been an associate member of the European Economic Community since 1969.

POPULATION

Population	10.4 million in 1994 (a rise of 0.5% per annum from 1984)
Land area	132,000 sq. km
Population density	79 per sq. km

ECONOMY

GDP	$73 billion (1994)
GDP per capita	$7,100 (1994)
In employment	3.8 million (1994)
Spending on education	6.5% of GDP (4.2% public expenditure, 2.3% from private sources) (1992)

In terms of GDP per capita, Greece is the poorest country in Western Europe. It also has a much higher percentage of its workforce employed in agriculture than any other Western European country. (See Section Two, Figures 2 and 3.)

RELIGION

There is no state religion – indeed religious freedom is guaranteed and proselytising forbidden by the constitution – but almost all of the population (96%) belong to the Greek Orthodox Church.

LANGUAGE

Two varieties of modern Greek are in use. *Katherevousa* (purist) Greek represents a deliberate attempt to return to classical Greek, and is used mostly in official documents. *Demotiki* (demotic) Greek, which exists in a number of dialects, is the one generally used in everyday speech and in literature. About 98% of the population speak Greek in one or other variety (or a mixture of the two); the main minority language is Turkish.

GOVERNMENT

Greece has four levels of government – *national, regional, prefecture* and *municipal/communal*. Control of education is highly centralised, with detailed prescriptions in laws and government directives. There has been some decentralisation in recent years, with prefects (see below) now locally elected and prefectures given more autonomy in spending money allocated to them. But educational administrators at prefecture level remain directly responsible to the national government.

There are numerous committees at national, prefecture, municipal/communal and institutional levels with a variety of rights and duties – to be consulted, to make recommendations, and at school level to exercise some managerial responsibilities.

Educational policy is determined in detail by the national government; administration and operational matters are the responsibility of the prefectures (see below). The Ministry of National Education and Religious Affairs (hereafter Ministry of Education) has ultimate responsibility for most education at all levels, but some types of vocational education and training are the responsibility of the Ministry of Labour, and some are shared between the two ministries (see below). Some specialist vocational schools are the responsibility of other ministries, such as the Ministry of Agriculture. Some units for children with special educational needs are run by the Ministry of Health and Social Security. Funding for schools is provided through the Ministry of the Interior.

In practice, however, the Ministry of Education delegates many of its responsibilities to autonomous public organisations. They include the following.

- The Pedagogical Institute, which issues guidance and direction on such matters as curriculum and timetables, teaching methods, textbooks, and the inservice training of teachers.
- The Organisation for Vocational Education and Training, established in 1992, which has general responsibility for vocational education and training. This includes assessing the training needs of each sector of the economy, and monitoring and recognising the qualifications offered by different training organisations, in Greece and abroad. The Organisation is also directly responsible for the Institutes of Vocational Training (see below). It is itself run by a board consisting of representatives of the Ministry of Labour and the economic ministries as well as the Ministry of Education, together with representatives of employers and employees.

In addition, there are a number of national advisory bodies. The most general is the National Education Council, which advises the Ministry of Education on education at all levels. Its members include representatives of other government ministries, local government, the Pedagogical Institute, political parties, the Church, teachers, parents, students and employers. There are also more specialised advisory bodies, with several advising on various aspects of universities and technological education.

Greece is divided into 13 regions (peripheries), but these do not have major educational responsibilities. The most important level of local government, for educational as for other matters, is that of the 54 prefectures (nomoi), under the direction of prefects (nomarchai). These were originally modelled on the

French prefect system, and until 1994 the prefects were appointed by the national government. Now, however, they are directly elected by the population of the prefecture, for a term of four years. Each prefecture has two education directorates, one in overall charge of primary and the other of secondary schooling. Their directors are responsible directly to the Ministry of Education as well as to the local prefect.

Each prefecture has its own advisory body, the Prefectural Education Committee (and larger prefectures may have Sub-prefectural Education Committees), which advises the prefect (or sub-prefect) on educational matters. Its membership includes representatives of parents and employers as well as of the educational administration itself. Each prefecture also has a regional council with responsibility for the teaching profession. Its members include teachers' representatives, in addition to local government officials.

The urban municipalities and rural communes have some educational responsibilities, mainly for the construction and maintenance of school buildings (as planned by the prefecture). Each has its own advisory body, the Municipal/Communal Education Committee, to advise on local education matters: its members include representatives of head teachers, parents and employers.

EDUCATION

Education in Greece is compulsory for nine years between the ages of five-and-a-half and 15. It may take place in state or private schools. It is divided into six years of primary school (*dimotiko scholio*) and three years of lower secondary school (*gymnasion*). Before compulsory education, children may attend preschool education (*nypiagogea*) from the age of three-and-a-half; and after it, they may attend a range of secondary schools or vocational training courses and eventually a range of tertiary institutions.

State education at all levels – including the provision of textbooks – is free. Private schools are closely regulated by the Ministry of Education, especially concerning their curricula, fees and buildings, but they receive no financial support from the state. The private sector is small and declining.

Substantial changes were made to education in Greece by legislation during the 1980s.

INSTITUTIONS

Schools at all levels have a similar administrative structure. Each establishment has a *head teacher* who has overall responsibility for the management of the school and its finances, supervision of the teachers and pupils, and ensuring that the relevant laws and regulations governing its operation are followed. He or she is assisted by a *deputy head teacher*, and they work in association

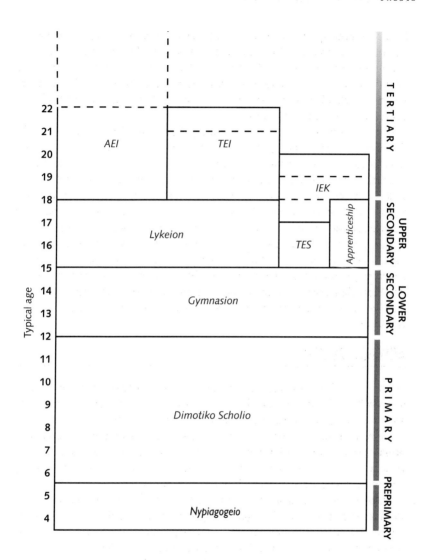

Note: This diagram is simplified and should be used in conjunction with the text

Greece's education system

with a number of administrative and advisory bodies described below. These include:

- the *Teachers' Council*, the main administrative body supporting the head and deputy head in their educational duties, including pupils' attendance and discipline;

- the *School Committee*, which consists of the head teacher plus representatives of local government, the parents and, in secondary schools, the students. It is responsible for the budget and operational matters;
- the *School Council*, which consists of the teachers' council plus representatives of local government, parents and, in secondary schools, students. Its role is advisory, and concerned especially with relations between the school and its pupils' families;
- the *Parents' Association*, which places parent representatives on other bodies, as described above;
- the *Pupils' Committees*, which allow pupils to contribute directly to the running of the school, and also place pupil representatives on other bodies, as described above.

Preprimary

Preprimary education in Greece is for children between the ages of three-and-a-half and five-and-a-half, in nursery schools (nypiagogea).

Nypiagogea

Attendance is voluntary. Most nursery schools are state-run and free; but there is a small private sector (catering for 4% of pupils), charging fees whose level must be approved by the government.

Most nursery schools are small, with either up to 30 pupils and one teacher (*monothesia*) or 31 to 60 pupils and two teachers (*dithesia*). The rare larger nursery schools (*polythesia*) must have one teacher for every 30 pupils.

There is a nationally defined nursery school curriculum, with opportunities for children to play, and other activities designed to help them develop physically, emotionally, intellectually and socially.

Nursery schools normally operate for about 34 weeks per year (September to June), five days per week, and three-and-a-half hours per day, either in the morning or in the afternoon.

In 1993–4, there were 5,600 nursery schools in Greece, with 8,100 teachers and 134,300 pupils (about 60% of the age-group). About 96% of the pupils attended state-run schools, 4% private schools. (European Commission)

Primary education

The six years of primary education (dimotiko scholio), from age five-and-a-half until 12, form the first stage of compulsory schooling.

Dimotiko scholio

Primary education may be provided in state-run schools or private schools (of which there are very few). Pupils are divided into classes by age. Class sizes are limited to 25 in schools with just one or two teachers, and to 30 in larger schools.

The primary curriculum, timetable and choice of textbooks are laid down by the Pedagogical Institute. In the first two years, pupils study the following subjects.

- environmental studies
- Greek
- arithmetic
- aesthetic education
- physical education

In the later years, the curriculum also includes the following.

- religious knowledge
- history
- geography
- civics
- the natural world
- physics and chemistry with hygiene
- geometry
- music
- a foreign language

Each class has a class teacher, who normally teaches all subjects except foreign languages, music, art and physical education, which are taught by specialists (who are sometimes secondary teachers too).

Pupils are assessed orally every day, and their attainments recorded and reported to parents in descriptive form. In the upper years, a four-point scale is also used. However, progress from one class to the next is automatic (except when a pupil has been absent for more than half of the year, when an examination must be taken). At the end of their final year, pupils whose attainment is satisfactory are given a certificate, but all primary school leavers are automatically admitted to lower secondary school.

Primary schools normally operate for about 35 weeks per year (September to June), five days per week, and five to six hours per day. Lessons normally take place in the morning (8.15 am – 1.30 pm), but sometimes a primary and a lower secondary school share the same building, in which case they alternate a morning and an afternoon timetable (2.00 – 7.00 pm).

In 1993–4, there were 7,400 primary schools in Greece, with 39,800 teachers and 744,500 pupils. About 93% of the pupils attended state-run schools, 7% private schools. (European Commission)

Lower secondary education

The lower secondary school (gymnasion), for pupils from age 12 to 15, completes the years of compulsory education.

Gymnasion

Gymnasia are co-educational and comprehensive, with children grouped into classes by age, not ability or attainment. Teachers are subject specialists.

All pupils study the same curriculum, specified by law in 1985, with some subsequent modifications. Textbooks are also centrally prescribed, and provided free. The subjects include the following.

- religion
- classical Greek literature
- modern Greek language and literature
- mathematics
- physics
- chemistry
- biology
- computing
- history
- geography
- foreign languages (English/French/German)
- physical education
- art education
- social education
- domestic science
- careers guidance

Assessment is by teachers, by oral and written tests at the end of each of the three terms of the school year. Those whose marks are satisfactory proceed to the next year; others must resit their examinations in September, and if they still fail, must repeat the year. Those who pass their examinations in the final year are awarded the lower secondary school leaving certificate (*Apolytirio Gymnasiou*), which is used for admission to upper secondary education, or when seeking employment. Decisions about repeating a year and about the award of a leaving certificate are made by the teachers' association.

Legislation in 1985 permitted specialist sports and music gymnasia to be established in a number of cities for children with particular talents; 80 sports gymnasia and 15 music gymnasia have now been established. In both types, pupils study the range of general subjects as well as their musical or sporting specialisms. They often therefore have a longer school week than others pupils (about 46 hours as against 35).

In 1993–4, there were 1,900 gymnasia in Greece, with 29,500 teachers and 444,000 pupils. About 96% of the pupils attended state-run schools, 4% private schools. (European Commission)

Upper secondary education

Upper secondary education is for students between the ages of 15 and 18. It is free (including the provision of textbooks) but not compulsory. There are three main kinds of schools for this age group, the *lykeia* (of different types), the technical/vocational schools (TES), and the apprenticeship schools (*scholes matheteias*). The distribution of students among these is illustrated in Figure 1.

Lykeion
Lykeia are under the direction of the Ministry of Education. Anyone holding a gymnasion leaving certificate has a right to be admitted to any lykeion. Attendance is free, and textbooks are also supplied free. Several different types of lykeion were established by legislation in 1985, but all offer a three-year general academic education, some with additional specialist studies.

- General (GEL – *Geniko Lykeion*): prepares students for higher education, in a university or institution of technological education (see below)
- Technical/Vocational (TEL – *Tecniko-Epagelmatiko Lykeion*): prepares students for higher education in an institution of technological education, or direct entry into employment in a particular technical field
- Integrated (EPL – *Enaio Polykladiko Lykeion*): prepares students for either higher education or employment in a particular technical field

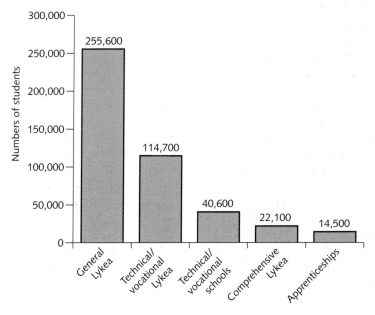

Greece figure 1   Numbers of students in the main types of upper secondary education, 1993–4 (European Commission)

- Specialist: combines general education with a specialist course of study; there are Ecclesiastical, Sports, Classical and Music lykea.

However, the first two of these types between them account for 94% of the 393,500 lykea students – 65% in the General lykeia and 29% in the Technical/Vocational lykea. In both of these, students in the first two years follow a common curriculum. The following subjects are common to both types of school, and occupy roughly two-thirds of the students' time.

- religion
- modern Greek
- history
- foreign language (English/French/German)
- mathematics
- physics
- chemistry
- physical education
- vocational guidance

For the rest of their time in these two years, students in the GEL study a further set of academic subjects.

- ancient Greek
- art
- music
- geology
- biology
- psychology
- astronomy

In their third year, students in the GEL study a common core of subjects

- religion
- philosophy
- political science
- foreign languages
- physical education

plus a range of 'preparatory' subjects according to which of four 'option streams' (mathematics and physical sciences; natural sciences; arts and languages; social studies) they have chosen with a view to higher education.

Students in the TEL, however, use the time not taken up by the common subjects listed above to study vocational subjects. In their first year, these are the same for all students – a set of 'orientation' courses in agriculture, design, economics, electricity, mechanics or medicine. These are the basis for their choices in subsequent years.

The EPL offers the choice of vocational or academic courses within the same school. The Ecclesiastical, Sports, Classical and Music lykea are similar to the GEL, but replace some of its subjects with their own specialised courses.

Assessment is by teachers, by oral and written tests at the end of each of the three terms of the school year, and by a written examination at the end of the year. Those who fail may be required to repeat the year. Those who pass their examinations in the final year are awarded a leaving certificate (*Apolytirio Lykeiou*), which is used for admission to tertiary education, or when seeking employment. Decisions about repeating a year and about the award of a leaving certificate are made by the teachers' association.

The GELs have 255,600 students (65% of the 393,500 students in the lykea sector), taught by 17,700 teachers in 1,200 schools. About 6% of GEL students are in private schools.

The TELs have 114,700 students (29% of all lykea students), taught by 8,600 teachers in 350 schools. About 14% of TEL students are in private schools.

The other types of lykea are much fewer in number. There are 25 EPLs, with 22,100 students and 1,900 teachers. And there are 16 Ecclesiastical, 15 Sports, 12 Classical and two Music lykea. (1993–4 figures; European Commission)

TES

Technical/Vocational Schools (TES) are under the direction of the Ministry of Education. They offer courses normally lasting two years (three years for evening courses), as compared with the three years of the TELs. For admission, students require the gymnasion leaving certificate. TES may be state-run or private. They train students for such occupations as car mechanic and refrigerator technician. The TES week has 30 teaching hours, 24 spent on the students' specialisation and workshop training, six on general subjects (Greek, mathematics, physics, a foreign language and civics). On successful completion of their studies, students are awarded a certificate (*Ptychio*) in their specialist subject. This is used when seeking employment, but it also qualifies students who wish to continue their studies for admission to the second year of the TEL.

There are 265 TESs, with 3,500 teachers and 40,600 students. Almost 80% of the schools are private, but they are mostly small, and cater overall for only 12% of TES students. (1993–4 figures)

Apprenticeship

Apprenticeships combine practical training in a firm with attendance at scholes matheteias (apprenticeship schools), which are under the direction of the Ministry of Labour in association with employers' and trade union organisations. Apprentices are normally aged 15 to 18 on beginning their apprenticeships, which last three years. In the first year, they attend school every day. Thereafter, they attend only one day per week, spending the remaining four days working for their employer. At school, they study a compulsory curriculum, three-quarters of which is devoted to theoretical subjects, one-quarter to practical work.

Apprentices are assessed by an examination at the end of their apprenticeship. Those who pass are awarded a certificate (Ptychio), which is equivalent to the certificate awarded by the TES.

At any time, there are between 14,000 and 15,000 young people on apprenticeships. They are taught by about 700 full-time teachers in the apprenticeship schools, and about 1,300 part-time trainers working for various firms.

Special education

The official policy is to integrate pupils with special educational needs into mainstream schools, and the Ministry of Education believes that most are being taught in this way, whether in ordinary classes with individual help or in special classes. There are also special schools for severely handicapped children, and for blind and deaf children. In 1990–1, some 16,000 pupils were in special education programmes (mainstream and special schools combined), 80% of them in programmes run by the Ministry of Education, 20% in units run by the Ministry of Health and Social Security. The provision of special education is unevenly distributed: it is greatest in Athens, and rare in isolated rural areas and smaller islands. (O'Hanlon, 1995)

Tertiary education

Tertiary education takes place mainly in three types of institution.

- universities (AEI) concerned with the advancement of knowledge through academic research and teaching
- institutions of technological education (TEI): concerned with the assimilation and practical application of scientific knowledge
- institutes of vocational training (IEK) offering post-secondary vocational training at a variety of levels

For admission to either AEI or TEI, candidates must hold a lykeion leaving certificate, and also take an entrance examination in the option stream they have followed in the lykeion (see above). In both AEI and TEI, the Ministry of Education operates a *numerus clausus* policy, limiting student numbers across the entire range of subjects, and the available places go to the candidates with the highest overall marks; 75% of this mark is based on performance in the entrance examination, and 25% on graduation marks from the lykeion.

Universities

There are currently 18 universities in Greece, and an Open University is also to open shortly. They are all state-run, and supervised by the Ministry of Education. Though their autonomy is guaranteed by the Greek Constitution, they are in practice subject to detailed government control. Tuition, including the supply of textbooks (which are often centrally prescribed), is free. The universities were reformed by legislation of 1982. This established the Council of Higher Education (SAP), to advise the Ministry on university matters. Its members are drawn from the Ministry, political parties, employers, trade unions and the universities themselves.

At the same time, the universities' internal structures and decision-making procedures were democratised. Though there are higher officers and administrative bodies (the rector, the rector's council, the senate, and the faculties), it is the *academic departments* that became the policy-making units of the university. Within departments, the traditional professorial chair was abolished, and its powers transferred to a departmental council. These councils now make their own decisions about research, teaching and assessment in their department – deciding, for example, which courses will be compulsory for students and which offered as options, and what the balance will be between written and oral examinations. A degree (Ptychio) is awarded as the degree of a particular department.

The academic year runs from September to August, and is divided into two semesters. Degree courses normally last four years, but in some subjects (notably medicine and dentistry) they last five.

A recent OECD study (OECD, 1995) made a number of criticisms and observations about university education in Greece; these included the following.

- there is too great a gap between universities and the economy, and between academic and technical/vocational studies. The latter are too often regarded as a second-best option for students who fail to gain admission to university
- provision and financial support for students' accommodation and living expenses are too generous and paternalistic
- courses are often too rigid, and too dependent on a single, centrally-prescribed textbook
- assessment and the award of degrees are insufficiently rigorous, and one-third of registered students do not attend classes
- about 45% of degrees are in the humanities
- between 60% and 80% of university graduates are employed in the public sector. A further 8% are unemployed

Institutions of technological education

There are currently 14 institutions of technological education (TEI) in Greece. They are all state-run, and supervised by the Ministry of Education, but their autonomy in teaching and academic matters is guaranteed by legislation of

1983, under which they operate. Tuition, including the supply of textbooks, is free. The legislation also established a *Council for Technological Education* (STE) and an *Institute for Technological Education* (ITE) – advisory bodies to the Ministry of Education, concerned respectively with general policy and more detailed matters such as the curricula and internal organisation of the TEI, and the equivalence of their qualifications.

Each institution has at least two faculties from the following range (the total numbers of existing faculties are shown in brackets).

- technological applications (16)
- health and caring professions (14)
- agricultural technology (8)
- administration and economy (7)
- graphic arts and fine arts (5)
- food technology (2)

The numbers and distribution of these faculties are determined, and changed from time to time, by the Ministry of Education, with advice from the STE.

Assessment is by tests (including practical work) and assignments set by the departments. A degree (Ptychio) is awarded as the degree of a particular department.

The academic year runs from September to July, and is divided into two semesters each of 15 weeks. Degree courses normally last between three and four years.

There are about 46,000 students in the TEI, with 1,800 permanent and 3,500 temporary teaching staff.

Institutes of vocational training

The institutes of vocational training (IEK) were established by legislation of 1992 to provide vocational training of a wide variety of types and levels. Thus their entrants may have been only to lykeia of any type, to TESs or to the gymnasion. They are admitted according to whatever criteria are considered appropriate, such as leaving certificate marks or work experience. They may come to IEK straight from compulsory education, or be adults of any age. IEK may be state-run or private, but tuition is free in either case. The IEK year consists of two semesters, and courses vary in length from one semester to two years.

The institutes do not normally have premises of their own, but operate from those of lykeia. They organise both theoretical instruction and practical training in firms; the latter occupies between a quarter and half of a typical IEK course. The institutes also try to place students in employment at the end of their courses.

Students are assessed by tests throughout their training, and a final examination. Those who are successful are awarded a certificate of vocational training (*Vevaiosi Epagelmatikis Katartisis*), specifying the subject and the length of their course. IEK qualifications do not give their holders access to AEI or TEI.

The teachers are very varied in the kind and extent of their qualifications and experience. Many are part-time, with their main jobs either as practitioners in industry or as teachers in other sectors of education.

In 1993, there were 57 state-run IEKs, with 12,900 students and 4,300 teachers (full- and part-time).

Adult education

State adult education, under the General Secretariat for Adult Education and Services of the Ministry of Education, concentrates mainly on literacy and vocational training. Other ministries sponsor their own specialist adult education programmes, again concentrating on vocational training: for example, the Ministry of Agriculture.

Adult education in liberal studies (including art, music, dance and foreign languages) is provided by private institutions.

Funding

Greece spends 6.5% of its GDP on education – 4.2% public expenditure, 2.3% from private sources. (1992 figures, CERI) The building and operating costs of state schools are funded by the Ministry of the Interior, which decides on their distribution among prefectures, which in turn decide on their distribution among communes/municipalities, which finally decide on their distribution among schools. Each school's budget is managed by the school committee (see above). Private schools receive no state funding.

Universities and ITEs are funded by the Ministry of Education, but they can also have other sources of funding, such as business sponsorship or payments for commissioned research.

Education is free in state educational establishments at every level, and textbooks are also provided free. Students in AEI and TEI may also receive support with board and lodging, according to their own and their families' circumstances, and they are eligible for free medical care and reduced fares on public transport.

Teaching profession

The permanent teachers in state schools are civil servants, though temporary teachers are sometimes employed to cover shortages. Most teachers in every type of school must have taken a four-year university course. For teachers in nursery and primary schools, who each teach almost all subjects, these courses are in university departments of nursery and primary education, respectively.

For teachers in the gymnasion and the lykeion, who are subject specialists, these are courses in their specialist subjects.

Teachers in TELs or EPLs, however, may instead have taken a three-year course in their subject at an ITE, supplemented by a one-year teacher training course at the college for technical education.

The requirement for nursery and primary teachers to be university graduates came into operation only in the mid-1980s. Previously, they took two-year courses at colleges of nursery or primary education. Many nursery and primary teachers currently in post have qualified by this older route.

Teachers at all levels of school are required to take inservice training courses every five or six years. These last three months, and most teachers can expect to take them three or four times in their career.

Parent/school relationships

Parents participate in the running of education through being represented on advisory bodies at prefecture and municipal/communal level, and on both advisory and decision-making bodies at school level (see above). In particular, the school committee, with parents' (and in secondary schools, students') representatives, is responsible for the school's budget and all operational matters. On purely educational matters, the parents' role – through the parents' association and the school council – is advisory.

Education inspectorate

Since 1982, Greece has had school advisers, based in the educational directorates or offices of each prefecture. Their duties include assessing teachers' performance, advising on teaching methods, arranging inservice training and encouraging educational research. There are separate advisers for primary and secondary education. The secondary advisers are subject specialists, and are responsible for teachers of their subject.

School advisers must have had at least 15 years' experience of teaching or related employment in education, and many also hold postgraduate degrees.

ACRONYMS AND ABBREVIATIONS

AEI	university
EPL	integrated lykeion
GEL	general lykeion
IEK	institute of vocational training
ITE	Institute for Technological Education
SAP	Council of Higher Education
STE	Council for Technological Education

TEI	institution of technological education
TEL	technical/vocational lykeion
TES	technical/vocational school

ACKNOWLEDGEMENT

We are very grateful to Dr N. Voliotis, Educational Counsellor at the Greek Embassy in London, for providing us with descriptive notes on *The Structure and Operation of the Greek Education System.*

REFERENCES

Archer, E. G. and Peck, B. T. (no date) *The Teaching Profession in Europe*, Glasgow: Jordanhill College of Education.

CERI (1995) *Education at a Glance: OECD indicators*, Paris: Organisation for Economic Co-operation and Development.

European Commission (1995) *Structures of the Education and Initial Training Systems in the European Union*, second edition, Luxembourg: Office for Official Publications of the European Commission.

OECD (1995) *OECD Educational Policy Review of Greece*, Athens: Organisation for Economic Co-operation and Development.

OECD (1996) *OECD Economic Surveys: Greece: 1995–1996*, Paris: Organisation for Economic Co-operation and Development.

O'Hanlon, C. (1995) 'Inclusive education in Spain and Greece', in Potts, P., Armstrong, F. and Masterton, M. (1995) (eds) *Equality and Diversity in Education 2: National and International Contexts*, London: Routledge.

BACKGROUND

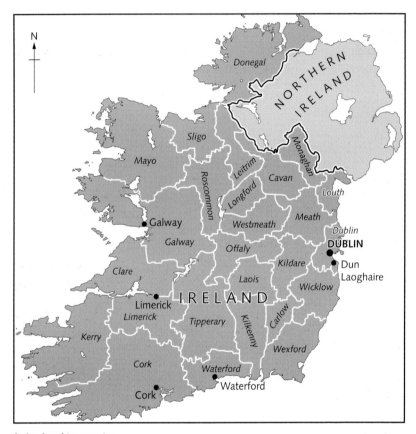

Ireland and its counties

The Republic of Ireland occupies most, but not all, of the island of Ireland – 83% of its area and 69% of its population. The remainder, Northern Ireland, is part of the UK.

Ireland was gradually conquered, partially lost and reconquered by the English from medieval times until the 17th century, when the conquest was completed. Ireland was formally united with Great Britain in 1801 to form the United Kingdom of Great Britain and Ireland. This lasted until 1921–5, when, after decades of struggle over home rule, Ireland was divided between the six counties of Northern Ireland, which remained part of the UK, and the

26 counties which became independent as the Irish Free State. In 1949, the Irish Free State became the Republic of Ireland (and left the British Commonwealth).

Ireland is a member of the EU and the Council of Europe.

POPULATION

Population	3.6 million in 1994 (an average annual rise of 0.1% since 1984)
Land area	70,000 sq. km
Population density	51 per sq. km

ECONOMY

GDP	$52 billion (1994)
GDP per capita	$14,600 (1994)
In employment	52% of working age population (1991)
	– 80% of men/39% of women aged 25–54
	– 37% of young people (15–24)
Part-time employment	8% of all employment (1990)

In the early 1990s, the Irish economy avoided the recession affecting most of the rest of Europe, with economic growth faster than in any other country in the EU.

However, it remains one of the poorest countries of Europe (see Section Two, Figure 2). Unemployment fell to 14.8% in 1994, having reached a peak of 15.8% in 1993. Unemployment levels are inversely related to levels of education: at the extremes, the unemployment rate in 1992 was 24% for those with only a primary education, and 4% for those with a university degree. (OECD, 1995)

RELIGION

In the 1991 Census, 92% of the population identified themselves as Roman Catholic, and 3% as belonging to the various Protestant churches, with 4% professing no adherence to any religion.

An unusual feature of education in Ireland is that most schools – almost all those at primary level, and most of those at secondary level – are owned and run not by the state but by the Roman Catholic Church and other religious bodies. However, almost all private schools receive state funds, and all are subject to detailed state regulation and inspection.

LANGUAGE AND ETHNICITY

Irish is the national language, but it is the mother tongue of only a minority of the population, mainly in the west of the country, and English is also recognised as an official language. Irish is no longer a compulsory school subject.

In 6% of all primary schools (207 in all), only Irish is used.

GOVERNMENT

Ireland has two levels of government, *national* and *local*. At present, most educational functions and powers are centralised, but the local authorities have some educational responsibilities, exercised through 38 vocational education committees (VEC). However, proposals are under discussion to create a new tier of eight regional educational councils (REC). The RECs would assume all the current responsibilities of the VECs, some of those currently held by the national government, and perhaps some currently held by individual schools. (See Bhreathnach, 1994.)

The Minister for Education is ultimately responsible for most education in Ireland, though responsibilities for vocational education and training are shared with the Minister for Enterprise and Employment, and certain other ministers (such as those for Agriculture and Food, and for Tourism and Trade) have responsibilities for training in their particular areas.

There is little legislation concerning education, and the Minister and the Department for Education operate largely by issuing regulations. Through these regulations, they control the school curriculum and examinations, and school management, resources and staffing. Universities and other institutions of higher education have a high degree of autonomy, but the Department funds them individually through the Higher Education Authority.

Ireland has over 100 local authorities, of a variety of forms. Of these, 38 currently have important educational responsibilities – the counties and county boroughs plus a small number of urban district councils – but even their functions are relatively limited, for two main reasons. First, most of Ireland's schools are privately owned and run – usually by religious bodies. Secondly, Ireland is a small country, and so the national government can exercise quite direct supervision at local level. The local authorities' main responsibilities are for the vocational schools and (together with religious and other bodies and the Department of Education) for the community and comprehensive schools in their area (see below). They exercise these responsibilities through VECs, each covering a particular local authority area. Each VEC has 14 members, elected by the appropriate local authority; between five and eight VEC members must themselves be members of that authority. The VECs range in size from those of the City of Dublin and County Cork, each with 21 schools, to those of Dun Laoghaire and the towns of Sligo and Wexford, each with one. (1993 figures)

EDUCATION

Education in Ireland has expanded greatly in the last thirty years, with the numbers of secondary level pupils more than doubling, and the numbers of students in tertiary education rising by almost 50%. There are a number of

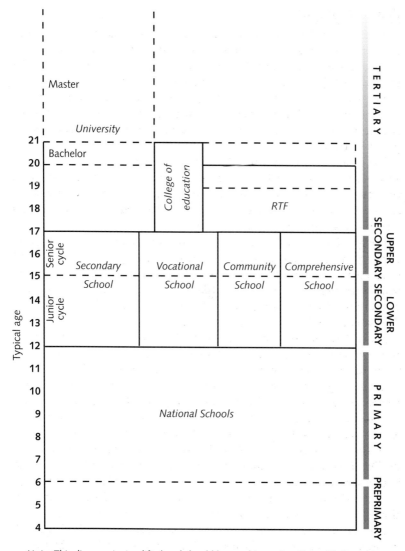

Note: This diagram is simplified and should be used in conjunction with the text

Ireland's education system

proposals under discussion for reform of education in Ireland. As well as describing current arrangements, we mention some of the most important of the proposed changes.

Education is compulsory and available free for nine years, between the ages of six and 15. (It is possible but uncommon for parents to educate their children at home.) Compulsory schooling is divided between primary level schools (six years) and the junior cycle (three years) of secondary level schools. In practice, however, most children and young people start school earlier and leave later than the compulsory ages. Over half the four-year-old and virtually all the five-year-old children have begun full-time education. And over 90% of 16-year-olds, three-quarters of 17-year-olds and half of 18-year-olds are still at school. There are proposals under discussion to raise the leaving age to 16.

Most schools in Ireland are privately owned and run, usually by the Roman Catholic Church and other religious bodies. These include almost all those at primary level, and about 60% of those at secondary level. However, over 95% of private schools receive state funds, and all are subject to detailed state regulation and inspection.

About 12% of men and 11% of women in the population leave full-time education at the age of 15. At the other extreme, about 10% of men and 7% of women aged over 20 have been to university.

INSTITUTIONS

Ireland has just over 4,000 educational institutions at primary and secondary levels, with 880,000 pupils and full-time students. Schools at primary level (with an average of 157 pupils) are smaller than those at secondary level (an average of 457). (1992–3 figures)

Preprimary education

Ireland has no system of preprimary education. However, national schools (i.e. primary schools: see below) may admit pupils from the age of four, and in practice just over half the four-year-olds and virtually all the five-year-olds are in 'full-time' education (generally mornings only).

Preprimary education is free, and provides formal learning, planned in an integrated way with primary schooling proper, and not just child-care. The teachers are primary teachers, with the same training, conditions and salaries.

Primary education

Primary schooling is compulsory for children between the ages of six and 12, but in practice (see above) over half of all four-year-olds and virtually all five-year-olds also attend. Schools at this level are called *national schools*.

National schools
There are just over 3,200 national schools; all but ten are denominational in character. About 93% are Roman Catholic and 6% belong to the (episcopalian) Church of Ireland. The remaining 1% comprise 18 Presbyterian schools, and one Jewish, one Methodist and one Muslim school. About 83% of schools are co-educational, 11% are boys' schools and 6% girls'. (1992–3 figures)

Almost all national schools (98%) are at present financed jointly by local religious organisations and the national government's Department of Education, and provide free education. (The other 2% are wholly private and may charge fees.) When a new school is built, the site is locally provided, but the Department contributes most (85–95%) of the costs of building and furnishing it. The Department allocates teachers to individual schools, and pays their salaries in full. In addition, the Department pays up to 75% of the recurrent costs, such as heating and cleaning, in the form of a grant paid according to the number of pupils.

Since 1975, national schools are run by boards of management (previously, they were run by a single manager, usually the local priest or other clergyman). The board members represent the 'patron' of the school (usually a bishop or corresponding high authority of the denomination owning the school), parents, the principal and other teachers.

Although the national schools are private, the main components of their curriculum, and the time devoted to each, are laid down by the government, although flexibility is allowed in teaching methods and timetabling. These are shown in Figure 1.

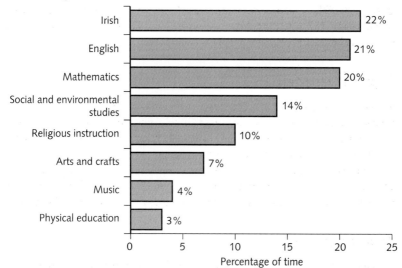

Ireland figure 1   *Percentage of time devoted to compulsory subjects in national schools*
Note: *Social and environmental studies include history, geography and science*

There are proposals under discussion to increase the science component in the curriculum, to set national targets for mathematics and perhaps to introduce a foreign language.

There is currently no national system of assessment at this level; tests are chosen or devised by teachers, who report to parents, usually in writing at the end of the year. At the end of primary schooling, each teacher writes a formal report on each pupil, which is passed on to the secondary school. However, there are proposals under discussion to introduce a system of national tests, possibly at ages seven and 11.

In total, there are about 3,300 national schools, with 521,000 pupils and 21,000 teachers. Most of the schools (54%) have between 50 and 200 pupils; 20% have fewer than 50, and 26% over 200. (1992–3 figures) About 51% of national school pupils are boys, 49% girls. (1990–1 figures)

Lower and upper secondary education

There are four main categories of secondary school in Ireland. All four combine the lower (compulsory – three years) and upper (postcompulsory – two years) stages of secondary education: these are called the *junior* and *senior* *cycles*. The numbers of students at junior and senior level are shown in Figure 2.

Parents may choose any type of junior school for their children, subject to availability of places. Traditionally, the different categories of school offered very different kinds of education. The differences were particularly marked between the oldest two, those called secondary schools (or voluntary

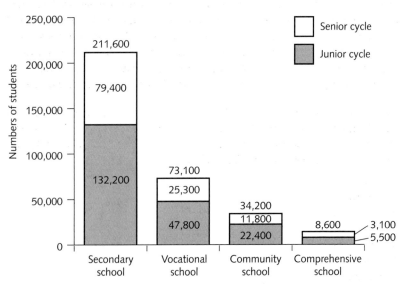

Ireland figure 2   Numbers of pupils/students in secondary education, 1992–3

secondary schools) offering an academic education and the vocational schools providing training in manual skills and preparation for trades. In recent years, however, they have become much more similar, especially in the junior cycle, with the secondary schools adopting practical elements from the vocational schools, and the secondary school academic curriculum becoming a model for all other types of school.

From 1994, any type of school may offer a three-year senior cycle, with the first year as an optional *transition year*, to help the students move from the highly structured junior cycle to the senior cycle proper where they are allowed more autonomy, and have to make subject and vocational choices. The transition year is to be distinct from the senior cycle proper, and must not be used to spread the two-year leaving certificate course (see below) over three years. It is to include such studies as: critical thinking; problem solving; moral education; education for parenthood, employment and leisure; media education; communication skills; and work experience. By 1995, about 60% of all secondary level schools offered a transition year.

Secondary schools
Secondary schools are privately owned, mostly by the Roman Catholic Church, though there are a few Protestant and non-denominational schools. However, the schools are subject to governmental regulations, and receive substantial government funding, especially those schools (95%) that do not charge fees. Even in the fee-charging schools, most of the teachers' salaries are paid by the government. The schools are run by boards of management, representing the patron, parents and teachers; the school principal is also a member. There are proposals under discussion to reduce the representation of the patron, and increase that of parents and teachers; and also to give both the boards and the principals more autonomy, especially concerning the hiring and appraisal of teachers. In Catholic schools (the great majority), the principal was traditionally a priest or nun, but the numbers of lay principals are increasing.

Junior cycle – The junior cycle of secondary schools lasts three years, and completes compulsory education. Schools are required to include the following subjects in their junior cycle curricula; the first six form the 'core'. (Physical education and singing must also be taught.)

- Irish
- English
- mathematics
- history
- geography
- civics
- science
- classical languages

- modern European languages
- business studies
- home economics

The content of these subjects and students' choices among them are strongly influenced by the junior certificate examinations, set by the Department of Education, and taken at the end of the junior cycle. To gain a certificate, students must study the six core subjects plus two others from the list – or from art, music and craft and design, where a school offers them. Grades are awarded in each subject on a seven-point scale. (Previous assessments by teachers are not taken into account.) Irish, English and mathematics have alternative examinations of different levels of difficulty.

Fifty-four per cent of students in the junior cycle of secondary school are girls, 46% boys. (1990–1 figures)

Senior cycle – The senior cycle of secondary schools lasts two years. It prepares students for the leaving certificate, set by the Department of Education, which thus strongly influences the curriculum and students' subject choices. The leaving certificate qualifies its holders for entry to universities and other tertiary institutions, and is also used by many employers. It may be taken in about 30 subjects, which the Department classifies into five groups.

- *language* (including Irish, English, Latin, Greek, Hebrew and certain modern European languages)
- *science* (including mathematics, physics, chemistry and biology)
- *business studies* (including accounting, business organisation and economics)
- *applied science* (including engineering, technical drawing and agricultural science)
- *social studies* (including history and geography – and also art and music)

In addition, there are plans to introduce a vocational course as part of the leaving certificate.

The Department recommends that each student should take at least five subjects, including Irish. Where the student takes five, three should be from their 'best' group, and the other two from another group or groups.

Leaving certificates may be taken at three levels – *ordinary, higher* and (from September 1995) *applied* level. (The last of these may be used as a qualification for vocational education and training but not for higher education.) Examinations are held at the end of the senior cycle. Grades are awarded in each subject on a seven-point scale. Previous assessments by teachers are not taken into account.

Fifty-five per cent of students in the senior cycle of secondary school are girls, 45% boys. (1990–1 figures)

Ireland has 467 secondary schools, with 12,300 teachers and 211,500 students, 62% of them in the junior cycle. The average secondary school has some 450 students; most (69%) have between 300 and 800. Most are single-sex schools: 36% are for girls and 28% for boys; the remaining 36% are co-educational.

Vocational schools

Traditionally, vocational schools trained their students in manual skills in preparation for trades. Now, however, they have become much more like the secondary schools, especially in the junior cycle. Unlike secondary schools, however, vocational schools are publicly owned, and currently run by the local VEC.

Junior cycle – In this cycle, students now follow academic courses similar in their curricula and assessment with those of the secondary school junior cycle (see above).

Sixty-four per cent of pupils in the junior cycle of vocational school are boys, 36% girls. (1990–1 figures)

Senior cycle – In this cycle, students may take one of a number of programmes, which include the following (which are also available in some secondary, comprehensive and community schools).

The *Vocational Preparation and Training Programmes* (VPT) are designed for those who will leave school at 15 or 16 without qualifications. They offer a combination of general studies (with a practical emphasis), vocational studies and work experience.

The *Leaving Certificate Vocational Programme*, which is at present under reconstruction, combines subjects from the leaving certificate (see secondary school senior cycle above) with vocational studies. Students must take five leaving certificate subjects, including Irish and two from the 'applied science' group. The vocational studies available are being expanded, and are to include compulsory 'modules' on enterprise education, preparation for work and work experience. It is hoped that the restructuring will increase the overall numbers of students, and the proportion of female students.

Fifty-eight per cent of students in the senior cycle of vocational school are boys, 42% girls. (1990–1 figures)

Ireland has 248 vocational schools, with 5,000 teachers and 73,000 students, 65% of them in the junior cycle. Most (66%) have between 200 and 800 students; 9% have under 100 students, and 7% over 800. (1992–3 figures)

Community schools and comprehensive schools

Community schools and comprehensive schools are both publicly owned, and very similar in the education they offer, combining the academic education characteristic of the secondary school with the vocational education characteristic of the vocational school (see above). The community schools also provide facilities for adult education and aim to serve the local adult community as well as their own students. They are both relatively new. The comprehensive schools (16 in number) were established in the late 1960s and early 1970s. Community schools were first established in the early 1970s and are still being created, usually by the amalgamation of existing secondary and vocational schools; there are now 54. The two categories differ in the composition of their boards of management. Both have representatives of the Department of Education, the local VEC and the Roman Catholic Church; but in addition, the community school boards have elected representatives of parents and teachers as well as the principal.

The 70 community and comprehensive schools have 2,600 teachers and 42,800 students, about two-thirds of them in the junior cycle. Between them, community and comprehensive schools have 13% of all secondary students. Most (71%) have between 300 and 800 students; 24% have over 800, and 4% (i.e. three schools) have under 300. (1992–3 figures)

Fifty-four per cent of students in community and comprehensive school are boys, 46% girls. (1990–1 figures)

Apprenticeships and Post Leaving Certificate courses

Ireland has an *apprenticeship* system, which has recently been reformed. Traditionally, people qualified as practitioners of a trade by serving a specified length of time as apprentices. From 1995, however, apprenticeship has consisted of a regulated and assessed combination, in successive phases, of training on the job with education in schools, technical colleges or government training centres. Those who complete an apprenticeship successfully are awarded a National Craft Certificate in their occupation.

Currently, apprenticeships last about three years. At any one time, there are about 10,000 apprentices, and 3,000 successfully complete apprenticeships every year.

Another 18,000 young people take part in *Post Leaving Certificate* (PLC) courses after completing their formal schooling. These courses are provided by participating schools in line with the local labour market, and regulated by the National Council for Vocational Awards (NCVA).

Special education

The integration of children with handicaps into ordinary schools and classes is encouraged where possible. Otherwise, special provision is made in special schools and special classes attached to ordinary schools. Class sizes there are small, and programmes tailored to the needs of the particular child.

There are 117 special schools, with 8,100 pupils, and about 340 special classes, with 3,400 pupils. (1992–3 figures) About 60% of the pupils in special schools and 55% of those in special classes are boys. (1990–1 figures)

Tertiary education

There are plans to increase the numbers entering tertiary education, in the medium term, to 45% of the age group.

Tertiary education takes place in three main types of institution, the *universities* (to which the *colleges of education* are attached) and the *regional technical colleges*. They are state-funded but self-governing. Entry to any of them is normally on the basis of the leaving certificate, and highly competitive. Candidates apply not to individual institutions but through the Central Applications Office. There are also a number of specialist colleges of various kinds, some of them private.

Tuition fees have traditionally been charged in higher education institutions (this was to cease in 1996), but there was a system of grants available for these fees and for living expenses, on the basis of the means-testing of students and their parents. The grants were administered by local authorities, but reimbursed by central government, and the process was closely regulated and supervised by the Department of Education.

Universities

Ireland has four universities: the University of Dublin (Trinity College); Dublin City University; the University of Limerick; and the National University of Ireland (NUI), which is a federation of three partially autonomous colleges in different parts of the country. They conduct research and offer degrees at bachelor, master and doctoral level, across the entire range of academic disciplines. First-degree courses normally take three or four years (five or six in architecture, medicine, dentistry and veterinary medicine). Each university awards its own degrees, but with external examiners from other universities to help achieve uniformity of standards.

In 1990–1, the universities had 37,900 students, 51% female, 49% male. The numbers of degrees awarded in the main subject areas are shown in Figure 3.

Colleges of education

There are five colleges of education, which train teachers for the national (i.e. primary) schools, though two (one in Dublin, the other in Limerick) are much larger than the others, and account between them for 85% of all students. All five are owned and run by the Roman Catholic Church, but are financed by the state, and each is associated with a university for the award of degrees.

In 1990–1, the colleges of education had just over 1,000 students, 91% female, 9% male.

Regional Technical Colleges (and other colleges of technology)

There are 11 Regional Technical Colleges (RTC), plus the Dublin Institute of Technology (DIT), which train students in a wide range of vocational and

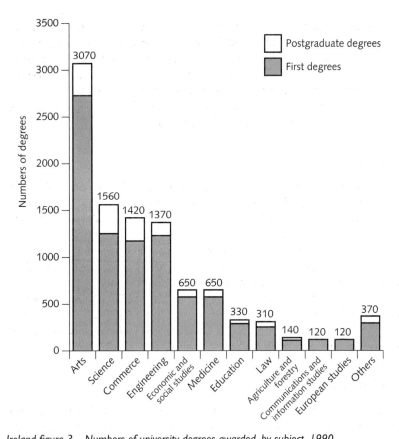

Ireland figure 3   Numbers of university degrees awarded, by subject, 1990

technical subjects, at a wide range of levels. They offer certificates (after two-year courses) and diplomas (after three years). They are not degree-awarding bodies in their own right, but students in some subjects can (after four-year courses) take degrees of the National Council for Educational Awards (NCEA).

The RTCs were established from the 1970s, first under the auspices of their local VEC (as was the DIT), but since 1993 they have been autonomous.

In 1990–1, the RTCs had 16,800 students, 59% male, 41% female. Other, more specialist technological colleges, had 10,500 students, 58% male, 42% female. Their most popular subject areas are business studies, with 9,200 students, and engineering, with 7,400 (93% male).

Adult education

The VECs, established in 1930, had adult education (or 'continuation education') as one of their responsibilities. They set up adult education boards and appoint adult education organisers – about 50 throughout the country, all qualified teachers – to identify adult education needs in their areas, and co-ordinate its provision. In recent years, community schools also provide evening classes and other extramural classes for adults, and many comprehensive schools and tertiary colleges also provide adult education facilities.

Grants for adult education are available from the Department of Education, through the National Association of Adult Education.

Funding

Public expenditure on education amounts to about 6.5% of GNP and 20% of all public expenditure (1993). Those sectors of education that are largely privately owned and run (national schools, voluntary secondary schools and colleges of education) are at the same time for the most part publicly financed.

Of the total spending by the Department of Education, 36% is on primary level, 37% on secondary level and 20% on tertiary education. A further 2% is spent on transport and 1% on administration. (1990 figures)

Compulsory education is free; higher education traditionally charged tuition fees, but this was to cease in 1996. Means-tested grants were available, administered by local authorities but funded by the national government, and about 50% of students received these.

Teaching profession

Teachers are currently employed by individual schools, though they are actually allocated to schools by the government, and qualifications and salaries are set nationally. There are proposals under discussion to reverse this position, so that teachers would be formally employed by the proposed RECs, but would actually be hired and appraised by the principals and boards of management of individual schools.

National school teachers (i.e. preprimary and primary) are trained in colleges of education (see above). Their courses combine three or four academic subjects with educational theory and teaching practice. They normally last three years, and lead to a pass degree (Bachelor of Education – BEd) of the university with which the college is associated. (Colleges associated with the University of Dublin also offer a four-year honours degree.) In 1991, there were 20,410 teachers in national schools, 76% of them women.

Secondary school teachers of academic subjects must normally be graduates in their own teaching subjects, and have taken a one-year postgraduate course leading to the Higher Diploma in Education (HDE). This combines educational theory with teaching practice.

Secondary level teachers of practical subjects take four-year degree courses, combining educational theory, training in their specialism and teaching practice.

In 1991, there were 11,600 teachers in secondary schools, all full-time; 2,500 in community and comprehensive schools, 97% full-time; and 11,600 in vocational schools, 79% full-time.

Inservice training is available at every level (in courses ranging from one day to four weeks), but is not compulsory at any level.

Parent/school relationships

Parents are represented on the boards of management of most schools, and there are proposals under discussion to increase their representation (and that of teachers) and reduce that of the churches. At the same time, these boards would be given increased powers, notably concerning the hiring and appraisal of teachers.

A programme has been introduced to improve the links between parents and primary schools through the use of *liaison teachers*.

Education inspectorate

There is an inspectorate, part of the Department of Education, with separate sections for primary education (including special education), postprimary education and the psychological service. Generally speaking, primary inspectors are responsible for particular areas of the country, and secondary inspectors for particular subjects.

Their responsibilities include inspection and evaluation of teachers, giving advice about curriculum and assessment, organising inservice education, informing the Department about activities at local level and advising the government about policy.

The proposals under current discussion to increase the responsibilities of schools' boards of management and principals would also alter the functions of the inspectorate. Under these proposals, the board and principal of a school would be responsible for the appraisal of individual teachers, and the inspectorate would assess the quality of the school as a whole.

ACRONYMS AND ABBREVIATIONS

Bed	Bachelor of Education
DIT	Dublin Institute of Technology
HDE	Higher Diploma in Education
NCEA	National Council for Educational Awards
NCVA	National Council for Vocational Awards
NUI	National University of Ireland
PLC	Post Leaving Certificate
REC	Regional Educational Council

RTC	Regional Technical College
VEC	Vocational Education Committee
VTP	Vocational Preparation and Training Programmes

ACKNOWLEDGEMENT

We are grateful to the Irish Department of Education and Central Statistical Office for supplying us with information about current arrangements and proposals.

REFERENCES

Bhreathnach, N. (1994) *Position Paper on Regional Education Councils*, Dublin: Department of Education.

Central Statistical Office (1993) *Statistical Abstract 1992*, Dublin: Central Statistical Office.

European Commission (1995) *Structures of the Education and Initial Training Systems in the European Union*, second edition, Luxembourg: Office for Official Publications of the European Commission.

Hunter, B. (ed.) (1995) *The Statesman's Year Book, 1995–1996*, London: Macmillan.

OECD (1995) *OECD Economic Surveys: 1994–1995: Ireland*, Paris: Organisation for Economic Co-operation and Development (especially Chapter IV: Education and Training).

BACKGROUND

Italy and its regions

After centuries of division and foreign rule (mainly by Spain, Austria and Napoleonic France), Italy became a unified country, within more or less its present borders, in 1870. It was originally a monarchy, the king of Piedmont and his descendants becoming kings of Italy. But after the period of Fascist government (1922–43) and defeat in the Second World War, Italy chose to become a republic in a referendum in 1946.

Italy is a member of the EU, having been a founder member of the European Economic Community.

POPULATION

Population	57.2 million in 1994 (no net change from 1984)
Land area	301,300 sq. km
Population density	190 per sq. km

ECONOMY

GDP	$1,000 billion (1994)
GDP per capita	$17,800 (1994)
In employment	60% of working age population (1991)
	– 89% of men/47% of women aged 25–54
	– 31% of young people (15–24)
Part-time employment	6.2% of all employment (1994)
Unemployed	2.6 million (11% of the labour force) (1994)
Spending on education	5.1% of GDP (1992, public expenditure only)

The overall unemployment percentage masks significant variation by region as well as by gender and by age. Unemployment is much higher in the south (19%) than the centre (10%) or the north (7%). It is twice as high for women (16%) as for men (8%). And it is almost three times as high for young people aged 16–24 (32%) as for the population as a whole (11%). The majority of unemployed people (58%) have been unemployed for more than a year. (1994 figures, OECD)

In the early 1990s, the Italian economy experienced its most severe recession since the mid-1970s. In 1993, Italy began a programme of privatisation and creation of a more market-oriented economy.

RELIGION

There is now no state religion, but almost all of the population belong to the Roman Catholic Church. Religious teaching of a Roman Catholic character is offered in schools during the years of compulsory education, but is not compulsory for pupils.

LANGUAGE AND ETHNICITY

Italian is the official language of the country, but French speakers in the region Valle d'Aosta and German speakers in the region Trentino-Alto Adige have the legal right to use these languages as well as Italian.

GOVERNMENT

Italy has four levels of government – *national, regional, provincial* and *communal*. The division of educational responsibilities among these is complicated. In addition, a system of participatory committees (*organi collegiali*) was established in 1974 at national, local and institutional levels. These have a variety of rights and powers – to be consulted, to make recommendations, and at school level to exercise some managerial responsibilities.

Educational policy is determined by the national government, though (since 1972) some of its administration is in the hands of the regions, provinces and communes, and many governmental powers are exercised by national government officers in the regions and provinces. Three government ministries have major educational responsibilities:

- the Ministry of Education (MPI – *Ministero della Pubblica Istruzione*), responsible for preprimary, primary and secondary education, and tertiary education outside the university system;
- the Ministry of Universities and of Scientific and Technological Research (MURST – *Ministero dell'Università e della Ricerca Scientifica e Tecnologica*), responsible (since 1989) for university education;
- the Ministry of Labour and Social Security, responsible for the co-ordination of vocational training outside the education system, though it is actually provided by the regions.

At national level, the participatory committee is the National Education Council (*Consiglio Nazionale della Pubblica Istruzione*). It has 71 members, representing the various educational professions, local authorities and employers. Its role is advisory.

Italy is divided into 20 regions; some regions have more autonomy than others. Generally speaking, the regions are responsible for planning and establishing new schools and maintaining existing school buildings (with centrally provided funds); medical and psychological services; vocational training outside schools and universities; and school transport, textbooks and meals, though these last are usually delegated to the provincial or communal levels of government.

Each region also has a regional education superintendency (*sovrintendenza scolastica regionale*), which is a regional branch of the national government, responsible for the co-ordination of national and regional policy, the recruitment of upper secondary school teachers, and the co-ordination of the provincial directorates.

Each region is divided into a number of educational districts, each intended to be an area of uniform social, economic and cultural characteristics. Each has its own participatory committee, the educational district committee (*consiglio di distretto scolastico*). Its members are representatives of staff, parents, students, trade unions, employers and political parties. It is an advisory body mainly on matters of educational planning, and makes recommendations to regional and other education authorities.

The provinces are responsible for providing buildings, equipment and services for primary, lower secondary and scientific and technical upper secondary schools. Each province also has a provincial directorate of education (*provveditorato agli studi*), which is a provincial branch of the national government, responsible for the general administration of schools, the enforcement of national government policy and the recruitment of primary and lower secondary school teachers. The head teachers of schools are responsible directly to their provincial director.

Each province also has a participatory committee, the provincial education committee (*consiglio scolastico provinciale*). Its members are elected representatives of staff, parents and employers. It is an advisory body, and makes recommendations to the provincial directorate and other education authorities.

There are just under 2,000 communes in Italy, each with its elected council. They are responsible for providing buildings, equipment and services for classical upper secondary schools, and for many educational support services to ensure that children from even the poorest families can benefit from education. These include free school transport, free or subsidised school meals, assistance with the purchase of textbooks and financial grants. In addition, some functions may be delegated to communes by regions and provinces.

EDUCATION

Education in Italy is compulsory for eight years from the ages of six to 14. It may take place in state or private schools, or at home. The compulsory stage of schooling is divided into five years of primary education (*scuola primaria*) and three years of lower secondary or intermediate education (*scuola media*). Before compulsory education, children may attend preschool education (*scuola dell'infanzia*) from the age of three; and after it, they may attend a range of secondary schools or vocational training courses.

Compulsory education is free in state schools, which cater for more than 90% of pupils at every level. It is also free in private primary schools, but tuition fees may be charged in private lower secondary schools. Fees are normally charged in upper secondary schools, whether private or state schools, though in state schools, students from poor families and students of high achievement are exempt. All upper secondary students pay for their textbooks.

At primary level, private schools need the authorisation of the Ministry of Education. They are mostly subsidised (*scuole sussidate*) and established in places where the state has decided not to set up its own schools; they must be free and open to everyone. Completely private primary schools (*scuole parificate*) are rare, and must fulfil stringent conditions, including being free and open to everyone, following the national curriculum and having formally qualified teachers.

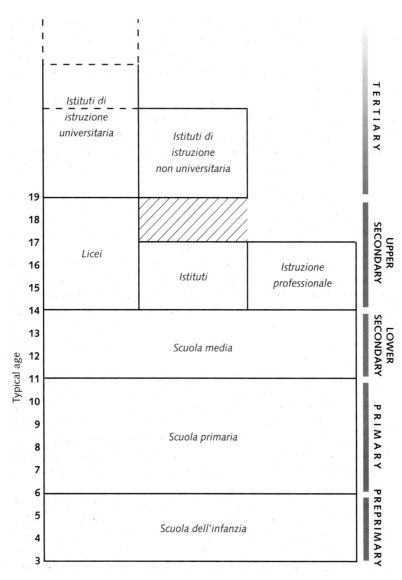

Note: This diagram is highly simplified and should be used in conjunction
with the text

Italy's education system

At secondary level, authorisation from the Ministry of Education is not
required for private schools to be opened, but they may seek legal recognition,
as *scuole legalmente riconosciute* or *scuole pareggiate* – the latter category
confined to those set up in association with the Catholic Church. Legally

recognised private schools may use the same titles as state schools (such as *liceo classico*), and offer qualifications officially recognised as equivalent to those from state schools. In return, they must follow the same educational programmes as state schools, have formally qualified teachers and admit only properly qualified students.

Lower secondary education was reformed at the end of the 1970s, and primary education in the latter half of the 1980s. The structure of upper secondary education has not been altered for several decades.

Schools and colleges at all levels (other than universities) share a common administrative structure, and have a high degree of autonomy in their administration and budgeting.

Each establishment has a principal (*preside*) or head teacher (*direttore didattico*), who has overall responsibility for the management of the school, in association with a number of bodies described below; he or she is in turn responsible to the provincial director of education.

Responsibility for the budget and all non-educational matters rests with a participatory committee, the school committee (*consiglio di istituto*), which consists of between 14 and 19 elected representatives of teachers and other staff, parents and (in upper secondary schools) students, and is chaired by one of the parents. In turn, it elects an executive board (*giunta esecutiva*) of six members. The principal/head teacher is an ex-officio member of the committee, and chairs the board.

Responsibility for educational matters is shared by the principal/head teacher and another participatory committee, the teachers' committee (*collegio dei docenti*), consisting of all the teachers and chaired by the principal/head teacher. It decides – or makes recommendations to the principal/head teacher – on teaching policy and plans for the school as a whole, choice of textbooks and educational materials and evaluation of teachers' performance, while working within the nationally specified guidelines and respecting teachers' autonomy.

Finally, a class committee (*consiglio di classe*) at secondary level or interclass committee (*consiglio d'interclasse*) at primary level – consisting of the teachers of a class or group of parallel classes, plus representatives of parents and, in upper secondary schools, students – decides on teaching policy and plans for the class or classes, monitors teaching and discipline, and conducts assessment.

There is a strong emphasis on oral (as against written) examinations at all levels of Italian education.

INSTITUTIONS

In 1990–1, Italy had a total of 69,900 preprimary, primary and secondary schools, with 874,700 teachers and 9.7 million pupils. (MPI)

Preprimary

Preprimary education in Italy (scuola dell'infanzia) caters for about 1.5 million children – just over 90% of three- to six-year-olds – with roughly equal numbers in state-run and local or private schools. (Private schools may receive some state funding if they meet certain conditions.)

Scuola dell'infanzia

Attendance at a scuola dell'infanzia is recommended by the MPI, but not compulsory. All were privately run until 1968, when the state system was established. State schools are formally the responsibility of the MPI, but in practice the administration of most of them is delegated to local authorities. The state schools are free (though parents may pay part of the costs of transport and school meals), but private schools usually charge fees.

Normally, a preprimary school is co-educational, and divided into three age-groups (three-, four- and five-year-olds), each group consisting of 14 to 28 children with two teachers. In 1991, the MPI issued guidelines about the subjects to be covered in preprimary schools, through activities appropriate for the children's ages.

- body and movement
- speech and words
- space, order and measure
- things, time and nature
- messages, forms and media
- the self and others

In 1992–3, there were 27,300 preprimary schools, with 1.6 million pupils and (in state schools only) 75,600 teachers. (European Commission) The pupil/teacher ratio has fallen from 26/1 in 1970–1 to 11/1 in 1990–1. (MPI)

Primary education

The five years of primary education (scuola primaria), from age six until 11, form the first stage of compulsory schooling.

Scuola primaria

The current scuola primaria system was established by legislation in 1990. Primary education may be provided in state-run schools, subsidised private schools, or authorised private schools (of which there are very few), but is free in every category. Class sizes are limited by law to 25 (20 if the class contains a pupil requiring special education).

Primary schooling is divided into two cycles, the first of two and the second of three years. In both cycles, a number of subjects must be taught – by multidisciplinary methods in the first, and by subject-based methods in the second. These subjects are divided into three groups, as listed below.

- Italian
- a foreign language (from the second year)
- art
- sound and music
- physical education

- mathematics
- sciences

- history
- geography
- social studies

In addition, the Catholic religion must be offered as a subject by schools, but is optional for pupils. The choice of textbooks for all these subjects is left to the teachers.

Teaching is organised on a 'module' (*modulo*) system, with more than one teacher per class – either three teachers for every two classes or four for every three. Teachers specialise in one of the subject groups, not in individual subjects.

Assessment is by teachers, and (except at the end of the primary stage) based on course work throughout the year. Pupils' achievements are described in words, not indicated by numerical marks. It is possible, but very rare, for pupils whose achievement is low to be required to repeat a year. At the end of the 5th Year, pupils sit examinations for the *Licenza Elementare*, which qualifies them for admission to the scuola media. This consists of two written papers (one in the language group and the other in the mathematics and sciences group of subjects), and an oral examination covering all the subjects. Pupils who fail (which is again very rare) may repeat their final year.

In 1992–3, there were 22,700 primary schools, with 2.96 million pupils and (in state schools only) 264,000 teachers. (European Commission) The pupil/teacher ratio has fallen from 21/1 in 1970–1 to 11/1 in 1990–1. (MPI)

Lower secondary education

The lower secondary school (scuola media), established in 1962 for pupils aged 11–14, completes the years of compulsory education.

Scuola media
State-run schools are comprehensive and free, and account for more than 90% of pupils. Pupils are grouped into classes by age, not ability or attainment. Class sizes are limited by law to 25 (and schools are limited to 24 classes).

The subjects of the curriculum were laid down by the government in 1979;

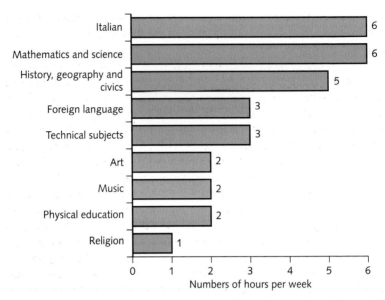

Italy figure 1   Number of hours per week for compulsory subjects in the third year of the scuola media
Notes: (i) Science consists of physics, chemistry and biology; (ii) the study of religion is optional

they must be taught separately by specialist teachers, but otherwise teaching methods and choice of textbooks are left to teachers' committees, class committees and individual teachers. The subjects are shown in Figure 1, with the number of hours per week allocated to each in the third year. (The other years are only slightly different.)

Assessment is by teachers, and (except at the end of the lower secondary stage) based on course work throughout the year. Pupils' achievements are (since 1977) described in words, not indicated by numerical marks. Pupils whose achievement is low may be required to repeat a year. At the end of the third year, pupils sit an examination for the *Diploma di Licenza Media* which qualifies them for admission to the upper secondary schools.

In 1992–3, there were 9,900 lower secondary schools, with 2.06 million pupils and (in state schools only) 233,000 teacher. (European Commission) The pupil/teacher ratio has fallen from 12/1 in 1970–1 to 8/1 in 1990–1. (MPI)

Upper secondary education

Upper secondary education is for students aged 14–19, and is not compulsory. (However, the raising of the upper age of compulsory education to 16 is under discussion, and at present 75% of 16-year-olds are still at school.) Tuition fees are charged and textbooks must be paid for, but students from poor families or of high attainment can be exempted from the former in state-run schools (about 91% of all upper secondary schools).

In 1992–3, there were 7,600 upper secondary schools, with 2.79 million students and (in state schools only) 230,700 teachers. (European Commission) The student/teacher ratio has fallen from 12/1 in 1970–1 to 8/1 in 1990–1. (MPI)

There are several different types of upper secondary school, with a fundamental distinction made between those preparing students for university or its equivalent (the *liceo*) and those preparing them for employment (the *istituto*). The licei are attended by about a third of the population aged 14–19, and the istituti by just under two-thirds of the population aged 14–17.

To qualify for entrance to any of them, students must hold the Diploma di Licenza Media. Along with this diploma, students leaving lower secondary education are given recommendations about the type of upper secondary education most appropriate for them (see above), but in practice they can gain admission to the school of their choice subject to the availability of places. In all types of school, grouping into classes is normally by age and subject, not ability. The numbers of students in the different types of school are illustrated in Figure 2.

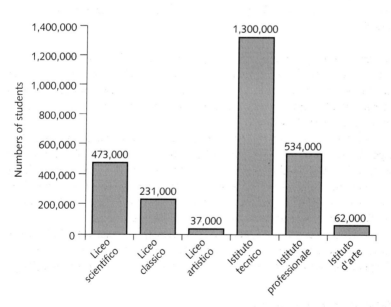

Italy figure 2   Numbers of students in upper secondary schools, 1992–3 (Adapted from European Commission, 1995)
Note: The istituti professionali and the istituti d'arte offer three-year courses; the other schools, five-year courses

Liceo

The liceo prepares students for university and other types of higher education. There are three main kinds, each preparing predominantly but (since the liberalisation of university entry in 1969) not exclusively for studies in particular areas.

- *liceo classico* – humanities, social sciences and education
- *liceo scientifico* – sciences and medicine
- *liceo artistico* – fine arts and architecture

In addition, there are several experimental music licei (*licei musicali sperimentali*) and one experimental dance liceo (*liceo coreutico sperimentale*), attached to music and dance academies.

In 1993, there were 1,000 licei scientifici, with 473,000 students (about 21% of the age-group); 750 licei classici, with 231,000 students (10%), and 135 licei artistici, with 37,000 students (under 2%). (European Commission)

The five years of study in the licei are divided into two *cycles*: the first is of two years, and the second of three years for the liceo classico and the liceo scientifico, and either two or three years for the liceo artistico. The first cycle is still referred to as *ginnasio* classes and the second as the liceo classes. (This terminology stems from the older structure of Italian education, when the now-abolished ginnasio catered for pupils aged 11–16, and the liceo only for those aged 16–19.)

Each type of liceo has a compulsory curriculum. A number of subjects are compulsory in all three, though there are differences in the amounts of time spent on them, and the ages at which they are studied. These are as follows.

- Italian
- history
- geography
- mathematics
- physics
- chemistry
- biology
- physical education

Religion is also available in all three licei as an optional subject.

In addition, the following subjects are compulsory in both the liceo classico and the liceo scientifico.

- Latin
- a modern foreign language
- philosophy

In the liceo classico alone the following are compulsory.

- ancient Greek
- history of art

In the liceo scientifico alone the following are compulsory.

- drawing
- astronomy

And in the liceo artistico alone, a range of specialist artistic subjects are compulsory, for example still life, architecture, perspective and anatomy for artists. (The five-year course in the liceo artistico qualifies students for entry to any university faculty; the four-year course only for entry to higher education in art or architecture.)

Istituti tecnici

The *istituti tecnici* (technical schools) also offer five-year courses, preparing students aged 14–19 for employment. In 1993, there were just under 3,000 technical schools, with 1.3 million students (about 36% of the age group). (European Commission)

Each technical school specialises in a particular sector, such as agriculture, commerce, industry, surveying, tourism and nautical occupations.

The five years of study in the technical school are divided into two cycles: the first of two and the second of three years. In the first cycle, all institutes have the same basic compulsory curriculum, with the following subjects.

- Italian
- history and civics
- geography
- foreign languages
- mathematics
- physics
- chemistry
- biology
- drawing
- physical education

Religion is also available as an optional subject.

In the second cycle, most of students' time is devoted to the specialisms of their institute, but a core of the general subjects above remains compulsory in them all.

Istituti professionali

The *istituti professionali* (vocational schools) normally offer three-year courses, preparing students aged 14–17 for employment – though courses can be as short as two or as long as five years. Traditionally, they were highly specialised and practical, aimed at preparing students as quickly as possible to enter a specific occupation. However, this aim has been modified since 1988–9, with courses being made more general, and the number of qualifications available being drastically reduced from about 150 to 20. In 1993, there were 1,700 vocational schools, with 534,000 students (about a quarter of the 14–17 age-group). (European Commission)

Each vocational school specialises in a particular sector, such as agriculture, commerce, industry and hotels.

Curricula are more flexible than in other upper secondary schools, but since 1992 are being divided into three areas of study as follows, with the weekly hours devoted to each averaged over the three years of study.

- general studies in the arts and sciences (19)
- technical and practical studies in the vocational area (17)
- in-depth study (4)

The last of these is entirely at the discretion of each school, and may be geared for example to the circumstances of the local community or the needs of individual students.

Istituti d'arte

The *istituti d'arte* (art schools) have traditionally offered three-year courses, preparing students aged 14–17 for employment and artistic production in such areas as ceramics, textiles, printing wood and glass – usually tailored to local needs and materials. On successful completion, the student receives a diploma in applied art (*Diploma di Maestro d'Arte Applicato*). Recently, some art schools have established an experimental two-year course to follow this, leading to a diploma (*Diploma Maturità d'Arte Applicato*) that qualifies them for entry to higher education in the arts.

In 1993, there were 165 istituti d'arte, with 62,200 students (about 3% of the 14–17 age-group). (European Commission)

Assessment

A similar system of assessment operates in all types of upper secondary school. Assessment is based on both written and oral tests and more general observation by teachers. Students who fail a subject must take a special examination in it the following September.

At the end of their final year, students take a final examination, which is externally set and marked, and is usually a combination of written and oral tests. Success leads to the award of a leaving certificate, the *maturità* – which is, according to the type of school, *classica*, *scientifica*, *artistica*, *tecnica* or *professionale*. The classical, scientific and artistic maturità certificates – but not the technical or vocational ones – qualify for admission to higher education.

Vocational training

In addition to the technical and vocational schools described above, Italy has a wide variety of courses and training schemes outside the school system.

Istruzione professionale
A range of initial vocational training courses (regulated by legislation of 1978) are provided by the regions or by private but non-profit making organisations contracted by the regions. They cover all the main sectors of employment – industry, agriculture, services and craft – and are usually highly specific and (in association with employers and trade unions) geared to the economic needs of each region. Most of them last one or two years. Traditionally, these courses were taken by students at the end of compulsory education who had obtained poorer marks than those going on to upper secondary education, and some courses are still aimed at such students. But in recent years, specialised courses have also been established to attract students who have been more successful in school. There is a regionally organised system of examinations and qualifications for these courses.

There were 262,000 students on initial training courses in 1989–90, 88% in central and northern Italy, and 59% male. Of these students, 19,000 (just over 7%) were on specialised courses. 91% of these were in central and northern Italy, and 72% were male. (Istituto Nazionale di Statistica, 1993)

Apprendistato
The historic apprenticeship system (*apprendistato*) was regulated by law in 1955, to set conditions for both apprentices and employers and establish a system of examinations and qualifications. Apprenticeships are for those between the ages of 15 and 26. The apprentice is a paid employee, working a 40-hour week, of which eight hours are devoted to theoretical studies. It is the responsibility of the employer to ensure that the apprentice acquires the necessary skills for the occupation concerned.

There are about 600,000 apprentices, over three-quarters in northern and central Italy, and just over half in traditional craft occupations.

Contratti di Formazione-Lavoro
Through *Contratti di Formazione-Lavoro* (CFL – work/training contracts), established in 1983–4, firms employ people between the ages of 15 and 32 for an initial period of two years, after which time the employer may but need not renew the contract. The students' time is to be divided between training and work, but the legislation does not specify in what proportions it is to be divided.

About 500,000 people participate in CFL every year, mostly aged 15 to 18 and holding only a compulsory school leaving certificate. Most of the employers involved are small firms, and the industrial sector is predominant.

Special education

The government encourages the teaching of children with disabilities in ordinary schools and classes, and the maximum permitted pupil/teacher ratio is reduced where a class contains a disabled child receiving special education, in preprimary (from 28 to 20), and primary (from 25 to 20) schools.

Tertiary education

Tertiary education is divided between the university system (*istituti di istruzione universitaria*) and non-university education (*istituti di istruzione non universitaria*). Non-university tertiary education remains the responsibility of the Ministry of Education, but the university system is now the responsibility of a separate ministry established in 1989, the MURST.

Istituti di istruzione universitaria

The MURST is responsible for planning university development, promoting and co-ordinating research, and distributing funds among institutions – though the distribution must be according to legally defined criteria, and the institutions have considerable autonomy in the way they spend these funds.

The 'university system' includes the following institutions – not all called 'universities'.

- 45 state universities (*università degli studi*)
- 5 private universities (*libere università*)
- 2 universities for foreigners (*università per stranieri*)
- 7 university institutes (*istituti universitari*)
- 3 polytechnics (*politecnici*)
- 3 higher schools (*scuole superiori*)

They all have autonomy in teaching, research, organisational and financial matters, and are run by a hierarchy of elected officers and representative committees. The head of a university is the rector (*rettore*), a member of the full-time teaching staff (*professori ordinari*) elected for a three-year term by his or her colleagues. The rector chairs the university's two governing bodies. For academic matters, there is the academic senate (*senato accademico*), consisting of the deans of faculties. For administrative and financial matters, there is the administrative council (*consiglio di amministrazione*), made up of representatives of staff, students, local and national government, and sometimes private sponsors. Each faculty is run by its own council (*consiglio di facoltà*), headed by the dean (*preside*), who is elected by his or her colleagues for a three-year term. And each department too has its council (*consiglio di dipartimento*), and enjoys a large measure of academic, administrative and financial autonomy.

For admission to university, the *maturità* is necessary and normally sufficient. Only in dentistry are national limits set on student numbers (*numerus clausus*). However, local limits (*numero programmato*) have been set in new universities, new courses and some established courses where overcrowding has been particularly severe – notably in medicine, surgery and veterinary medicine.

The most important qualification offered by Italian universities is the *Diploma di Laurea* (DL) – so named from the crown of laurel leaves traditionally worn by graduates. The DL is a non-professional academic qualification, available in 93 different subject areas. For each, there is a set of courses, with lectures and seminars, and an allotted number of years of study decided by the department concerned; most last from four to six years, but individual students can continue their studies for longer periods, and many do. In 1991–2, 31% of all laurea students were *fuori corso* – that is, they had overrun the allotted time for their course. (ISTAT)

To obtain the DL, students must pass examinations in all their courses (*Esami di Profitto*) and a final examination (*Esame di Laurea*), as well as submit a dissertation based on research (*Tesi di Laurea*). Holders of the DL may call themselves 'doctor' – *Dottore/Dottoresa*, abbreviated to *Dott./Dott.ssa*. This is not the same as the research doctorate awarded after further studies, which is comparable to the doctorates awarded in most other European countries.

In the academic year 1991–2, there were over 1.4 million students enrolled in Laurea courses, distributed among the different sectors as shown in Figure 3. In 1991, 327,000 new students enrolled on Laurea courses, and 87,000

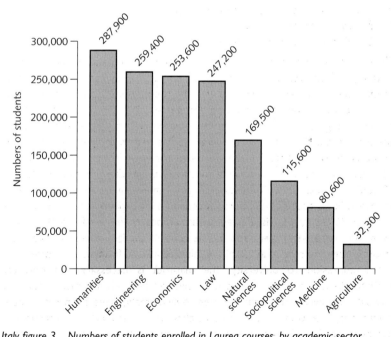

Italy figure 3   Numbers of students enrolled in Laurea courses, by academic sector, 1991–2 (MURST)

students obtained the DL – figures suggesting that roughly a quarter of students complete the course successfully.

Partly because of the low rate of successful completion of Laurea courses, a less demanding qualification has been progressively introduced since 1990, the *Diploma Universitaria* (DU). Courses leading to the DU last three years, and it has become generally known as the '*Laurea Breve*' ('Short Laurea'). This nickname is officially discouraged, however, because DU courses are intended to be different in character from those for the Laurea as well as shorter – less theoretical and more vocationally oriented.

The highest qualifications offered in the university system are available only to holders of the Laurea (or equivalent foreign qualifications), who must also sit a competitive entry examination, as numbers of students at this level are limited nationally. They are of two kinds.

The first is the specialist diploma (DS – *Diploma di Specialista*), awarded after two to five years' further study, on the basis of taught courses and examinations. About 67,000 students enrol on specialist diploma courses each year – mostly in the medical sector – and each year about 16,000 specialist diplomas are awarded.

The second is the research doctorate (DR – *Dottorato di Ricerca*), awarded on the basis of three to four years' research resulting in an original thesis. About 4,000 research doctorates are awarded annually, in a wide range of fields.

Istituti di istruzione non universitaria
Non-university higher education is the responsibility of the Ministry of Education, and consists mostly of academies for the arts, including fine arts, music, drama and dance. All admit students on the basis of the maturità and/or an entrance examination, which may include practical tests. Courses last four years.

Funding

Italy spends 5.1% of its GDP on education (1992, public expenditure only; CERI, 1995). The national government is responsible for most, though not all, of the funding of state education; it also provides partial funding for recognised private education. Through the MPI, it funds the training and salaries of teachers in preprimary, primary, lower secondary and most upper secondary schools. (Teachers in state schools are civil servants.) It funds the universities through the MURST. It pays the costs of its own administrative offices in the regions and provinces.

The regions fund school medical and psychological services; vocational training outside schools and universities; and school transport, textbooks and meals. The provinces provide buildings, equipment and services for primary, lower secondary and scientific and technical upper secondary schools. The communes provide buildings, equipment and services for classical upper secondary schools, and for many educational support services to ensure that children from even the poorest families can benefit from education, including free school transport, free or subsidised school meals, assistance with the purchase of textbooks and financial grants. In addition, some functions may be delegated to communes by regions and provinces.

Education is free in state schools at preprimary, primary and lower secondary levels, which cater for more than 90% of pupils at every level. It is also free in private primary schools, but tuition fees may be charged in private preprimary and lower secondary schools. Fees are normally charged in upper secondary schools, whether private or state schools, though in state schools, students from poor families and students of high achievement are exempt. All upper secondary students pay for their textbooks.

University students must pay fees – registration fees (set by the national government) and contribution fees (set by the individual universities). They are also eligible for financial assistance from the state, both grants and interest-free loans.

Teaching profession

Teachers in state schools are civil servants, with rights and duties defined by law. They have a legal right to freedom in teaching and cultural expression, and their working hours and conditions, salaries, career development and leave are also specified in detail. To become a permanent teacher, they must, *after* obtaining the academic and teacher training qualifications described below, pass a national competitive examination (*concorso*) for their chosen level of school.

A teacher in preprimary schools teaches all the subjects, a teacher in primary schools specialises (under the module system) in a group of subjects, and a secondary school teacher is a subject specialist.

Teacher training was reformed by legislation in 1990, for implementation beginning from the school year 1993–4. Previously, teachers in preprimary and primary schools had training only at upper secondary level, in specialist teacher training schools. Now, however, teachers at both levels are trained at university, in four-year courses combining academic education with teacher training.

Before the 1990 legislation, secondary school teachers, at both upper and lower secondary levels, first obtained a university or equivalent education in their specialist subject, then began on-the-job training in a probationary teaching year. Since 1993–4, they proceed after their degrees to postgraduate teacher training schools, to obtain a diploma qualifying them for the teaching profession.

To become a principal/head teacher or inspector, teachers must have been in the profession for a specified period (five years for a principal/head teacher, nine years for an inspector) and succeed in a further concorso, with both written and oral examinations on the educational and administrative duties involved.

Parent/school relationships

Parents participate in the running of education through being represented on participatory committees (organi collegiali) at various levels (see above). At local authority level, parents are represented on advisory bodies – the educational district committees and the provincial education committees. At institutional level, there are elected parents' representatives on bodies with decision-making powers as well as advisory functions. The school committee of each establishment not only has parents' representatives, but is chaired by a parent. It has final responsibility for the budget and all non-educational matters, and for day-to-day management elects an executive board from among its members. The class or interclass committee, again containing representatives of parents, decides on teaching policy and plans for a class or classes, monitors teaching and discipline, and conducts assessment.

Education inspectorate

The inspectorate (Ispettorato Tecnico) is part of the Ministry of Education, with some inspectors working at the centre and others allocated to regions. Their role is partly to advise schools, especially on inservice training and innovation; and partly to check that government and school policy is being implemented satisfactorily, and human and material resources are being used appropriately. The inspectorate also produces an annual report on education in Italy.

Inspectors are former teachers or principals/head teachers of at least nine years' standing, who have succeeded in a concorso with both written and oral examinations. The inspectorate is headed by a central co-ordinator (coordinatore centrale) assisted by regional co-ordinators (coordinatori regionali).

ACRONYMS AND ABBREVIATIONS

CFL	Contratti di Formazione-Lavoro (work/training contracts)
CL	Corso di Laurea (course leading to the Laurea)
CNPI	Consiglio Nazionale della Pubblica Istruzione (National Education Council)
CUD	Consorzio per l'Università a Distanza (Consortium for Distance University Education)
DL	Diploma di Laurea (university first degree)
Dott./Dott.ssa.	Dottore/Dottoressa (holder of a Diploma di Laurea, the university first degree)

DR	Dottorato di Ricerca (research doctorate)
DS	Diploma di Specialista (post-Laurea specialist diploma – mostly medical)
DU	Diploma Universitaria (university diploma) – commonly but unofficially known as 'Laurea breve' (short Laurea)
MPI	Ministero della Pubblica Istruzione (Ministry of Education)
MURST	Ministero dell'Università e della Ricerca Scientifica e Tecnologica (Ministry of Universities and of Scientific and Technological Research)
SDAFS	Scuole Dirette a Fini Speciali (specialist vocational schools, attached to universities but with courses lower in level than the Laurea)
SS	Scuole delle Specializzazione (post-Laurea specialist schools – mostly medical)

ACKNOWLEDGEMENT

We are grateful to the Italian Embassy in London for supplying us with extensive information about education in Italy.

REFERENCES

CERI (1995) *Education at a Glance: OECD indicators*, Paris: Organisation for Economic Co-operation and Development.

European Commission (1995) *Structures of the Education and Initial Training Systems in the European Union*, second edition, Luxembourg: Office for Official Publications of the European Commission.

Istituto Nazionale di Statistica (1992) *Conoscere l'Italia/Introducing Italy*, Rome: Dipartimento per l'informazione e l'editoria, Presidenza del Consiglio dei Ministri.

Istituto Nazionale di Statistica (1993) *Italian Statistical Abstract*, Rome: Istituto Nazionale di Statistica.

Istituto Nazionale di Statistica (1993) *Le Regioni in Cifre*, Rome: Istituto Nazionale di Statistica.

MPI (1992) *L'Istruzione in Italia/Education in Italy*, Rome: Ministero della Pubblica Istruzione.

MURST (1993) *Higher Education in Italy: a guide for foreigners 1993*, Rome: CIMEA della Fondazione RUI.

OECD (1996) *OECD Economic Surveys: 1995–1996: Italy*, Paris: Organisation for Economic Co-operation and Development.

Richards, C. (1994) *The New Italians*, London: Michael Joseph.

BACKGROUND

The Netherlands and its provinces

The Netherlands are often referred to as 'Holland', but Holland is only part of the country. The provinces of North Holland and South Holland together have 38% of the population and 16% of the land area of the Netherlands.

The present-day Netherlands first came into being as an independent country in 1648, when the northern provinces of the Spanish Netherlands (low countries) won independence from Spain. In 1815 they were united with the southern provinces and the Grand Duchy of Luxembourg, as the kingdom of the Netherlands. This lasted only until 1830, however, when the southern provinces won independence as the kingdom of Belgium. Luxembourg became an independent duchy again in 1890. The Netherlands, Belgium and Luxembourg came together once more in 1948 to form a customs union ('Benelux'), and in 1957 were founder members of the European Economic Community, the forerunner of the EU.

The Netherlands is one of the smallest countries of Europe in area, and the most densely populated country in the world. It is exceptionally flat and low-lying. More than half of its land is below sea-level, having been reclaimed from the sea, and is maintained by an elaborate system of dykes and pumps. It has few natural resources, and its economy has always depended heavily on trade.

POPULATION

Population	15.4 million in 1994 (up 0.6% per annum from 1984)
Land area	33,900 sq. km
Population density	454 per sq. km

ECONOMY

GDP	$320.2 billion (1992)
Per capita income	$21,089 (1992)
In employment	63% of working age population (1991)
	– 91% of men/56% of women aged 25–54
	– 56% of young people (15–24)
Spending on education	4.6% of GDP (1991)

LANGUAGE

The national language is Dutch, but Frisian is also an officially recognised language in the province of Friesland, and both Dutch and Frisian are used in schools there.

RELIGION

Thirty-four per cent of the adult population are Roman Catholic, and 25% belong to various Protestant denominations. Just over 3% are Muslim, and just under 1% are Hindu or Buddhist. The remaining 37% have no religious affiliation. (1991 figures)

GOVERNMENT

The Netherlands has three levels of government, each with its own responsibilities for education: *national, provincial* and *municipal.*

The national government, and specifically the Ministry of Education, Culture and Science (hereafter called the Ministry of Education) sets the detailed legislative framework within which schools and other educational institutions operate – both those that are publicly run and those in the (very large) private sector. There are four central 'umbrella' organisations, one representing state education, and the others Catholic, Protestant and secular private education. The national government is also the competent authority for all but one of the publicly run universities, and some other institutions of higher education.

There are 12 provinces. Provincial governments are responsible for adult education, but their main educational duty is that of supervising the municipalities within their boundaries, and ensuring that they provide an adequate number of schools.

There are about 650 municipalities which are the competent authorities for all the publicly run schools and some institutions of higher education within their boundaries. For each private school, its own school board is the competent authority, but the municipality has a duty to oversee the private schools within its boundaries and ensure that they comply with legal requirements. There is one municipal university, in Amsterdam.

EDUCATION

Education is compulsory. Children must attend an educational establishment that complies with legal requirements and meets government standards, full-time between the ages of five and 16, and part-time for a further year for those who do not continue full-time education. Part-time education is normally two days a week, but one day a week for those who have taken up apprenticeships. Full-time education is normally for seven or eight years in a primary school (most children actually start at four), and four years in one of a variety of types of secondary school.

The educational institutions attended at any level may be publicly run or private. In the Netherlands, the private sector of education is considerably larger than the public: 70% of primary schools and 80% of secondary schools are private, accounting overall for almost 70% of pupils. However, the private sector in the Netherlands is not as independent as in some other countries. The same legal requirements concerning curriculum and assessment apply to publicly run schools and private schools, and both sectors are equally eligible for support from public funds, which are disbursed according to the same criteria for both. Though many private schools are funded in part by parental contributions, such contributions must not be a condition of pupils' admission. Where private schools may differ from publicly run schools is in such matters as religious or political orientation, and moral values.

Historically, private education based on religious divisions was one aspect of the general division of Dutch life into religious 'pillars', with not just separate

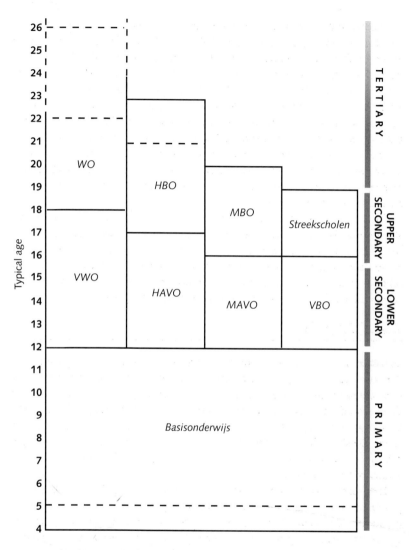

Note: This diagram is highly simplified and should be used in conjunction with the text

The education system of the Netherlands

schools and colleges for Catholics and Protestants, but separate hospitals, social services, trade unions, employers' organisations, newspapers and television channels. However, these divisions have weakened since the late 1960s, partly as a result of a decline in religious belief and practice. (Walford, 1995)

The Netherlands has just over 11,400 schools, with 2.7 million pupils; and 14 universities and 296 vocational colleges, with 378,000 students in all. In these establishments, there is a total of some 207,000 teaching staff. (1991–2 figures)

INSTITUTIONS

The various types of school described below encompass both private schools (*bijzondere scholen*) and publicly run schools (*openbare scholen*), and the statistics attached to them are for private and public schools taken together, except where otherwise stated. Primary schooling is comprehensive, but secondary schooling is selective, with a clear distinction between general and vocational education.

Preprimary education

Since 1985, there is no separate, formal nursery education. Although education is compulsory only from five, almost all children start primary school at four.

For children aged two to three (and those four-year-olds who do not go to school), there are playgroups (*peuterspeelzaal*), which cater for about a fifth of all two-year-olds and half of all three-year-olds. They may be state-funded or private, but in either case parents must make a financial contribution. Staff are often voluntary workers.

There are also day-care centres (*kinderdagverblijven*), which take preschool children from as early as six weeks, but they cater for only some 1% of children under five. (European Commission, 1995)

Primary education

Primary education (*basisonderwijs*) is governed by the 1985 Primary Education Act. It lasts seven or eight years, from the ages of four or five to 12. (Education is compulsory from five, but almost all children start school at four, and classes are provided specifically for four-year-olds.) Primary education is not selective; there is no streaming within schools, or differentiation between types of school. Primary schools are co-educational, and run separately from secondary schools. Pupils in the state system must attend a school in the catchment area specified by their local authority; there is no such restriction for private schools.

The primary school year runs from 1st August to 31st July, with six weeks' summer holiday (staggered across the country). The school week involves an average of from 22 hours (for younger pupils) to 25 hours (for older pupils) of teaching, spread across usually five but sometimes six days. There is a maximum of 5.5 hours of teaching per day.

There are just over 8,400 primary schools in the Netherlands, with 1.4

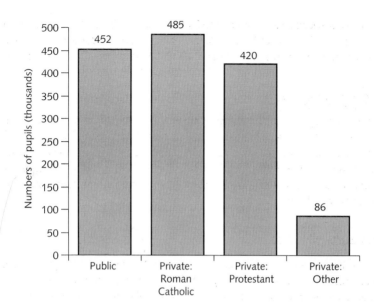

*Netherlands figure 1   Basic education: numbers of pupils in public and private schools,
1990–1*

million pupils and 80,000 teachers, two-thirds of whom are women. (1991–2 figures) They may be public or private, as Figure 1 illustrates.

The following subjects must be taught in both public and private primary schools, preferably as an integrated curriculum.

- Dutch
- English
- arithmetic and mathematics
- factual subjects (including history, geography, science, social structures and religious movements)
- creative activities (including language use, drawing, music, handicrafts, movement and play)
- sensory co-ordination and physical exercise
- health instruction
- self-reliance/social and life skills (including road safety)

In addition, Frisian is compulsory in the province of Friesland.

Normally classes are organised by age, and one teacher teaches all or most subjects.

There is no formal certificate or diploma at the end of primary education. Instead a report is drawn up for each child, usually based on a test as well as class work. It describes the child's abilities, interests and level of achievements, and recommends suitable forms of secondary education.

Lower and upper secondary education

This stage is governed by the 1968 Secondary Education Act, with some subsequent modifications, notably the Basic Education Decree of 1993. The full-time compulsory component lasts four years, normally from the ages of 12 to 16. For those not continuing in full-time education, part-time education is compulsory for a further year. But many do continue full-time study in secondary schools, to the ages of 17, 18 or even up to 20, depending on the type of institution.

There are just over 2,000 secondary schools in the Netherlands (60% of them academic, 40% vocational), with 1.2 million students and 89,000 teachers, of whom 70% are women. About 20% of them are public, 80% private. (1991–2 figures)

Secondary education is selective and usually based on the child's report at the end of primary education. The structure of secondary (and tertiary) education in the Netherlands is complicated, and the account here omits many details. (See the text of European Commission, 1995, or the diagram in CERI, 1995, for more detail.) There are three main types of secondary education.

- pre-university education (VWO – *Voorbereidend Wetenschappeljik Onderwijs*)
- general secondary education (AVO – *Algemeen Voortgezet Onderwijs*)
- vocational education (BO – *Beroepsonderwijs*)

And there are subdivisions within these types. Thus the AVO category is divided into MAVO and HAVO – intermediate (*Middelbaa Algemeen Voortgezet Onderwijs*) and senior (*Hoger Algemeen Voortgezet Onderwijs*) general secondary education. As the diagram shows, this distinction refers not to age differences, but to the different academic levels of institutions attended by students of the same age. Similarly, the BO category is divided into VBO and MBO – preparatory (*Voorbereidend Beroepsonderwijs*) and intermediate (*Middelbaa Beroepsonderwijs*) vocational education. But as the diagram shows, this distinction does refer to age. (MBO spans upper secondary and lower tertiary levels; there is also HBO – higher (*Hoger Beroepsonderwijs*) vocational education, which is of tertiary level.)

There are standard routes through the system from institution to institution – denoted by movement upwards on the diagram. As the diagram shows, these are not always what the names of the different schools might suggest. Thus 'intermediate general secondary education' (MAVO) is designed to lead not to 'senior general secondary education' (HAVO) but to 'intermediate vocational education' (MBO). And it is 'senior general secondary education' (HAVO), not any type of vocational education (BO), that is designed to lead to 'higher vocational education' (HBO).

These standard routes are not rigid, however; the system has considerable flexibility, with many opportunities to transfer between different types of institution. This has been extended in recent years, as a result of government policy. Firstly, an increasing number of schools offer courses of more than one type, and sometimes even combined classes of different types (such as VBO with MAVO; MAVO with HAVO; HAVO with VWO). Secondly, since 1993 the first three years of all types of secondary school consist of a similar basic education (*basisvormingp*), designed to delay choice and facilitate movement between schools of different type, if this is appropriate. Fifteen compulsory subjects for the basic education curriculum are laid down centrally, with attainment targets and recommended minimum hours of study for each.

- Dutch
- English
- French or German
- mathematics
- biology
- physics
- chemistry
- computing
- history and civics
- geography
- economics
- technology
- social and life skills
- arts
- physical education

These compulsory subjects are to occupy 80% of students' time, leaving the remainder for optional subjects. The latter include other languages (ancient and modern), religious studies, astronomy, film, theatre, law, health care, nutrition and clothing. (European Commission, 1995)

A similar, though not identical, range of subjects continues to be taught in all types of secondary school after the three years of basic education. The main differences lie in the level at which the subjects are taught, the other subjects added, and the distribution of time among the subjects.

In all types of secondary school, there is a final examination with two components: a national examination for all schools of each type; and an examination set by each school. Those who pass receive a national diploma in the appropriate type of education.

Pre-university education (VWO)

There are three traditional types of VWO, the *gymnasium*, the *atheneum* and the *lyceum*. In the gymnasium, Latin and classical Greek are compulsory, in the lyceum they are optional and the atheneum does not teach them. All three have a six-year course, and are normally entered directly from primary school.

They are primarily intended to prepare students for entry to university, but students can and do transfer to other types of school or proceed to higher vocational education.

Traditionally, all three types of school are divided after the fourth or fifth year into an 'A side' and a 'B side'. The A side of a gymnasium concentrates on Latin and Greek, and that of an atheneum on economics and modern languages. The B side of both types of school concentrates on mathematics and science. But the curriculum is broadly based for everyone. At the end of their secondary education, students sit a leaving examination in seven subjects, between two and four compulsory (according to the type of school and side) the others of their choice, for the VWO certificate. In addition, there are compulsory non-examination classes in social studies, creative arts and physical education.

However, the distinctions between these three types of school and between the two 'sides' within them have become less rigid in recent years, and many schools now offer 'integral VWO' courses, with the classics as optional subjects, and less restricted (though still not unrestricted) choice of combinations of subjects. There are over 700 VWO schools with over 160,000 pupils – 53% in the atheneum, 29% in the lyceum and 18% in the gymnasium. There are equal numbers of boys and girls in each. (1990–1 figures)

General secondary education (AVO)
General secondary education is academic education of a lower level than VWO. It encompasses two types of school, senior general secondary education (HAVO), and intermediate general secondary education (MAVO).

As the diagram of the Education System shows, 'senior' and 'intermediate' here refer to the different academic levels of institutions attended by students of the same age. There are about 1,000 MAVO schools, with 180,000 students and 500 HAVO schools with 140,000. Each type has a majority (55%) of girls. (1990–1 figures) Both HAVO and MAVO are entered directly from primary school. The HAVO course lasts five years from the age of 12, and is primarily designed to prepare students for higher vocational education (HBO). The MAVO course lasts four years from the age of 12, and is primarily designed to prepare students for intermediate vocational education (MBO). But there are other possibilities. For example, students who have gained a MAVO leaving certificate may then transfer to the fourth year of a HAVO school; and students who have gained a HAVO leaving certificate may go on to study for a VWO certificate.

The curriculum in AVO schools is broadly based, and similar in the range of subjects to that of basic education. For the leaving certificate, students must sit examinations in six or seven subjects, which must include Dutch and one foreign language. In addition, students have non-examination classes in physical education and a creative or expressive arts subject.

Vocational education (BO)
Vocational education has recently been re-organised. At present, secondary vocational education is provided at two types of school, preparatory (VBO) and intermediate (MBO); MBO also extends into tertiary education. VBO courses are entered directly from primary school; MBO courses are for students with an appropriate MAVO or VBO leaving certificate. About 90% of BO schools are private.

Preparatory vocational education (VBO)
Unlike other types of secondary school, VBO schools lay down no conditions for admission. VBO courses last four years, with an increased emphasis on vocational training as against general subjects after the first year. The vocational areas covered include the following. (European Commission, 1995)

- technical subjects
- home economics/domestic science
- trades
- commerce and administration
- agriculture

Students who pass the VBO examination may proceed to apprenticeships, or to MBO courses.
In 1991–2, there were 220,900 students on full-time VBO courses.

Intermediate vocational education (MBO)
MBO – which straddles the upper secondary/tertiary division – prepares students for middle-ranking positions in industry, the service sector and government. In the late 1980s and early 1990s, MBO was re-organised. MBO schools were amalgamated (reducing the number catering for full-time students from about 380 to about 140), and MBO courses were made more flexible in content, level and length, and involved closer consultation with industry. They may be full- or part-time, and 'long' (up to four years), 'intermediate' (up to three years) or 'short'. Admission to the longer courses requires higher grades in MAVO or VBO leaving certificates than admission to the shorter ones.

There are four main sectors in MBO education – *economics, technical, social services/healthcare* and *agriculture*. MBO schools may specialise in one sector, or cover a range of sectors. In 1990–1 there were 259,000 students on full-time long MBO courses. Male students take 87% of places in the technical sector, and female students 89% of those in social services/healthcare.

The MBO final examination has two components, one set nationally by an examination board for each of the four sectors, the other set by each school.

Apprenticeship

Apprenticeships are governed by the 1993 Part-time Vocational Courses Act. They combine general education and theoretical vocational training in a training school (*streekscholen*) with practical vocational training in a training workshop or with a firm. There are three levels of apprenticeship training – 'tertiary', 'advanced' and 'elementary' (comparable in level with long, intermediate and short MBO courses respectively). Apprentices must be over 16, and courses last between one and three years. Those who successfully complete their theoretical and practical examinations are awarded a recognised vocational diploma.

The apprenticeship system is divided into 31 occupational sectors (though this number is likely to be greatly reduced), each with a national board whose members are representatives of employers' organisations, trade unions and the education system, to oversee its curriculum and assessment arrangements. The theoretical component of apprenticeships is funded by the Ministry of Education (28 sectors) or the Ministry of Agriculture (three sectors). The practical component is funded by employers, but they receive financial assistance from the Ministry of Social Affairs and Employment.

There were about 130,000 apprentices in 1990 – an increase of 65% since 1980.

Special education

Special education is governed by the 1985 Special Education Interim Act, which was planned to remain in force for ten years. In 1990–1, the Netherlands had just over 1,000 special schools, with 109,000 pupils (68% boys, 32% girls). Pupils in special schools constitute 4% of all pupils in primary and secondary education.

Special schools may be primary or secondary. Special primary schools cater for pupils of the same age as mainstream primary schools (i.e. four or five to 12), but special secondary schools can have pupils aged from 12 to 20.

Special schools – primary and secondary – are divided into 15 categories, according to the type of children's learning difficulties for which they cater. The great majority are for either *children with learning and behavioural difficulties* (40% of all children in special schools) or *mentally handicapped children* (39%). (1990–1 figures)

Numbers of pupils in special schools have grown in recent years – by 20% between 1980 and 1990, despite a reduction by 15% in the overall primary school population during the same period. Official policy is now to reverse this trend, educating children in mainstream schools and returning pupils in special schools to mainstream schools where possible. To assist this, there are schemes of co-operation between special and mainstream schools, including *peripatetic supervision* of pupils in mainstream schools by teachers from special schools, and *split placements* of pupils between a special and a mainstream school.

Tertiary education

Tertiary education is governed by the 1993 Higher Education and Research Act. It comprises higher vocational education (HBO), in 70 colleges with 261,000 students (full- and part-time); and university education (WO – *Wetenschappeljik Onderwijs*), in 13 conventional universities with 162,000 full-time students, plus the Open University with 68,000 part-time students. (1992–3 figures, European Commission, 1995) Both HBO and WO have a two-level system of undergraduate and postgraduate work. Both have autonomy with regard to their curriculum, teaching and research.

Higher vocational education (HBO)
In the late 1980s and early 1990s, many HBO colleges were amalgamated; there are now 70, 70% private and 30% public. For admission, students require a VWO, HAVO or MBO certificate, in addition to any entrance requirements imposed by individual colleges. Full-time HBO courses of undergraduate level normally last four years, but students may take up to six years to complete them. (Part-time courses may last up to nine years.) The first stage of any course (up to two years) is a foundation stage, consisting of general education; thereafter students specialise in one of seven vocational sectors. The courses have an important practical training as well as theoretical component. There is a foundation examination at the end of that stage, and a final examination at the end of the course. Graduates in the technical or agricultural sectors are awarded the title of *ingenieur* (*ing.*), and in the other five sectors that of *baccalaureus* (*bc.*) For use abroad, both may take the title *bachelor* (*B.*).

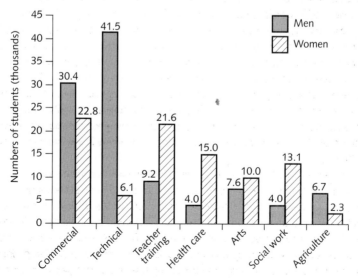

Netherlands figure 2   Numbers of students in the different HBO sectors, 1990–1

There are seven HBO sectors: in 1990–1, these had just under 200,000 full-time students, distributed as shown in Figure 2.

University education (WO)
The Netherlands has 14 universities. Ten are state universities – nine (including the Open University) run by the Ministry of Education, and one by the Ministry of Agriculture; one is a municipal university (in Amsterdam); and three are private. There are also eight teaching hospitals, each attached to a university.

Admission to university is normally with a VWO certificate, but students may also be admitted after passing an HBO foundation examination, or on the basis of a university entrance examination. There is a central admission system, which divides courses into three types, on the basis of the number of places available and the state of the labour market:

- courses for which no restrictions are necessary. All qualified candidates are admitted to the university of their choice;
- courses for which some restrictions are necessary. All qualified candidates are admitted, but not necessarily to the university of their choice. A placement committee is established, which allocates students to universities;
- courses for which a maximum number (*numerus clausus*) is set by the Ministry of Education. Not all qualified candidates can be admitted, and the choice among them is made by lot.

Most degree courses are designed to last four years (five or six in medicine), but students may take up to six years to complete them. After successfully passing their final examinations, graduates take the title of *doctorandus* or *meester* (*ingenieur* in technical or agricultural subjects).

The distribution of full-time students across university faculties is shown in Figure 3.

Adult education

Adult education in the Netherlands is of two main kinds, 'basic education' and 'evening-class education'. Basic education is intended to provide adults with the minimum knowledge and skills necessary to function in Dutch society, such as literacy and numeracy. 'Evening-class' education (which may take place during the day, in what are termed 'day-evening classes') is intended to provide the equivalent of ordinary primary and secondary schooling for adults who have missed them. These classes are held in ordinary schools.

Since 1984, the Open University (OU – *Open Universiteit*) has offered distance education at university level for adults (over 18). No education qualifications are required for admission, but in practice most OU students do have some. It offers courses in cultural studies, science and technology, social science, economics, business management, public administration and law.

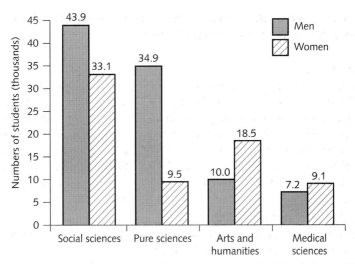

Netherlands figure 3   Full-time university students by faculty, 1990–1

In 1990–1, about 115,000 adults participated in basic adult education, 80,000 in general secondary education, 229,000 in secondary vocational education, 55,000 in tertiary vocational education, and 15,000 in universities (plus another 36,000 in the OU). A further 396,000 took part in various other types of adult education, including non-formal oral education and correspondence courses.

Funding

Whether public or private, educational institutions are eligible for funding on the same basis by the Ministry of Education (apart from those in agricultural education, which are funded by the Ministry of Agriculture). To qualify, private institutions must be non-profit making, follow government regulations on admissions, and accept the authority of an external appeals committee on disputes between the school board and members of staff. The level of funding varies between the sectors of education, but within each sector it depends on the number of pupils, the length of time for which they attend, the class sizes, and the teachers' salary scales. There are several different systems of funding in operation, which allow schools different degrees of autonomy in the way their funds are spent.

Education is free up to the age of 16, though parents contribute to the cost of books and other teaching materials, and where necessary of travel. After 16, fees are payable, in secondary, tertiary and adult education, and in apprenticeships. There are means-tested grants for students aged between 12 and 17. All full-time students over 18 but under 27 are entitled to a basic grant, and there are means-tested supplementary grants and loans.

Total government expenditure on education was 4.6% of GDP in 1991. This declined during the 1980s (from 6.5% in 1979), which is partly but not wholly explained by a decline in the proportion of young people in the population. (OECD, 1996) Of this expenditure, 37% is on secondary, 29% on primary, 28% on tertiary and 6% on special education. Expenditure per pupil or student varies greatly from sector to sector, as Figure 4 shows.

Parent/school relationships

Every school has a *participation council* and a *parents' council*. The participation council consists of elected representatives of parents, staff and, in secondary schools and above, students. It has powers defined for each individual school or institution. The parents' council co-ordinates parents' activities, and advises the parent members of the participation council.

Teaching profession

There are three main categories of qualified teacher: primary teacher, secondary teacher grade one and secondary teacher grade two.

Primary teacher
For all age-groups in the primary school, all but a few specialist subjects (such

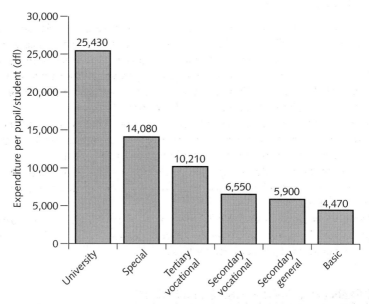

Netherlands figure 4   Expenditure per pupil/student in different sectors of education,
1989

as physical education and music) are taught by the same teacher. Primary teachers are trained in HBO courses, which last four years full-time or six years part-time, to teach both general subjects and one specialist subject.

Secondary teacher
Grade two secondary teachers are qualified to teach only the first three years of VWO and HAVO schools, but all age-groups at MAVO, VBO and MBO schools. To teach one general (i.e. academic) subject, they are trained for four years full-time (or six years part-time) in HBO colleges or universities. To teach technical subjects, they are trained for five years full-time (or seven years part-time) in the Dutch Technical Teacher Training College.

Grade one secondary teachers are qualified to teach all age-groups at all secondary schools. They must normally be university graduates, who take a further one-year postgraduate training course at a university. This qualifies them to teach one subject. In addition, holders of grade two qualifications can obtain grade one status by taking an additional three year part-time course. And for teachers of physical education, a four year full-time course in an HBO college gives grade one status.

Inservice training is available for all teachers, but not compulsory.

All teachers, in private as well as public schools, are classified as civil servants.

Education inspectorate

The Education Inspectorate, headed by the Inspector-General of Education is responsible to the Minister of Education for the inspection of all primary and secondary educational institutions, public or private (apart from those in agricultural education, which have their own inspectorate, responsible to the Minister of Agriculture). Though centrally controlled, the Inspectorate is distributed throughout the country, with 14 regional offices.

Its duties are to ensure that schools and other institutions meet their statutory obligations; to monitor the state of education; to promote the development of education; and to report to and advise the Minister.

In addition to the national Inspectorate, the larger municipalities often have their own inspectors, who are concerned with the publicly run schools within their boundaries.

Tertiary institutions – WO and HBO – are not monitored by the Education Inspectorate. They have a system of internal quality control, with periodic external monitoring by 'visiting committees'.

ACRONYMS AND ABBREVIATIONS

| AVO | Algemeen Voortgezet Onderwijs (general secondary education) |
| BO | Beroepsonderwijs (vocational education) |

HAVO	Hoger Algemeen Voortgezet Onderwijs (senior general secondary education)
HBO	Hoger Beroepsonderwijs (higher vocational education)
LBO	Lager Beroepsonderwijs (lower vocational education) – now replaced by VBO
MAVO	Middelbar Algemeen Voortgezet Onderwijs (intermediate general secondary education)
MBO	Middelbar Beroepsonderwijs (intermediate vocational education)
OU	Open Universiteit (Open University)
VAVO	Voortgezet Algemeen Volvassenonderwijs (general secondary adult education)
VBO	Voorbereidend Beroepsonderwijs (preparatory vocational education)
VWO	Voorbereidend Wetenschappeljik Onderwijs (pre-university education)
WO	Wetenschappeljik Onderwijs (university education)

ACKNOWLEDGEMENTS

We are grateful to the Embassy of the Netherlands in London for supplying us with extensive information, and to Dr Robert van der Zwan.

REFERENCES

Central Bureau of Statistics (1993) *Statistical Yearbook 1993 of the Netherlands*, The Hague: SDU Publishers.

CERI (1995) *Education at a Glance: OECD Indicators*, Paris: Organisation for Economic Co-operation and Development.

European Commission (1995) *Structures of the Education and Initial Training Systems in the European Union*, Luxembourg: Office for Official Publications of the European Commission.

James, E. (1989) 'The Netherlands: benefits and costs of privatised public services – lessons from the Dutch education system', in Walford, G. (ed.) (1989) *Private Schools in Ten Countries: policy and practice*, London: Routledge.

OECD (1966) *OECD Economic Surveys: 1995–1996: Netherlands*, Paris: Organisation for Economic Co-operation and Development.

Römkens, L. and Visser, K. (1994) *Vocational Education and Training in the Netherlands*, Berlin: CEDEFOP.

van Dorp, A. and van Opdorp, J. (no date) *The Kingdom of the Netherlands: facts and figures: education and science*, The Hague: Ministry of Foreign Affairs/Central Directorate for Information.

Walford, G. (1995) 'Faith-based grant-maintained schools: selective international policy-borrowing from the Netherlands', *Journal of Education Policy*, Vol. 10, No. 3.

BACKGROUND

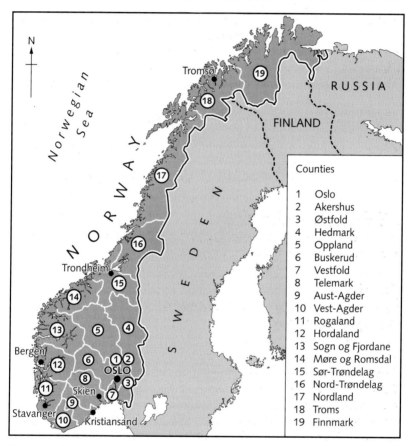

Norway and its counties

Norway first became a united and independent kingdom around 900 AD. But it was ruled by the kings of Denmark from 1380 until 1814, when it was united instead with Sweden under the Swedish crown. It regained independence in 1905.

It is a member of the Nordic Council (with Denmark, Finland, Iceland and Sweden), and of the European Free Trade Association. Despite negotiating three times to enter the EU, it remains outside.

Norway is one of the largest countries in Europe. It is long (north to south) and narrow (west to east), with numerous fjords, extensive mountain ranges and thousands of islands.

POPULATION

Like its Nordic neighbours, Norway is sparsely populated, with most of the population concentrated in the south of the country.

Population	4.3 million in 1994 (up 0.5% per annum from 1984)
Land area	324,000 sq. km (mainland only)
Population density	13 per sq. km (mainland)

ECONOMY

GDP	$110 billion in 1995
Per capita income	$25,400 in 1995
In employment	73% of working age population (1991)
	– 89% of men/77% of women aged 25–54
	– 51% of young people (15–24)
Spending on education	7.6% of GDP (1992)

RELIGION

Freedom of religion is guaranteed by the constitution, but Norway has a state church, the Church of Norway, to which 89% of the population belong; it is evangelical Lutheran. Of the remainder, most (150,000) belong to other Protestant denominations. In addition, there are 62,000 members of humanist organisations, 41,000 Muslims, 34,000 Roman Catholics and 1,000 Orthodox Jews. (1995 figures, Statistics Norway)

LANGUAGE AND ETHNICITY

Two varieties of the Norwegian language are officially recognised. *Bokmal* ('book language') is the language as it developed during the centuries of Danish rule, and is heavily influenced by Danish. *Nynorsk* ('new Norwegian') is a 19th century invention, based on rural Norwegian dialects and intended to restore a traditional Norwegian purified of Danish influences. All official documents are published in both varieties, and both are used in the press and broadcasting. All children must learn to read both, and to write either one. Ability to write both is required for entry to university. However, Nynorsk remains largely a rural language. Bokmal is the main language for about 80% of Norwegian school children. About 85% of Norwegian books are in Bokmal, and it is the language usually taught abroad as 'Norwegian'. Bokmal and Nynorsk (and Danish and Swedish) are mutually intelligible.

In addition, Sami is spoken by the Sami (Lapp) population, who live mostly in the northernmost country, Finnmark. They are about 20,000 in number. They may choose whether to study Sami at school as their first or second language.

GOVERNMENT
Norway has three levels of government – *national, county* and *municipal.*

Since 1990, all education (apart from preschool) is the responsibility of a single government ministry, the Ministry of Education, Research and Church Affairs (hereafter called the Ministry of Education), assisted by numerous advisory councils. Preschool institutions are not part of formal education in Norway, and are under the authority of the Ministry of Consumer Affairs.

While the national government has ultimate responsibility for education at all levels, and sets the general framework of educational policy, immediate responsibility for upper secondary education has been devolved in recent years to the counties, and for lower secondary and primary education to the municipalities – though the curriculum subjects, the division of time between them and the major examinations are still set nationally. The national government retains immediate responsibility only for tertiary education.

There are 19 counties, mostly rural. County councils are responsible for upper secondary education (see below). Each county has a county education committee, appointed by the county council. There is also in each county a director of schools, appointed by the national government, who is responsible for overseeing the educational work of the county and of the municipalities within it, and ensuring that they fulfil their statutory obligations. A county vocational training committee is responsible for administering apprenticeship contracts with companies and organising vocational examinations and the issuing of certificates.

The counties (apart from Oslo) are divided into municipalities, some 450 in all. They vary enormously in size from 250 to 400,000 inhabitants; the average size is 10,000. The municipalities have a great deal of autonomy, though they have certain statutory duties, and are supervised by the county governor on behalf of the national government.

Municipalities are responsible for primary and lower secondary education. Each municipality has an education committee (appointed by the municipal council) and a chief education officer (appointed by the education committee).

EDUCATION

Education is compulsory between the ages of six and 16, and everyone aged 16 to 19 has a right to three further years of academic or vocational education. The current compulsory period is divided into two stages: primary (6–13) and lower secondary (13–16). Upper secondary education normally covers the 16–19 age-range.

Public education is free. In addition, pupils in primary and lower secondary schools are entitled to free transport if they live more than 4 km from the nearest school, and to free accommodation if they live too far from the

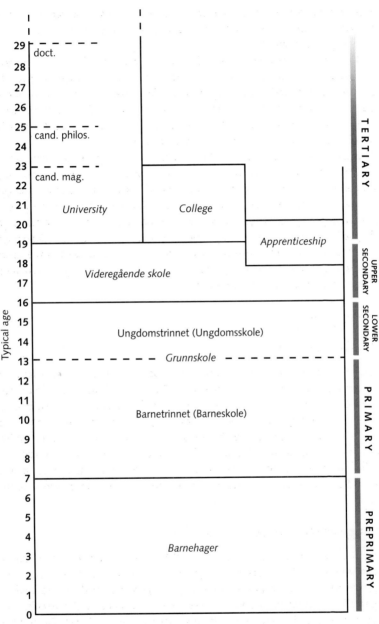

Note: This diagram is simplified for clarity, and should be used in conjunction with the text

Norway's education system

nearest school to travel daily. Students in upper secondary education and in tertiary education may be granted scholarships on the basis of a means test, and are eligible for state loans.

In 1993–4, Norway had some 3,900 schools (just over 3,300 primary and lower secondary, and just under 600 upper secondary), with almost 680,000 pupils and 77,000 teachers (20% part-time). At higher education level, there were four universities, six specialist university colleges and 26 state colleges, with 160,000 students in all in 1993–4 – almost twice as many students as in 1985. (European Commission/Ministry of Education)

The private education sector in Norway is small, though it has increased in size in recent years. It now caters for 1.5% of primary and lower secondary pupils, and 4% of upper secondary students. The government acknowledges the right of private schools and higher education institutions to exist, but encourages (and gives financial support to) only those that do not compete with public education, for example because they are based on alternative educational philosophies. Normally, government grants cover 85% of the costs of primary and lower secondary and 75% of the costs of upper secondary private schools; the rest is covered by fees.

INSTITUTIONS

Preprimary education

Preprimary institutions – *barnehager* – are not part of formal education in Norway, and are under the authority of the Ministry of Consumer Affairs, not the Ministry of Education. There were 6,000 in 1994, about half provided by municipalities, half by private organisations or by groups of families in a private home (but with a qualified preschool teacher). About 43% of children under seven attend barnehager – 422,000 in 1994. Over 90% of barnehager staff are female. The teachers must have three years' college training, but no formal qualifications are required of teaching assistants. (Statistics Norway/European Commission)

Primary and lower secondary education

Compulsory education is governed by the 1969 Education Act (and subsequent amendments). It takes place in the *grunnskoler*, which are divided into two stages: *barnetrinnet* (primary – ages 6–13) and *ungdomstrinnet* (lower secondary – ages 13–16). Sometimes these are separate establishments (*barneskoler* and *ungdomsskoler*), and sometimes the two stages are combined (*kombinerte skoler*). About a third of Norway's grunnskoler are combined schools.

There are some 3,350 grunnskoler, with 470,000 pupils and 47,000 full-time equivalent teachers – a pupil/teacher ratio of 10/1. (1993 figures, Ministry of Education)

Compulsory education is comprehensive: classes are kept together as mixed-ability units, except for elective subjects at the lower secondary stage. In the primary stage, each class is taught by one class teacher. At the lower secondary stage, there are some specialist subject teachers, for such subjects as foreign languages and physical education.

Because of Norway's large size, sparse population and difficulties of transport, many schools are small: about a third of primary schools have pupils of different ages in the same class.

The 1969 Education Act laid down that teaching should be in accordance with national curriculum guidelines. These list the subjects to be taught, and the number of lessons to be devoted to them. Currently (since 1987) these are as shown in Figures 1 and 2.

Special provision is made for Sami pupils, and also to ensure that all Norwegian pupils are familiar with Sami history and culture.

There is no formal assessment in primary schools, but parents must be informed about their children's progress at least twice a year, whether by written reports or personal meetings. In lower secondary school, pupils are given marks on a five-point scale in all the compulsory national curriculum subjects twice a year, and for a final examination set nationally by the Council for Primary and Lower Secondary Education.

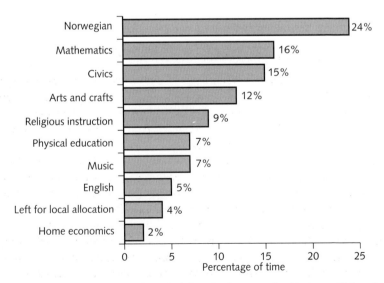

Norway figure 1   Percentage of time laid down by the national curriculum guidelines for compulsory subjects in the barnetrinnet

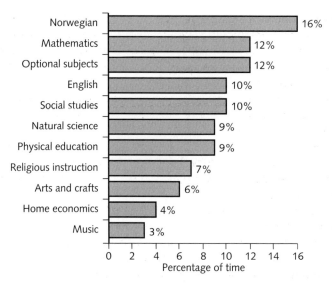

Norway figure 2   *Percentage of time laid down by the national curriculum guidelines for compulsory subjects in the ungdomstrinnet*
Notes: (i) The percentage figures are for the entire primary and lower secondary stages respectively; (ii) at the primary stage, English and home economics are taught only from the fourth year; (iii) at the secondary stage, the optional subject is usually German or another foreign language

Upper secondary education (including apprenticeship)

This stage follows compulsory education, and normally covers the age-range 16–19, but about a quarter of students are over 20. Since the 1974 Education Act, the upper secondary school – *videregående skole* – has combined academic and vocational education. Extensive reforms were introduced in 1994 to the structure, curriculum and subject syllabuses, with an Upper Secondary Education Act and a Vocational Training Act – a process referred to as *Reform '94*. Employers' and employees' organisations were actively involved in the planning of the new syllabuses in vocational education. Extensive inservice training is provided to enable teachers to follow the new syllabuses.

As part of Reform '94, all Norwegians now have the right to continue their education until the age of 19 (and over 95% of 16–19-year-olds do so), taking courses that qualify them either to enter higher education or to follow an occupation. This right does not depend on a student's marks at lower secondary school, but these marks can determine admission to the most popular subjects.

There are some 700 upper secondary schools in Norway, with 210,000 students and 23,700 teachers. (1993 figures, Ministry of Education)

Upper secondary education now consists of courses at three levels, each level normally occupying one year.

Foundation course

Students take a foundation course at school, in their first year of upper secondary education. There are now 13 foundation courses, listed below. Students may not always be able to study their first preference among the courses, but they are guaranteed a place on one out of their first three preferences.

- general and business studies
- music, dance and drama
- sports and physical education
- health and social studies
- arts, crafts and design
- agriculture, fishing and forestry
- hotel and food-processing trades
- building and construction trades
- technical building trades
- electrical trades
- engineering and mechanical trades
- chemical and processing trades
- woodworking trades

Students who attend and pass their course are eligible to proceed to the next level in the same subjects.

Advanced course I

An advanced course I is also taken at school, normally in the student's second year of upper secondary education, and in the same subjects as they studied for their foundation course.

Advanced course II – academic

Courses at this level in academic subjects are taken in school, in the student's third year of upper secondary education. These courses may be either a continuation of the (academic) studies the student has followed at the lower levels, or supplementary academic studies for students who have taken vocational subjects at the lower levels. Both types of course lead to qualifications for entry to higher education.

To qualify for higher education, students following academic courses need to have studied a prescribed set of subjects throughout their three years of upper secondary education. These subjects, and the minimum number of hours per week to be devoted to them, are shown in Figure 3.

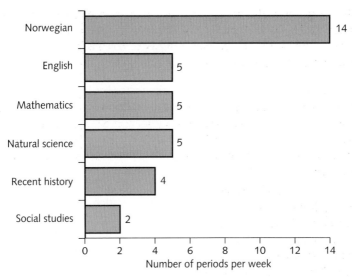

Norway figure 3   Minimum number of 45-minute periods per week in academic upper secondary education to qualify for entry to higher education (Ministry of Education)

Advanced course II – vocational
Vocational courses at this level occupy the third and sometimes a fourth year of upper secondary education. The one-year courses consist of training only; they are occasionally taken in school, but much more often at the workplace. The two-year courses combine training with productive work, at the workplace. Whether young people take their courses as students at a school or as apprentices at the workplace, they take the same tests and receive the same vocational qualifications, usually the craft or journeyman's certificate.

(Adults who have not followed the upper secondary course of training but who consider that they have obtained the requisite knowledge and skill by other means may also take these tests and, if successful, obtain the same certificate.)

Special education

The national policy is that pupils with special needs should as far as possible be integrated into ordinary schools, receiving where necessary special teaching in the mainstream classroom or in separate groups. Until recently, Norway also had some special schools, but those run by the state have now been replaced by 20 resource centres (13 national and seven regional) offering advice, information and training to municipalities, schools and teachers. (Ministry of Education, 1994)

Tertiary education

Tertiary education institutions fall into two sectors: the *university* sector and the *college* sector. There are approximately 160,000 students in tertiary education – about 45% of the 20–24 age-group. The two sectors have roughly equal numbers of students, but the university sector has been more generously funded by the government. (In 1992, it received 5 billion NKr, as compared with 3 billion NKr for the college sector.)

Tertiary education in Norway has recently been expanded and re-organised. The number of students increased by 88% between 1985 and 1993. Co-operation and co-ordination among universities and colleges is being encouraged through what is called 'Network Norway'. The aim is to provide a more closely integrated system, by closer co-operation and a clearer division of labour between institutions, with the establishment of national centres of competence in different disciplines. The college sector has been re-organised into a smaller number of larger institutions, whose regulations are being brought into line with those of the university sector.

Tertiary education receives about 90% of its funding from the state. The remainder comes from external sources, such as research foundations or research conducted under contract. For students, tertiary education is free (apart from a small fee payable to student organisations for welfare activities). There are no tuition fees, and financial assistance is available for living expenses and study materials. About a quarter of this assistance takes the form of grants, and the remaining three-quarters the form of loans repayable over 20 years. In addition, there are subsidised student accommodation, cafeterias and nurseries for students' children.

The language of instruction in tertiary education is Norwegian, but prospective students are advised by the authorities that much of the required reading in many courses is in English.

University sector

There are four universities, ranging in size from the University of Oslo with 34,600 students to the University of Tromsø with 5,900; they have some 78,000 students in total. There are also six specialist colleges at university level, devoted respectively to agriculture, economics and business administration, music, physical education, and veterinary medicine. They range in size from the Norwegian School of Economics and Business Administration with 2,300 students to the Oslo School of Architecture and the Norwegian State Academy of Music, with 270 each; they have about 6,000 students between them. (1993/4 figures, Statistics Norway/Norwegian Council of Universities)

These institutions are all run centrally by the state, but have considerable autonomy, especially in their curricula, research and admissions. Normally, a secondary school leaving certificate satisfies the formal entrance requirements, but it does not guarantee a place, as a university or college may, with the consent of the Ministry, limit access to particular subjects of study because of limited resources. At present, most subjects are affected by such limits and entrance is highly competitive. Criteria for admission are very varied, but the government plans to standardise them.

In academic subjects, degree courses are offered at two levels. There is a first degree, *cand. mag.* (*candidatus/candidata magisterii*) awarded after studies lasting three-and-a-half years (in the natural sciences) or four years (in the humanities or social sciences). Then there is a higher degree, awarded after one-and-a-half or two further years of study, *cand. philos.*, *cand. scient.* or *cand. polit.* – in arts, sciences and social sciences respectively (*candidatus/candidata philosophiae*, ... *scientiarium*, ... *rerum politicarum*). Most students who successfully take a first degree proceed to complete a higher degree too.

In professional courses (such as medicine, dentistry, law, theology, agriculture, business and psychology), degree courses typically last four-and-a-half to six years of study, with such degrees as *cand. med.*, *cand. odont.*, and *cand. jur.*

The first degree is based on a credit system, and students may transfer credit from one institution to another, including credits from regional colleges, private colleges and institutions abroad. The degree may cover a wide range of subjects, with students given considerable choice.

In both academic and professional subjects, doctoral programmes are offered, lasting three to four years. Most of these (e.g. *dr. scient.*, *dr. art.*, *dr. polit.*) combine obligatory training in theory and method with the completion of a thesis, but the 'general' degree of doctor of philosophy (*dr. philos.*) requires only a thesis, though more stringent criteria are applied to it. The number of doctorates granted each year has doubled between 1984 and 1993, from about 250 to about 500.

The students in the university sector consist of roughly equal numbers of men and women, but women predominate in arts (65%) and social sciences (55%), and men in engineering (75%) and science (60%).

College sector
Traditionally, tertiary education in Norway was influenced by the country's large size, sparse population and difficulties of transport and communications. Thus, as well as a few large universities and colleges in the major cities, there were numerous small colleges throughout the country. In recent years, however, the college sector has been radically re-organised, a process completed in 1994. There is now a much smaller number of larger state-run colleges, colleges are encouraged to offer a wider range of courses but with particular specialities and to co-operate with one another in a planned division of labour, and students have increased opportunities to combine courses from more than one college in their programme of studies. The colleges offer a wide range of academic and vocational courses in such fields as teacher training,

social work, nursing, business administration, engineering, science, languages, technology, computer science, hotel management, maritime studies and fisheries, journalism, opera and ballet.

There are now 26 state-run colleges, with about 70,000 students in 1994–5. In addition, there are a number of private colleges, with some 12,000 students. (Norwegian Council of Universities)

Non-university colleges typically offer one-, two- and three-year programmes, leading to the award of *Høgskolekandidat* (college graduate) certificates. In some cases, students can combine programmes to take a degree equivalent to the university first degree, or 'top up' their college qualifications to degree level with a university course. Though some students leaving college continue their studies at a university, most proceed directly to employment.

Adult education

This is governed by the Adult Education Act of 1976. County and municipal councils are required to provide appropriate education for adults in their areas. There is overall supervision by the Ministry of Education, which has the advice of the Council for Adult Education. The main aim of adult education is defined as the development of the individual. Those studying adult education courses should therefore have some control over their content and teaching, except where the courses lead to formal qualifications.

Adult education is extremely varied, but the following major types can be distinguished. (Ministry of Education)

- Adult education associations. There are 43 non-government but state-subsidised associations, which organise classes and study groups in a wide range of subjects, some academic, some occupational and some purely as leisure interests. These involve about 600,000 people each year, of whom 12% are studying at upper secondary level and 3% at university level.
- 'Labour market courses'. These offer occupational training and qualifications, and are aimed particularly at unemployed people. They are organised by the labour market authorities in association with schools and voluntary bodies, and are fully financed by the state. About 66,000 people participated in 1992, but the level of participation varies from year to year with variations in unemployment levels.
- Courses aimed at providing adults with education and qualifications normally obtained at school. At primary and lower secondary levels, this is the responsibility of the municipalities, and at upper secondary level of the counties – just as with schooling for children at these levels. About 50,000 people participate in these courses each year.
- Distance education. This caters for a wide range of levels and types of learning, up to university studies. About 30,000 people take part each year.
- 'Folk high schools'. Like the other Scandinavian countries, Norway has a

system of 'folk high schools', usually boarding schools, offering courses that do not lead to formal qualifications. Some are run by counties, some by churches and some by other independent organisations. There are currently 84 establishments, situated throughout the country, with places for about 8,000 students in all.

Much adult education – especially at school level and in labour market activities – is financed by the state. Voluntary organisations are also eligible for state support. But in some cases students have to pay fees to cover all or part of the costs.

Funding

Norway spends 7.6% of its GDP on education. (1992 figures) The municipalities are responsible for primary and lower secondary education, and the counties for upper secondary education – among other services. Since 1986, they themselves (rather than the national government) decide on the distribution of their income among their various responsibilities. About half of their income comes from local taxation, 40% from the national government, and the remainder from fees and charges.

Tuition is free at all state schools and higher education establishments. Private schools may charge fees, though they also receive state subsidies for about 80% of their costs.

Teaching profession

Teacher training is governed by the Teacher Training Act of 1973 (with later amendments). It takes place mainly at colleges of education and universities, who construct their own courses, but to standards set by the Act.

There are three grades of teacher, according to length of training and qualifications, and not necessarily related to the type of school in which they teach. Salary levels depend on the teacher's grade.

- *lærer* – three years in a college of education
- *adjunkt* – at least four years, for example a first degree from a university or college, including teaching subjects and pedagogy; or by training first as a lærer, then for a further year at a university or college
- *lektor* – at least six years, for example a higher degree from a university or college, including teaching subjects and pedagogy; or by training first as an adjunkt, then for a further two years at a university or college; or by training first as a lærer, then for a further three years study at graduate level at a university or college

Education inspectorate

Norway has no inspectorate.

ACKNOWLEDGEMENT
••••••••••••••••••••••

We are grateful to the Norwegian Embassy in London for supplying us with extensive information about education in Norway.

REFERENCES
•••••••••••••

European Commission (1995) *Structures of the Education and Initial Training Systems in the European Union*, Luxembourg: Office for Official Publications of the European Commission.

Ministry of Education, Research and Church Affairs (1992) *Vocational Training in Norway*, Oslo: Ministry of Education, Research and Church Affairs.

Ministry of Education, Research and Church Affairs (1994) *Education in Norway*, Oslo: Ministry of Education, Research and Church Affairs.

Ministry of Education, Research and Church Affairs (1994) *Reform '94: upper secondary education in Norway after the introduction of Reform '94*, Oslo: Ministry of Education, Research and Church Affairs.

National Academic Information Centre (no date) *Admission Requirements for Foreign Students to Universities, University Colleges and Regional Colleges in Norway*, Oslo: National Academic Information Centre, University of Oslo.

Norwegian Council of Universities (1994) *Higher Education in Norway: the university system*, Bergen: Norwegian Council of Universities.

OECD (1995) *OECD Economic Surveys 1994–1995: Norway*, Paris: Organisation for Economic Co-operation and Development.

Royal Ministry of Cultural and Scientific Affairs/Royal Ministry of Church and Education (1988) *Reviews of National Policies for Education: Norway: report to OECD*, Oslo: Royal Ministry of Cultural and Scientific Affairs/Royal Ministry of Church and Education.

Statistics Norway (1995) *Mini-Facts about Norway 1995–96*, Oslo: Statistics Norway/Royal Ministry of Foreign Affairs.

BACKGROUND

Portugal and its regional directorates of education

Portugal has been an independent country since the 12th century (apart from 60 years under Spanish rule in the 16th–17th centuries), as a monarchy until 1910, thereafter as a republic. From 1926 until 1974, the country was a dictatorship under Dr Salazar and (from 1968) his successor Dr Caetano. In 1974, the Caetano regime was ousted by a military coup, which set up a Junta of National Salvation. A new, democratic constitution was introduced in 1982.

Portugal had an extensive overseas empire, mostly in Africa, which it relinquished only after the revolution in 1974. It is a member of the EU, having joined the European Community in 1986.

POPULATION

Population	9.9 million in 1994 (including Madeira and the Azores) – a fall of 0.1% per annum during the previous decade
Land area	92,000 sq. km (including Madeira and the Azores)
Population density	107 per sq. km
Young people (15–24)	33% of population

ECONOMY

The 1982 constitution is explicitly socialist, permitting limited private economic activity but envisaging expansion of the public and co-operative ownership of land, natural resources and production. In practice, however, the country has been engaged since 1989 in privatisation and the development of a market economy.

GDP	$87 billion (1994)
GDP per capita	$8,800 (1994)
In employment	70% of working age population (1991) – 92% of men/67% of women aged 25–54 – 50% of young people (15–24)
Spending on education	5.5% of GDP (1995)

In terms of GDP per capita, Portugal is the second poorest country in Western Europe (only Greece being poorer).

RELIGION

Virtually the entire population is Roman Catholic, but the constitution guarantees freedom of worship.

LANGUAGE

Portuguese.

GOVERNMENT

Mainland Portugal has four levels of government, *national, district, municipal* and *parish*. The Azores and Madeira (each with a population of about a quarter of a million) are autonomous *regions* with their own legislatures and governments, whose responsibilities include education. It is intended that autonomous regions should be formed in mainland Portugal too, but at present it is divided, for the government and administration of education, into five regional directorates of education that are decentralised departments of the national Ministry of Education.

The Ministry of Education (ME – *Ministério da Educação*) is responsible for basic educational policy and the organisation of the education system throughout mainland Portugal, including issuing guidelines for the school curriculum. For all but higher education, much of the administration is carried out through the five regional directorates of education. Higher education is the responsibility of the ME's central Department of Higher Education.

The Ministry of Employment and Social Security (MESS – *Ministério do Emprego e da Segurança Social*) is responsible for some preprimary schools, for apprenticeships and for some types of vocational training, either alone or jointly with the ME.

There are 18 districts, over 300 municipalities and over 4,000 parishes. The districts and parishes have no major educational responsibilities, but the municipalities are responsible for funding the building, equipment and maintenance of preschool education and the first cycle of primary education, and partly responsible (along with the national government) for their running costs. They are also responsible for funding school transport and extracurricular activities.

EDUCATION

Education and training in Portugal were thoroughly re-organised by the Basic Law of the Education System of 1986 (the year the country joined the European Community), and subsequent legislation and decrees – the process being largely completed by the academic year 1994–5. Among the aims of the reforms were the following (see OECD, 1995, Chapter III and Annex III):

- increasing the period of compulsory education, to nine years from the ages of six to 15;
- reducing early leaving, particularly during the compulsory years;
- increasing the popularity of technical and vocational education, while making it less narrowly skills-based and more relevant to the economy;
- developing training alternatives to the school system (such as apprenticeship);
- decentralising the education system, creating regional authorities and giving greater autonomy to schools.

The compulsory stage of schooling is known as basic education (*ensino básico*), and is now divided into three successive 'cycles', each of which has its own category of school, though the second and third are sometimes combined in the one school. Before basic education, children may attend preschool education (*educação pré-escolar*) from the age of three; and after it, they may attend a range of secondary or vocational schools, or enter apprenticeships or other training schemes.

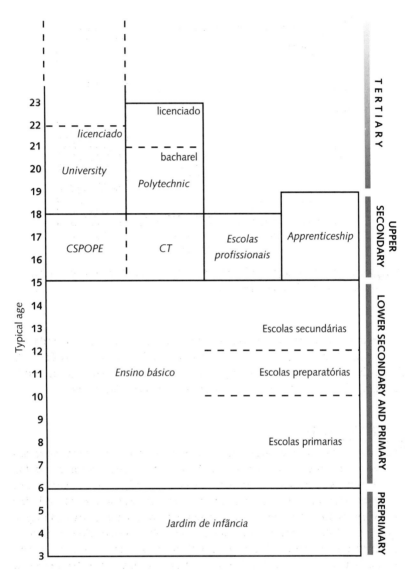

Note: This diagram is simplified and should be used in conjunction with the text

Portugal's education system

Basic education is free; some pupils are also entitled to free books, etc., transport, meals and, where appropriate, accommodation. However, there are enrolment and tuition fees for both secondary and higher education (though those for the secondary stage are small), and students must buy their books and other materials.

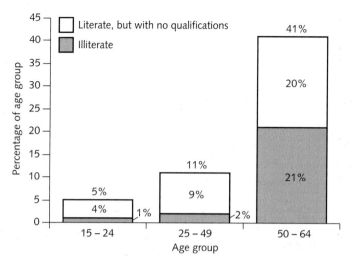

Portugal figure 1   Percentage of different age groups who are illiterate, or literate but with no educational qualifications, 1991 (OECD)

Portugal has dramatically increased levels of literacy in recent decades. In 1960, 34% of the population was illiterate; by 1991, the figure was 6.5%. By European standards, this is still a high level of illiteracy; however, most of it is accounted for by people over 50 years of age, as Figure 1 illustrates.

INSTITUTIONS

The recent reforms introduced a common management structure for state-run schools at all levels (below tertiary level). Each school has a *school council* (or several small schools may share a *school area council*), whose members are representatives of the staff, the parents, the municipal council and, for secondary schools, the students. It is responsible for general policy and overall supervision of the school, and appoints the school's executive director (who is an ex-officio member). More detailed planning and direction is the responsibility of the *pedagogical council*, whose members are the executive director and representatives of teachers, parents, the psychology and guidance services and, except in the first cycle of basic education, pupils.

There is no single management structure at tertiary level, and both universities and polytechnics have considerable autonomy in administrative and financial, as well as academic and pedagogical matters.

In addition to institutions run by the state, Portugal has a private educational sector. This sector is small at primary and academic secondary levels, with 7–8% of pupils; larger at tertiary level, with 33% of students; and largest of all

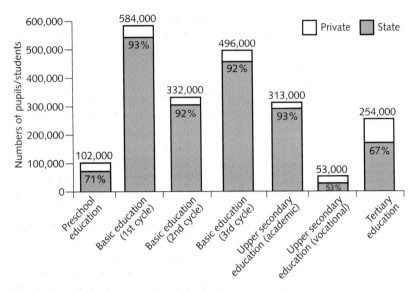

Portugal figure 2   Numbers of pupils/students, and percentage in state institutions, 1993–4 (European Commission, 1995)
Notes: (i) The preschool figures are for ME schools only: see below; (ii) the category 'Upper secondary education (vocational)' combines Cursos Tecnológicos (CT) courses (predominantly state-run) and vocational schools (predominantly private): see below

in vocational upper secondary education with 47%. (In vocational schools – see below – 99% of students are in private institutions.)

The numbers of pupils/students in different levels and types of educational institution, state and private, are illustrated in Figure 2.

Preprimary

Preprimary education is available, but not compulsory, for children from the age of three until six, when compulsory primary education begins. It is usually provided in a *jardim de infância* – (nursery school).

Jardim de infância

Nursery schools may be either state-run or private. But more significantly, they may be provided (in the case of state schools) or supervised (in the case of private schools) by either the ME or the MESS. In general, ME schools concentrate more on education, while MESS schools also engage in other types of social work, often in association with other social service departments. Admission is in principle available to all children, but where demand exceeds supply, priority for ME schools is given to older children, and for MESS schools according to criteria of social and financial need. Ministry of Education schools are free, but at MESS schools, parents may be required to contribute to costs on a means-tested basis.

The pupil/teacher ratio at ME schools is limited by law to a maximum of 25/1 for four- to six-year-olds, and 15/1 for three-year-olds. In practice, their overall pupil/teacher ratio is 17/1. (There is little difference between state and private schools in this respect.) These legal limits do not apply to MESS schools, where the average pupil/teacher ratio is in practice 27/1.

There is no compulsory curriculum in either category of school, but the ME provides curriculum guidelines for its schools (such as expression through movement, drama and music), with recommendations of activities (including painting, modelling, story-telling and 'pretending' games). Activities developing the skills needed for reading and writing may also be undertaken. Teachers are required to assess throughout how well their objectives are being met by the children, and if necessary to alter the teaching programmes.

About 185,000 children – very nearly half the three to six age-group – attend some 5,400 preprimary schools, where they are taught by 9,000 teachers. Of these children, 55% are in ME schools (40% state, 15% private) and 45% in MESS schools. (1993–4 figures, European Commission, 1995)

Primary/lower secondary

The compulsory stage of schooling (from age six to 15) is known as basic education (*ensino bàsico*), and is divided into three successive 'cycles', of four, two and three years respectively. Each cycle is taught in a particular category of school: the first in primary schools (*escolas primarias*); the second in preparatory schools (*escolas preparatórias*); and the third in secondary schools (*escolas secundárias*) – together with postcompulsory upper secondary education. However, the second and third are sometimes combined in the one establishment, which is then known as a preparatory/secondary school.

Basic education in state schools is free, but parents must normally pay for children's food and transport, books and other teaching materials. However, state financial assistance is available according to income, for pupils in both the state and private sectors.

Escolas primarias

The first cycle of basic education lasts for four years from age six to 10, and takes place in primary schools. Primary schools are mixed-sex. Pupils are grouped into classes by age. Each class is taught by the same teacher for all subjects, though with specialist assistance where necessary. There is no centrally determined timetable: the distribution and organisation of teaching time are decided by the teachers.

A compulsory curriculum is laid down by the ME, with the following subjects.

- expression (physical, musical, dramatic and visual)
- environment
- Portuguese
- mathematics
- personal and social development/moral and religious education (religious education may but need not be Catholic)
- a multidisciplinary area to be developed by each school with regard to its own environment and pupils.

In addition, if resources permit, a foreign language may be introduced.

The proportions of time for each of these are also laid down by the ME, but vary from year to year of the cycle.

Sports and games are extracurricular activities, and optional.

Assessment, both formative and summative, is conducted by the teachers and finalised at meetings of the school council. Pupils who fail in a large number of areas may have to repeat a year; those who fail in a few may proceed to the next year while receiving special support in those subjects.

About 584,000 pupils attend 10,000 primary schools, where they are taught by 41,000 teachers. Ninety-three per cent of the schools and pupils, and 97% of the teachers, are in the state sector. The pupil/teacher ratio in the private sector (33/1) is more than twice as great as that in the state sector (14/1). (1993–94 figures, European Commission, 1995)

Escolas preparatórias

The second cycle of basic education lasts for two years from age 10 to 12, and takes place in preparatory schools (or preparatory/secondary schools). To qualify for entry, pupils must successfully have completed the first cycle. Schools and classes are usually mixed-sex, with pupils grouped into classes by age. Now they are taught by specialist-subject teachers, where possible the same teacher for each subject in both years of the cycle. There is no centrally determined timetable: the distribution and organisation of teaching time are decided by teachers.

A compulsory curriculum is laid down by the ME, with the following multidisciplinary areas.

- language and social studies (Portuguese language, history and geography, plus a foreign language, either German, French or English)
- mathematics and natural sciences
- artistic and technological education
- physical education
- personal and social development/moral and religious education (religious education may but need not be Catholic)

- a multidisciplinary area to be developed by each school with regard to its own environment and pupils.

The proportions of time for each of these are also laid down by the ME.

Sports and games are extracurricular activities, and optional.

About 332,000 pupils participate in the second cycle of basic education, 92% of them in the state sector. Numbers of schools and of teachers are not recorded separately for the second and third cycles (see below). (1993–4 figures, European Commission, 1995)

Escolas secundárias
The third cycle of basic education lasts for two years from age 12 to 15, and takes place in secondary schools (or preparatory/secondary schools), together with postcompulsory upper secondary education. To qualify for entry, students must successfully have completed the second cycle. As in the second cycle, schools and classes are usually mixed-sex, with students grouped into classes by age, and taught by specialist-subject teachers.

A compulsory curriculum is laid down by the ME, with the following subjects and multidisciplinary areas.

- Portuguese language
- a foreign language (continued from the second cycle)
- human and social sciences (history and geography)
- mathematics, physical and natural sciences
- visual education
- physical education
- personal and social development/moral and religious education (religious education may but need not be Catholic)
- an optional area, with a choice for students between a second foreign language, music and technology
- a 'school area' to be developed by each school, but including civics education

The proportions of time for each of these are also laid down by the ME.

Sports and games are extracurricular activities, and optional.

About 496,000 students participate in the second cycle of basic education, 92% of them in the state sector. Numbers of schools and of teachers are not recorded separately for the second and third cycles, but both cycles together have 1200 schools and 101,000 teachers, 91% in the state sector. (1993–4 figures, European Commission, 1995)

Upper secondary education

Upper secondary education is divided into the following main categories.

- secondary school courses mainly oriented towards further study (CSPOPE

– *Cursos Secundários Predominantemente Orientados para o Prosseguimento De Estudos*)
- secondary school technology courses mainly oriented towards employment (CT – *Cursos Tecnológicos*)
- vocational school courses (*escolas profissionais*)

In addition, young people in this age-group may participate in training outside the school system, in apprenticeships or initial training schemes in various employment sectors.

Traditionally, technical and vocational education have been much less popular with students than general education (as Figure 2 above illustrates): in 1991–2, just over 13% of upper secondary students took vocational courses of any kind (OECD). The numbers on apprenticeships, though rising, are also very low (see below).

CSPOPE and CT

To qualify for entry to CSPOPE or CT, students must successfully have completed the third cycle of basic education. Students are normally grouped into classes by age, though this may be modified to obtain a balance of male and female students in classes. They are taught by specialist-subject teachers.

The current system of upper secondary education is new, stemming from legislation of 1986, but fully in operation only since 1993–4. Both CSPOPE and CT last for three years from age 15 to 18, and take place in secondary schools; every school must offer both types of course, though they may specialise in either one. They are not kept completely separate. There is a common core of general subjects that must be taken by CT as well as CSPOPE students, and CSPOPE students must take some technology courses.

The common core of general subjects is as follows. The proportion of students' time devoted to them varies considerably, but generally speaking it occupies between a third and a half of students' time in the first two years of CSPOPE or CT, and between a fifth and a quarter in the final year.

- Portuguese
- philosophy
- one or two foreign languages
- physical education
- personal and social development/moral and religious education (religious education may but need not be Catholic)

Both CSPOPE and CT students also have their own specialised studies.

Assessment is not only by teachers in the school itself, but has an external element. All students who successfully complete secondary school courses are awarded a diploma in secondary studies (*Diploma de Estudos Secundários*), which lists their subjects and marks. Successful CT students in addition are awarded a vocational qualification diploma (*Diploma de Qualificacão Profissional*).

Escolas profissionais
Vocational schools are a relatively new (established 1989) alternative to regular secondary schools, offering direct training for employment, with less demanding entrance requirements – normally completion of basic education. Courses normally last three years, with a 40-week year and a 30-hour week. They have more autonomy than secondary schools, in teaching as well as management, so as to enable them to meet local training needs, and are almost all privately run. But the basic curriculum is laid down by the ME. It has three components, as follows.

- technical, technological and practical (50% of students' time), with four to six subjects, geared to local training needs, taught either in school or in the workplace
- scientific (25% of students' time), two to four basic subjects, which must be linked to the students' technical, technological and practical studies
- socio-cultural (25% of students' time), including Portuguese, a foreign language and social integration

Assessment has two components, equally weighted – continuous assessment throughout each course, and an interdisciplinary vocational aptitude test. The same qualifications are available as for secondary school students, namely the diploma in secondary studies (Diploma de Estudos Secundários), and the vocational qualification diploma (Diploma de Qualificação Profissional).

There are around 22,200 students in some 200 vocational schools, taught by 5,500 teachers. There are only three state-run vocational schools, leaving just under 99% of the students, teachers and schools in the private sector. (1993–4 figures, European Commission, 1995)

Apprenticeships and pre-apprenticeships
The apprenticeship system is governed by laws of 1984 and 1988, and is under the auspices of the Institute of Employment and Vocational Training (IEFP – *Instituto do Emprego e Formação Profissional*) of the MESS. Apprenticeships are for those aged 14 to 24 who have completed at least six years of education. Training is provided jointly by training centres and companies, who sign a formal contract with each apprentice. Apprenticeships last between one and four years, and consist of:

- general studies (in a training centre), including Portuguese, a foreign language and current affairs;
- technological training (in a training centre) in the chosen vocational area;
- practical training (with a company) in the chosen occupation.

The proportion of apprentices' time devoted to practical training increases from about 10% in the first year to about half in the third and fourth years.

Apprenticeships are available in 27 vocational areas. Apprentices must pass tests and examinations each year in order to proceed to the next year. Those passing the final year tests and exams qualify for the certificate of vocational aptitude (*Certificado de Aptidão Profissional*). Overall pass rates are around 88%. In 1993, there were about 20,000 apprentices, supervised by about 10,000 trainers in all. (The supervision of apprentices was only a small part of the work of most of these trainers.)

Pre-apprenticeship training was established in 1991 for those aged 15 to 21 who do not qualify for admission to apprenticeships. The structure of pre-apprenticeship courses mirrors that of apprenticeships.

Formação profissional

In addition to apprenticeships, a number of shorter initial training schemes are available for unemployed people aged 18 to 25. Since 1993, these are of two basic kinds, the first aimed at those who have completed compulsory schooling, the second at those who have a university degree or its equivalent. They last at least a year, consist of roughly one-third theoretical and two-thirds practical training, and lead to a vocational qualification.

Special education

The 1986 Basic Law and subsequent legislation have laid down that all children with disabilities have a right to education, and that priority should be given to their education in mainstream schools.

Tertiary education

Two-thirds of Portugal's 261 tertiary institutions are state-run, one-third private or co-operative – with student numbers (about a quarter of a million in all) distributed in proportion.

The state-run institutions are of two types: *universities*, offering higher academic education; and *polytechnics*, offering higher vocational and professional training. The polytechnics have mostly come into being only since the mid-1980s.

Of the 103 private or co-operative institutions, four are universities, the others are colleges of various kinds, academic and vocational.

Admission to tertiary education is centrally regulated, and applications are centrally processed. To qualify for admission, would-be students must have completed CSPOPE, CT or their equivalent, and must also take a general aptitude test and a specific test for the course of their choice, both set by the individual institutions.

University courses last from four to six years, and lead to the *licenciado* degree. Polytechnic and other courses may lead to a *bacharel* degree after three years, or a *licenciado* degree after four or five years. Assessment is normally by examination; students who fail an exam may resit.

Funding

Portugal spends 5.5% of its GDP on education. This is slightly higher than the EU average (of 5.3%), but Portugal's annual expenditure per pupil/student ($2550) is 72% of the EU average. (1995, CERI)

Teaching profession

Teachers in state-run schools have the status of civil servants. All teachers above preprimary level are subject specialists.

All teachers must have a degree. Normally this is a specialist teaching degree. Those in preprimary education or the first cycle of basic education need a *bacharelato* degree, requiring three years of study. Those in the second cycle of basic education need in addition a specialised diploma, which requires one or two years. Those in the third cycle of basic education or in secondary education need a five- or six-year *liceniatura* degree. Preprimary teachers are trained at *escolas superiores de educação*, and secondary teachers at universities. Teachers in basic education may be trained at either type of institution.

In addition to these specialist teaching degrees, teachers in the upper two cycles of basic education and in secondary education may have purely academic liceniatura degrees, supplemented by a one- or two-year teacher training course.

Besides initial training, teachers must undertake inservice training as a condition of advancement through salary scales.

All teacher training courses include pedagogical training and teaching practice as well as academic work.

Education inspectorate

The General Inspectorate of Education (IGE – *Inspecção Geral da Educação*) is the section of the Ministry of Education responsible for monitoring the administrative and financial as well as the educational performance of all educational establishments in Portugal at every level, whether state-run or private, and of the education system as a whole. It is centrally co-ordinated, but operates through five regional delegations, corresponding to the five regional directorates of education.

ACRONYMS AND ABBREVIATIONS

CSPOPE	Cursos Secundários Predominantemente Orientados para o Prosseguimento De Estudos (upper secondary courses primarily oriented to further study)
CT	Cursos Tecnológicos (upper secondary technology courses)
IEFP	Instituto do Emprego e Formação Profissional (Institute of Employment and Vocational Training)

IGE	Inspecção Geral da Educação (General Inspectorate of Education)
ME	Ministério da Educação (Ministry of Education)
MESS	Ministério do Emprego e da Segurança Social (Ministry of Employment and Social Security)

REFERENCES

CERI (1995) *Education at a Glance: OECD indicators*, Paris: Organisation for Economic Co-operation and Development.

da Costa, A. M. B. (1995) 'Inclusive schools in Portugal', in O'Hanlon, C. (1995) (ed.) *Inclusive Education in Europe*, London: David Fulton Publishers.

European Commission (1995) *Structures of the Education and Initial Training Systems in the European Union*, second edition, Luxembourg: Office for Official Publications of the European Commission.

OECD (1995) *OECD Economic Surveys: 1994–1995: Portugal*, Paris: Organisation for Economic Co-operation and Development.

Rajan, A. and Grilo, E. M. (1990) *Vocational Training Scenarios for Some Member States of the European Community: a synthesis report for France, Greece, Italy, Portugal, Spain and the United Kingdom*, Berlin: CEDEFOP.

BACKGROUND

Spain and its autonomous communities

Spain took its modern form at the end of the 15th century, when the Christian kingdoms of the Iberian peninsula (apart from Portugal) had united and conquered the territories under the rule of the 'Moors', Muslims of North African descent. During the next two centuries, Spain was one of the strongest and wealthiest European powers. But the later 17th and the 18th century saw a long decline in Spain's wealth and power, culminating in its conquest in the early 19th century by France under Napoleon. After his defeat, the Bourbon monarchy was restored, and lasted until 1931, when the king abdicated and the Second Republic was established. Spain was polarised between left-wing forces, supporting the republican government, and right-wing forces, with the support of much of the army. In 1936, civil war broke out, ending in 1939 with the overthrow of the republic and the establishment of the Falangist regime of General Franco, which survived until his death in 1975. During this period, no other political parties were permitted, and any potential sources of opposition, such as trade unions, were suppressed. Powers were taken away from the regions and centralised in Madrid, and the use of regional languages was restricted. Education was kept under close control by the government, in collaboration with the Roman Catholic Church. In 1975, the monarchy was restored once more, and a parliamentary democratic system of government established. From 1978, a process of decentralisation began, with regional autonomy restored.

Spain is a member of the EU.

POPULATION

Population	39.2 million in 1994 – (up 0.2% per annum from 1984)
Land area	505,000 sq. km (including islands)
Population density	78 per sq. km

ECONOMY

GDP	$482 billion (1994)
GDP per capita	$12,300 (1994)
In employment	48% of working age population (1991)
	– 85% of men/38% of women aged 25–54
	– 34% of young people (15–24)
Spending on education	5.8% of GDP (1992)

RELIGION

The majority of the population are Roman Catholic, but since 1978 Spain has had no state religion, and the rights of religious minorities are guaranteed.

LANGUAGE

Castilian (or simply 'Spanish') is the official language of Spain, and the main language of about two-thirds of its population. But there are three other widely spoken languages.

- Catalan – closely related to Castilian and to French – spoken by 64% of the population of Cataluña (Catalonia), 49% of Valencia, 71% of the Balearic Islands, and a minority in Aragon just over the borders from Cataluña and Valencia

- *Galician* – related to Castilian but more closely to Portuguese – spoken by 90% of the population of Galicia
- *Euskara (Basque)* – not related to any other known language – spoken by a quarter of the population of País Vasco (Basque Country), and by 12% of Navarre, mostly in the north west (there is also a Basque-speaking population on the French side of the border)

In bilingual communities, both Castilian and the regional language are taught in schools and universities.

GOVERNMENT

Spain is a constitutional monarchy with four levels of government – *nation, community, province* and *municipality*. Since 1978, the system has been semi-federal, with a considerable degree of autonomy for the communities, which have their own parliaments. In and around the community of País Vasco (Basque Country), there is a movement for Basque unity and independence, some of whose supporters belong to an active terrorist organisation, ETA (*Euskadi ta Askatasuna* – Basque Homeland and Liberty).

The Ministry of Education and Science (MEC – *Ministerio de Educación y Ciencia*) is responsible for basic educational policy and the structure of the education system throughout Spain. In addition, it is responsible for detailed educational administration in ten of the communities, the other seven having assumed 'full powers' in education (see below).

The MEC's responsibilities throughout Spain include determining the number of years of compulsory schooling; the number and duration of the 'levels' and 'cycles' of schooling (see the diagrams below) and the standards of attainment required for each; the compulsory core curriculum; the minimum standards required of schools (facilities, teacher/pupil ratios, staff qualifications, etc.); and the criteria for the award and recognition of academic and professional qualifications. The MEC also supervises investment in education by the communities, and ensures that Castilian is taught in communities which also teach a local language.

In addition, the MEC is responsible in the ten communities that have not assumed 'full powers' for the financing, administration, management and inspection of educational institutions and their staff.

Spain has 17 autonomous communities, each with its own parliament and government. They are the basic unit of the semi-federal system, and have a wide range of responsibilities. Certain areas of responsibility are reserved exclusively to the communities by the constitution. In certain other areas – including education – the communities may assume 'full powers', though despite the terminology their responsibilities remain within limits set by national legislation. At present, seven communities have assumed full powers in education (those underlined on the map on page 203, plus the Canaries), and are responsible for the financing, administration, management and inspection of educational institutions and their staff. The other ten communities are expected to assume full powers in education during the next few years.

There are 50 provinces in Spain (the traditional unit of regional government, established since 1833) and over 8,000 municipalities. However, they now have no important educational responsibilities.

EDUCATION

Education in Spain is in the process of thorough re-organisation at every level. First, in 1983, legislation was passed reforming the universities (see below). Then in 1990, the Basic Law on the General Structure of the Education System (LOGSE – *Ley Orgánica de Ordenación General del Sistema Educativo*) initiated a nine-year period (1991–2000) of reform at every other level. This began with the youngest age-groups, and is proceeding year by year up the age-range. Diagram 1 shows the system as it was before the reforms, and Diagram 2 the system as it will be when they have been fully implemented. By 1997, the reform of the preprimary and primary stages should have been completed. For these stages (and for universities), therefore, we describe in detail only the new system. The changes to secondary education begin taking effect only in the year 1996–7, and for the later stages of schooling we describe both the pre-1996–7 arrangements and the new ones that are to replace them.

The main changes made by LOGSE are as follows.

- free, compulsory and comprehensive education is to last ten years (6–16), instead of eight (6–14); as a consequence, the division between general education and vocational training is delayed until age 16, instead of 14
- schooling is divided at age 12 between primary and secondary stages, whereas previously the compulsory years (6–14) comprised basic general education (EGB – *Educación General Básica*), with no distinction of primary and secondary stages
- the national government is to specify a minimum compulsory curriculum (*Enzeñanzas Minimas*) for each type and level of schooling, leaving some scope for communities, schools and pupils to make choices of their own
- guidance departments are to be established in all secondary schools to provide education and vocational counselling and advice

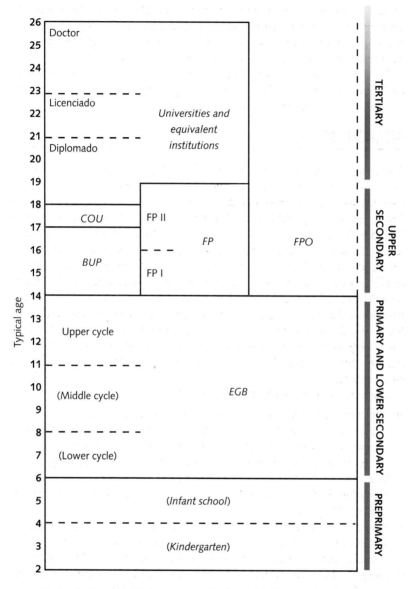

Notes: (i) The school system portrayed here is being replaced by that of Diagram 2. The preprimary stages and the lower and middle cycles of EGB have already been replaced (mid-1996)

(ii) This diagram is simplified for clarity, and should be used in conjunction with the text

Diagram 1: Spain's old education system

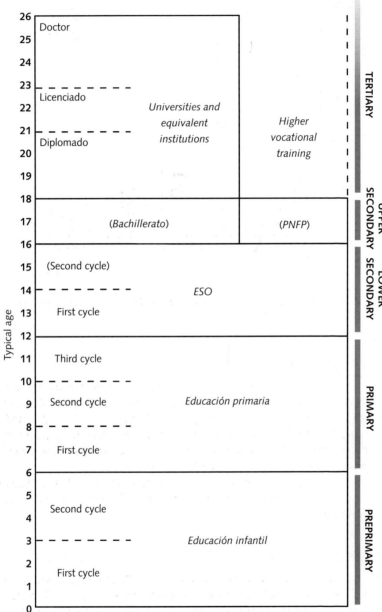

Notes: (i) The school system portrayed here is replacing that of Diagram 1.
The second cycle of ESO and the upper secondary stage have not yet
been introduced (mid-1996)

(ii) This diagram is simplified for clarity, and should be used in conjunction
with the text

Diagram 2: Spain's new education system

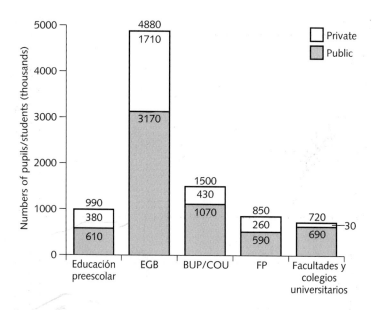

Spain figure 1 Numbers of pupils/students in private and public education of different categories, 1990–1

INSTITUTIONS

In addition to schools run by the state, Spain has a large private sector, with schools and colleges run by religious groups (such as the Roman Catholic Church) and other associations. Some private schools are publicly subsidised: to be eligible for public funds, they must provide free education, and meet similar requirements to those of state schools in curriculum, assessment, pupil admission, teacher recruitment, and pupil/teacher ratio.

The numbers of pupils/students in the main categories of educational institution, public and private, are shown in Figure 1. These categories are explained below.

Preprimary

With the implementation of the LOGSE of 1990, preprimary education (*educación infantil*) is divided into two three-year 'cycles', the first from age nought to three, and the second from three to six, when compulsory schooling begins. Preprimary schools may be public (*escuelas de educación infantil*) or private (*centros de educación infantil*). They may provide only one or other cycle, or both; but there are detailed regulations governing overall size and the numbers and distribution of children of different ages.

Publicly provided preprimary education is free (though parents must pay for children's food and transport, books and other teaching materials), and open to everyone, except where demand exceeds supply, in which case priority may be given by individual schools according to such criteria as how closely a child lives to the school and whether he or she has any brothers or sisters already there. The education system as a whole is committed to providing preprimary places for all children whose parents want it. Private schools set their own criteria for admission.

Under the LOGSE, educación infantil – public or private – must be primarily educational, and not merely provide child-care. Three curriculum areas are defined:

- identity and personal independence;
- the physical and social environment;
- communication and representation.

Timetables are not set nationally, but they are required to be integrated, and to take account of children's ages, and their rhythms of activity, play and rest. Assessment is by observation of children by teachers and interviews with parents. Grouping within a school by ability or attainment is forbidden. All public and most private schools are for both sexes.

Other establishments for under-six-year-olds are permitted to operate only until the year 2000, by which time they must conform to these requirements and become full escuelas or centros de educación infantil.

In 1990–1 (just before the new system was introduced), there were just under a million preprimary pupils in Spain, 60% of them in public institutions, 40% in private. They were taught by 40,000 teachers, 95% of them women. (INE) By 1994–5, 60% of three-year-olds and virtually 100% of four- and five-year-olds in Spain attended a preprimary establishment. (European Commission)

Primary education

Under the LOGSE of 1990, primary education (educación primaria) is divided into three two-year 'cycles' (6–8, 8–10 and 10–12). Primary schools may be public or private, though some private schools are publicly subsidised.

Primary education is compulsory. Publicly provided primary education is free; parents must pay for children's food and transport, books and other teaching materials, but financial assistance is available according to income. All public primary schools are mixed sex; some private schools are single sex. Pupils remain in the same class group throughout their primary school career, and are taught almost all subjects by their class teacher, who remains with them for an entire cycle.

A minimum core curriculum and annual timetable are laid down by the

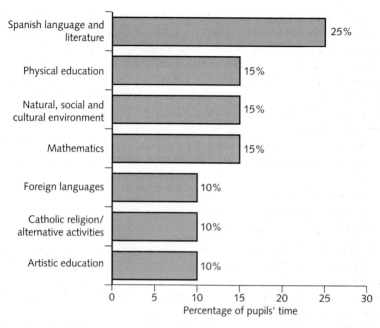

Spanish language and literature — 25%
Physical education — 15%
Natural, social and cultural environment — 15%
Mathematics — 15%
Foreign languages — 10%
Catholic religion/ alternative activities — 10%
Artistic education — 10%

Percentage of pupils' time

Spain figure 2   Percentage of pupils' time devoted to compulsory subjects in primary schools

MEC; schools must follow them with regard to the principles of comprehensive education and subject integration. This timetable is shown in Figure 2, with approximate percentages of time allocated to each subject in the second and third cycles. (The first cycle does not include foreign languages, and more time is therefore allocated to the other subjects.)

Bilingual communities may teach their own language for up to 10% of the total time devoted to languages.

Assessment takes place throughout primary schooling, with tests administered by teachers. Normally, pupils move automatically from one cycle to the next, but in exceptional cases they may spend an extra year in a cycle. Where a pupil's attainment is unsatisfactory, it is the teachers' responsibility to provide extra tuition or adapt the curriculum.

Secondary education

Under the LOGSE of 1990, the timetable for the reform of secondary education is from the school year 1996–7 (for students in their first year of secondary school) until 1999–2000. We shall therefore outline the older system, as well as describing the new system in more detail. (For more detail about the older system, see European Commission, 1995.)

The older system
Under the older system (see Diagram 1, above), 'secondary' education is divided at the age of 14 (when compulsory education ends) into two stages.

Below 14, there is the upper cycle of EGB – which is compulsory and comprehensive. The curriculum is set centrally by the MEC. Assessment is by teachers, but students who fail in any subject may take an examination in it. If they still fail, they may be required to have remedial lessons or repeat the year.

Above 14, there is a division between academic education and vocational training. Postcompulsory education is selective, with only those who have successfully completed EGB (or subsequently passed an examination of equivalent level) allowed to enter the basic postcompulsory academic course (BUP – *Bachillerato Unificado Polivalente*). However, the system is flexible, and students on vocational courses can transfer to academic courses or obtain university entry at a number of points (see below).

In 1990–1 (just before the beginning of the introduction of the new system) there were just under 4.9 million students in EGB, 65% of them in public institutions, 35% in private. They were taught by 240,000 teachers, 91% of them women. Of those completing the EGB stage, 77% were qualified to enter BUP. (Boys' success rate, 74%, was lower than that of girls, 81%.) (INE)

Academic education – The BUP lasts three years, and, together with a subsequent one-year university orientation course (COU – *Curso de Orientación Universitaria*) prepares students for university study. The BUP curriculum – set nationally – is the same for all students in the first two years, but offers options in the third. Assessment is by a mixture of continuous assessment and an examination at the end of each year (with opportunities for re-sitting, remedial classes or repeating a year). Those who complete the course are awarded the Bachillerato, and qualified to proceed to the COU.

The COU is a one-year course. Its curriculum was reformed in 1988–9, so as to give students greater flexibility in choosing subsequent university courses. It has three compulsory subjects (Spanish; a foreign language; philosophy) and four 'option streams' (science and technology; biology and health; social sciences; humanities and languages). Students choose one stream, but each stream itself offers a range of compulsory and optional choices. Assessment is similar to that for the BUP. To gain access to a university, students must successfully complete COU and also sit an entrance exam set by the university.

In 1990–1 (just before the beginning of the introduction of the new system) there were just under 1.5 million students in BUP and COU, 46% male, 54% female. 71% of them were in public institutions, 29% in private. They were taught by 96,000 teachers, 54% of them women. Of those completing the COU stage, about two-thirds qualified to enter university. (INE)

Vocational training – Vocational training is of two kinds: the first, called simply vocational training (FP – *Formación Profesional*) is provided under the auspices of the MEC, and includes academic education of the same type as in BUP, though at a lower level. The second, called occupational vocational training (FPO – *Formación Profesional Ocupacional*), is under the auspices of the National Employment Institute (INE – *Instituto Nacional de Empleo*) of the Ministry of Labour and Social Security, and is practical rather than academic.

A full FP course lasts four or five years, but is divided (at age 16) between a two-year FP I and a two- or three-year FP II stage (the latter more specialised). As well as leading to FP II, a successfully completed FP I course can allow students to transfer to the second year of BUP, or lead straight to employment. As well as leading to employment, a successfully completed FP II course can lead to university entry in a relevant field, or to a COU course and subsequent university entry.

At both stages, FP courses combine general education with practical training in a particular vocation, either in school or in an actual workplace. The general education element is similar to that of the BUP, but less demanding. The vocational element is in one of the following branches.

- administration and commerce
- agriculture
- automotive engineering
- chemistry
- community services
- construction
- electricity and electronics
- fashion and tailoring
- glass and ceramics
- graphic arts
- hairdressing and beauty

- health
- hotel and tourism
- image and sound
- marine and fisheries
- metal
- mining
- skins and leather
- technical drawing
- textiles
- wood

FPO courses are widely varied in length and kind, in degree of specialisation and in the type of institution or workshop where they are taught. Preference is given in admission to these courses to unemployed people. They are free, and maintenance and transport grants are also available.

In 1990–1 (just before the beginning of the introduction of the new system) there were just under 850,000 students in FP, 55% male, 45% female. 69% of them were in public institutions, 31% in private. They were taught by 63,000 teachers, 58% of them men. (INE)

The new system
Under the LOGSE of 1990 (see Diagram 2, above), secondary education is to be divided into three two-year cycles. The first two (12–14 and 14–16) are to be compulsory and comprehensive (ESO – *Educación Secundaria Obligatoria*). The third (16–18) is to be divided between academic education (Bachillerato) and vocational education (FP – *Formación Profesional*, and FPO – *Formación*

Profesional Ocupational). ESO was to be introduced for first-year students in 1996–7; the Bachillerato and the new FP system will be introduced for their first-year students in 1998–9. The final shape of the Bachillerato and especially of the new FP system are still being decided.

Educación Secundaria Obligatoria, the Bachillerato and FP may be taught in the same school or in different schools.

ESO – A minimum curriculum and timetable for the ESO are laid down centrally. It consists of compulsory and optional subjects. For the first cycle, the timetable is as shown in Figure 3.

The second cycle differs in allowing less time for natural sciences, technology, arts and music, more time for most of the other compulsory subjects and considerably more time (25–35%) for optional subjects. Optional subjects that every school must offer are Latin, Greek and a second modern foreign language.

Assessment is continuous, and though divided by subject is conducted collectively by a team of teachers, and expressed on a five-point scale. Successful completion of the ESO qualifies students for entry to the Bachillerato or FP. All leavers, whether judged successful or not, receive a certificate showing their attendance and attainments and giving recommendations for future education or work.

Bachillerato – The Bachillerato lasts for two years (16–18) and prepares students for university or higher vocational training.

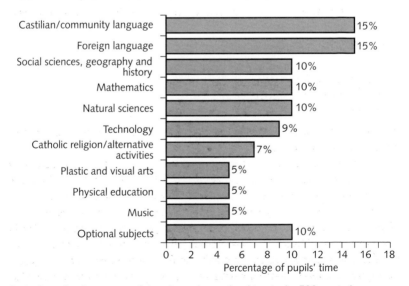

Spain figure 3   Percentage of time devoted to each subject in the ESO curriculum

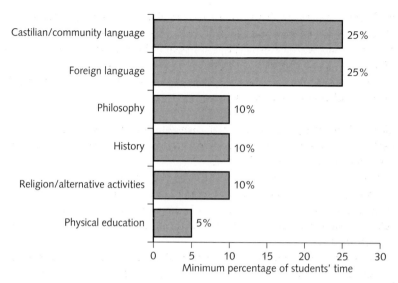

Spain figure 4   Percentage of time devoted to each subject in the Bachillerato common core curriculum

The curriculum falls into three categories: (i) common core subjects; (ii) 'option streams'; (iii) optional subjects.

The common core subjects are as shown in Figure 4, with approximate minimum percentages of time for each, which may be allocated over one year or two.

The option streams include at least the following.

- arts
- natural and health sciences
- humanities and social sciences
- technology

At least 5% of students' time is allocated to subjects from option streams. This leaves a further 10% or so for optional subjects.

The subjects are taught in ways that enable students to learn co-operatively as well as individually, to do research of their own, and to explore the relationship between theoretical understanding and practical application.

Assessment, which is by teachers, is a combination of continuous and end-of-year procedures. To progress from year to year, students may not fail in more than two subjects. They may repeat years, but not take more than four years to complete the course. To obtain the Bachillerato certificate and qualify for higher education, students must pass in all subjects. To enter a university, they must in addition pass an entrance examination set by the university.

FP and FPO – The final details of the new system of vocational education are still to be decided, but already steps are being taken to co-ordinate more closely the two existing systems of vocational training and qualifications – the more academic FP (run by the MEC) and the more practical FPO (run by the Ministry of Labour) – under a single National Vocational Training Programme (PNFP – *Programa Nacional de Formación Profesional*). The aim is to make vocational training better matched to the needs of the labour market, and more adaptable in the face of technological change.

Special education

Legislation in 1982 and 1987 as well as the LOGSE of 1990 have encouraged the integration of pupils with special needs into mainstream schools. The effects of the legislation are difficult to gauge, as official statistics are not kept of children with special needs outside special schools. However, research in the autonomous community of Cataluña found that between 1982 and 1992, the percentage of the school age population being taught in special schools fell from 0.71% to 0.55%. The researchers estimated that in the same period the percentage of the school age population with special needs being taught in mainstream schools rose from 1.39% to 1.45%. In Spain as a whole, just over 1% of all pupils and students are in special schools or other educational establishments. Of these, most (62%) are deemed to be mentally handicapped, and 7% to have emotional difficulties. (O'Hanlon, 1995)

Tertiary education

University education
University education in Spain was reformed in 1983 by the law known as the LRU (*Ley Orgánica de Reforma Universitaria*). It now consists of three 'cycles', the first normally lasting three years, the second two or three years, and the third two years (involving the writing of a thesis). Students may complete their studies at the end of the first cycle (with the qualification of *diplomado*), or the second (*licenciado*) or the third (*doctor*).

There are different types and levels of university institution. University faculties (*facultades universitarias*) and higher technical schools (*escuelas técnicas superiores*) teach all three cycles. University colleges (*colegios universitarios*) are attached to university faculties: the colleges themselves teach only the first cycle, but students can then transfer to the faculties and study the higher cycles. University schools (*escuelas universitarias*) teach only the first cycle, which completes the students' education with the diplomado or its equivalent.

The numbers of students graduating (at all levels) from university faculties and colleges in the most popular subjects are illustrated in Figure 5.

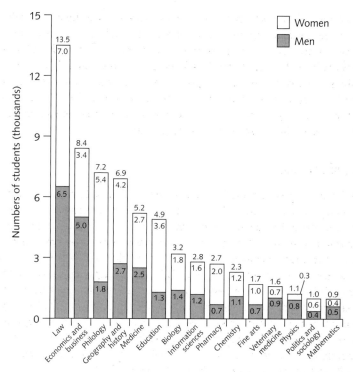

Spain figure 5   Numbers of students, and percentage of women, graduating in the most popular subjects from university faculties and colleges, 1990–1

Spain also has a National Distance Education University (UNED – *Universidad Nacional de Educación a Distancia*), which provides university education by correspondence, and also a range of short correspondence courses. The short courses are open to anyone, but admission to the university courses requires the same qualifications as conventional universities. The UNED is run by the national government.

To qualify for entrance to university faculties, higher technical schools and university colleges, students must currently have successfully completed COU and also passed an entrance examination conducted by the universities. In time, the COU requirement is to be replaced by the Bachillerato, but the additional requirement to pass the university entrance examination will remain. To qualify for admission to university schools, successful completion of the vocational FP II is an acceptable alternative to the COU or Bachillerato.

Whether a qualified candidate is actually admitted depends on the availability of places, and where these are insufficient to meet demand, on the admissions criteria set by individual universities. The number of places available in each university is set nationally by the university council; 70% of courses have restricted numbers.

Assessment is by examination, usually at the end of each university year (October to June), with two sessions (June and September) giving students two opportunities to pass.

Fees in those communities that have taken 'full powers' are set by the communities; elsewhere they are set by the MEC. There is a system of student scholarships, run jointly by the MEC, the communities and the universities.

In 1990–1, university faculties and colleges had 720,000 students, 45% male, 55% female, taught by 39,000 teachers. 96% of them were in public institutions. Higher technical schools had 75,000 students, four-fifths male, taught by 6,000 teachers. 95% of them were in public institutions. And university schools in various subjects had a total of 343,000 students, taught by 18,000 teachers. (INE)

Non-university education

Spain also has a range of officially recognised non-university institutions of higher education, some of whose qualifications are recognised as equivalent to the diplomado or licenciado.

Funding

Spain spends 5.8% of its GDP on education (public and private sources, 1992 figures; CERI)

Teaching profession

The training and the qualifications of school teachers are being reformed by the LOGSE of 1990.

Preschool and primary teachers must now have completed a three-year course, leading to the qualification of *maestro*, at university teacher training schools (*Escuelas Universitarias de Formación de Profesorado*). However, in the first cycle of preschool education, less thoroughly trained teaching assistants (*técnicos*) may also be employed. Preschool and primary teachers teach all subjects, other than music, physical education and foreign languages, for which specialist teachers are employed.

By contrast, teachers at secondary level are specialist teachers, normally of one subject. At present, teachers in BUP or COU must have obtained a licenciado or its equivalent, and also taken a teacher training course leading to a *certificado*. Teachers in FP need only have obtained a diplomado or its equivalent. However, after LOGSE, all secondary teachers – whether in the Bachillerato or the FP – will have to hold a licenciado or its equivalent, and also to have successfully taken a teacher training course of at least one year, which includes an element of teaching practice.

All teachers in public or private schools must have the appropriate initial qualifications for their level and, after LOGSE, must also undertake inservice training. Permanent teaching posts in state education, at all levels, are obtained by competitive examination. Teaching posts in private education, however, are filled by ordinary private contracts between an employer and employee.

The teaching profession is predominantly female, especially for the earlier years of schooling. Just before the LOGSE reforms, about 90% of teachers in EGB, 55% of those in BUP/COU and 45% of those in FP were female.

Education inspectorate

There are two levels of inspectorate in Spain. One (*Alta Inspección*) is organised by the MEC, to check that the regulations laid down nationally are being followed by the communities. The other (*Inspecciones Técnicas de Educación*) is organised by the communities themselves (where they have taken 'full powers', otherwise in the individual communities but by the MEC again) to monitor and support the work of schools and teachers.

ACRONYMS AND ABBREVIATIONS

BUP	Bachillerato Unificado Polivalente (the basic postcompulsory academic course under the older system)
COU	Curso de Orientación Universitaria (one-year university orientation course, after BUP, under the older system)
EGB	Educación General Básica (basic general education – the older system of compulsory primary/lower secondary education)
ESO	Educación Secundaria Obligatoria (compulsory secondary education under the new system)
ETA	Euskadi ta Askatasuna (Basque Homeland and Liberty – a separatist terrorist organisation)
FP	Formación Profesional (vocational training)
FPO	Formación Profesional Ocupacional (occupational vocational training – more practical, less academic than FP)
INE	Instituto Nacional de Empleo (the National Employment Institute of the Ministry of Labour and Social Security)
LOGSE	Ley Orgánica de Ordenación General del Sistema Educativo (Basic Law on the General Structure of the Education System)
LRU	Ley Orgánica de Reforma Universitaria (Basic Law on University Reform)
MEC	Ministerio de Educación y Ciencia (Ministry of Education and Science)

PNFP Programa Nacional de Foramación Profesional (National Vocational Training Programme)

UNED Universidad Nacional de Educación a Distancia (National Distance Education University)

ACKNOWLEDGEMENT

We are grateful to the Spanish Embassy in London for supplying us with information about education in Spain.

REFERENCES

Boyd-Barrett, O. (1990) 'Structural change and curricular reform in democratic Spain', *The Curriculum Journal*, Vol. 1, No. 3, pp. 291–306.

Boyd-Barrett, O. (1991) 'State and church in Spanish education', *Compare*, Vol. 21, No. 2, pp. 179–97.

CERI (1995) *Education at a Glance: OECD indicators*, Paris: Organisation for Economic Co-operation and Development.

European Commission (1995) *Structures of the Education and Initial Training Systems in the European Union*, Luxembourg: Office for Official Publications of the European Commission.

Hooper, J. (1995) *The New Spaniards*, Harmondsworth: Penguin.

INE (1994) *España: Annuario Estadístico 1993*: Madrid: Instituto Nacional de Estadística.

MEC (1992) *Education: National Report* (English version), document presented to the 43rd meeting, Geneva 1992, of the International Conference on Education, Madrid: Ministry of Education and Science.

OECD (1995) *OECD Economic Surveys: Spain: 1994–1995*, Paris: Organisation for Economic Co-operation and Development.

OECD (1996) *OECD Economic Surveys: Spain: 1995–1996*, Paris: Organisation for Economic Co-operation and Development.

O'Hanlon, C. (1995) 'Inclusive education in Spain and Greece', in Potts, P., Armstrong, F. and Masterton, M. (1995) (eds) *Equality and Diversity in Education 2: national and international contexts*, London: Routledge.

BACKGROUND

Sweden and its Skolverket *regions*

Sweden became a united and independent kingdom in the 10th century, and a constitutional monarchy in 1809; the present constitution came into force in 1975. At various times the Swedish kings have also ruled Finland (until 1809) and Norway (1814–1905).

Sweden is a member of the Nordic Council (with Denmark, Finland, Iceland and Norway), and of the EU, which it joined in 1995.

After the general election of 1991, a centre-right coalition government was formed, after many years of government by the Social Democratic Party, and extensive changes to the education system followed, which have not been reversed by the re-election of the Social Democrats in 1994 as a minority government.

Like its Nordic neighbours, Sweden is large and sparsely populated, with the population concentrated in the south of the country.

POPULATION

Population	8.8 million in 1994 (up 0.5% per annum from 1984)
Land area	450,000 sq. km (of which 9% are lakes)
Population density	21 per sq. km (of land area)
Urban/rural balance of population	83%/17% in 1991

ECONOMY

GDP	$197 billion (1994)
Per capita income	$22,400 (1994)
In employment	82% of the working age population in 1991
	– 94% of men/91% of women aged 25–54
	– 61% of young people (15–24)

The percentage of women in employment is high compared with other countries. About 35% of employed women and 5% of employed men are in part-time employment. (1990 figures)

RELIGION

All Swedish citizens are assumed to belong to the (evangelical Lutheran) State Church of Sweden, unless they specifically withdraw from it, which very few do – even among members of non-conformist denominations, who number over a quarter of a million. There are just under 150,000 Roman Catholics.

LANGUAGE AND ETHNICITY

The great majority of the population are Swedish speaking. (Swedish, Norwegian and Danish are mutually intelligible.) There is a small Sami (Lapp) speaking community of some 17,000 – and one Sami school, with 133 pupils in 1990. In addition, Sweden has about half a million residents of non-Swedish citizenship. About 110,000 of these are Finns, the largest single national group; a further 90,000 are from other EU countries (and Norway) and 135,000 are 'guest workers' from Eastern Europe and the Middle East. The Swedish authorities believe that the majority of Swedish people have a 'positive and progressive' attitude to immigrants, but acknowledge the existence of a hostile and sometimes violent minority as a problem yet to be solved. (See OECD, 1995, pp. 36–7.)

About 11% of pupils in primary and lower secondary education, and 7% of those in upper secondary education, come from homes where a language other than Swedish is spoken. (1989 figures, OECD, 1995)

GOVERNMENT

Sweden has three levels of government – *national*, *county* and *municipal*. Their respective educational responsibilities were altered after the 1991 election, when various powers were transferred from the counties to the municipalities, and a system of detailed allocation of resources for specific purposes by the national government was replaced by a system giving more responsibility for their allocation to the municipalities.

Swedish government ministries are limited in their powers and duties, in comparison with those of most other countries. On the one hand, decisions are made (at least formally) by the cabinet as a whole, not by individual ministers. On the other, these decisions are largely confined to policy-making and the preparation of legislation; actual administration is the responsibility of various national agencies (see below).

The Ministry of Education and Science sets national goals for education, and defines the school curricula, syllabuses and timetables. It also provides general financial support for these activities, though it no longer gives detailed direction as to how these funds are to be allocated. The national government is responsible for initial teacher training, but not inservice training, which is the responsibility of the municipalities; national government and the municipalities share responsibility for the management training of head teachers. The municipalities are responsible for the implementation of national educational goals and policies, but the national government retains responsibility for ensuring that this is carried out satisfactorily and to uniform standards throughout Sweden.

The actual monitoring and evaluation of the work of schools and municipalities, and the administration of the government's remaining direct educational responsibilities, are assigned to the national agencies.

There are 24 counties (*län*), with responsibilities divided between an elected county council (*landsting*) and a governor and county administrative board (*länsstyrelse*) appointed by the national government. Since 1991, the counties' educational functions have been much reduced, but they still have some responsibilities for colleges of agriculture, forestry and horticulture, and for training in the paramedical sector. In addition, county labour boards have responsibilities for labour market training (see below).

There are 286 municipalities, mostly small in population. (Three-quarters have fewer than 30,000 inhabitants; only 11 have more than 100,000 inhabitants.) Each has its own elected council, whose areas of responsibility include education. Since 1991, they are responsible for the allocation of educational resources, for school organisation and personnel and for the inservice training of teachers. Each municipality must draw up a municipal education plan, within the guidelines set by national goals and curricula, and in turn setting the framework in which head teachers and their staff develop and conduct school activities. In all these tasks, the municipalities are subject to monitoring and evaluation by the National Agency for Education on behalf of the national government.

EDUCATION

The administration of the national government's direct educational responsibilities, and its monitoring and evaluation of the work of schools and municipalities, are conducted, not directly by the Ministry of Education and Science, but by national agencies, including the National Agency for Higher Education (VHS – *Verket för högskolservice*) and the National Agency for Education (*Skolverket*). Skolverket has a central directorate in Stockholm, with three departments, responsible respectively for basic information, evaluation and development. In addition, it has a field organisation, with eight regions throughout Sweden, each with its own regional directorate, who maintain contact with the municipalities.

Education is at present compulsory and free for nine years, normally between the ages of seven and 16, in the municipally run compulsory basic school, the *grundskola*. (Parents may choose to let their children start at the age of six.) In addition, all children are entitled to at least one year of preschool education. During compulsory education, textbooks are free, free meals are provided, and free transport is also available for children who have to travel long distances to school. Pupils in compulsory education receive a basic child allowance.

Over 90% of pupils completing the final year of grundskola move on to the upper secondary school, the *gymnasieskola*. The gymnasieskola is also

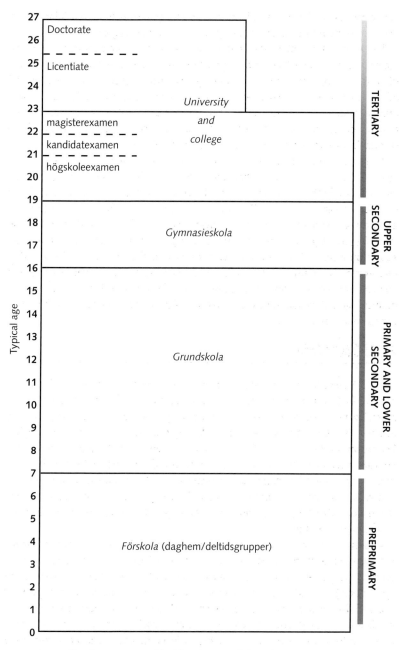

Note: This diagram is simplified for clarity, and should be used in conjunction with the text

Sweden's education system

municipally run, but each school normally serves several municipalities. Upper secondary schools may not charge tuition fees, but they may charge for school meals, books and other teaching materials – though most do not. Students in the gymnasieskola receive financial assistance, part of which is paid to all students, and part needs-tested.

INSTITUTIONS

Sweden has just over 1.2 million pupils and students at primary and secondary levels, with 123,000 teachers. (1993 figures)

Preprimary education

Municipalities are required to provide nursery facilities for children from six months old, to enable parents to work. All children are entitled to at least one year of preprimary education (whether they start school at seven or six), but in Sweden this is part of the public child-care system, not of the education system, and it concentrates on play and social education, with no formal instruction.

Some 376,000 children, about half of all children aged under seven, participate in publicly provided day-care – 84% in day-care centres (daghem), where the children can be looked after all day, throughout the year; and 16% in part-time groups (deltidsgrupper), which children attend for up to three hours per day during the school year. (European Commission, 1995)

Primary and lower secondary education

The primary and lower secondary stages are combined in the comprehensive and co-educational grundskola, which caters for the nine years of compulsory education, currently from age seven to 16. Until recently, the grundskola was divided into three levels (junior, intermediate and senior) each comprising three school years, with its own set curriculum and educational objectives. The different levels were sometimes housed in different buildings and even on separate sites. However, these levels were abolished by legislation of 1993, and the nationally prescribed curriculum now specifies targets to be reached by the fifth and the ninth year of schooling. This change has already taken effect (from 1995) for the first six years of the grundskola (the old junior and intermediate levels). For pupils now in the last three years, the older arrangements still obtain, but the new system will be fully in place by 1998.

In 1993, Sweden had 4,800 grundskola establishments, 60% with under 200 pupils, and 90% with under 400 pupils. Fewer than 2% had more than 600 pupils. These catered for a total of 907,000 pupils. In some smaller schools, it is necessary to combine pupils of different ages in the same class; overall, about

14% of pupils were in such classes. There were some 93,000 grundskola teachers (or whom 5% were on leave), giving a pupil/teacher ratio of 12:1. About 7% of these teachers are unqualified, but this figure varies considerably between different municipalities and different subjects. (Statistics Sweden, 1994)

Traditionally, teaching at the junior and intermediate levels was by class teachers, and at the senior level by subject teachers. Since 1988, however, the distinction between class and subject teaching has been blurred, and more emphasis placed on working as part of an integrated teaching team, with each teacher able to teach a range of subjects.

The grundskola is comprehensive, and takes virtually all the children in its area. Pupils normally attend a school near their homes, though their parents may choose another school, which may be municipal or private. Only 1.5% of Swedish children of compulsory school age attend a private school, though the numbers are increasing. (In 1985, the percentage was 0.7%.) There is no streaming in the lower years of the grundskola, and it is becoming less common in the upper years, but it can still be found there, especially in mathematics and English.

The grundskolan are run by the municipalities. The Ministry of Education and Science lays down guidelines concerning their overall educational values, aims, curricula, and time schedules, but the municipalities are otherwise free to organise them as they wish. They are financed jointly by the national government (55% overall) and the municipalities (45%). The government's grant to a municipality is based straightforwardly on the number of children of the relevant ages.

The curriculum (laroplan) of the grundskola is laid down from time to time by the national government, the current curriculum came into effect from 1995. Though the curriculum is now specified centrally in less detail than formerly, the government still decides the subjects to be taught, the syllabus for each subject and the minimum number of hours of teaching time to be devoted to each. On the basis of this, each municipality must draw up a municipal education plan, and each school a school working plan, in which teaching content, organisation and methods are adapted to local conditions.

The minimum teaching time for a pupil's entire grundskola career is 6,665 hours, divided between the different subjects as shown in Figure 1.

Throughout the grundskola, pupils must also be given study and vocational guidance (syo) about educational opportunities and vocational choices. In some schools, there are specialist guidance teachers.

No marks are given in the first six years of grundskola, but pupils and parents are given progress reports. At the end of the ninth year of compulsory schooling, a leaving certificate (grundskolabetyg) is available, which lists pupils' marks in the various subjects. These certificates used to be the basis for admission to the upper secondary school, but all grundskola leavers are now

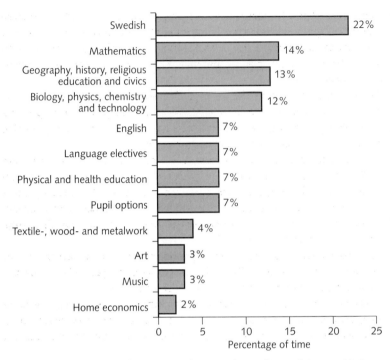

Swedish	22%
Mathematics	14%
Geography, history, religious education and civics	13%
Biology, physics, chemistry and technology	12%
English	7%
Language electives	7%
Physical and health education	7%
Pupil options	7%
Textile-, wood- and metalwork	4%
Art	3%
Music	3%
Home economics	2%

Percentage of time

Sweden figure 1   Division of time among the compulsory subjects of the grundskola curriculum, from 1995

entitled to enter. More than 90% of those who completed the ninth year in 1988 did so, and about 80% went on to complete their upper secondary education within four years.

Upper secondary education

There are about 314,000 students in upper secondary education, in 640 schools, with 30,000 teachers (of whom 5% are on leave), giving a student/teacher ratio of about 11:1. (1993 figures, Statistics Sweden, 1994)

Upper secondary education in Sweden has undergone extensive re-organisation, completed in the autumn of 1995. Compared with the older system, the new one offers less academic specialisation and more flexibility, with extensive vocational options. Academic and vocational education both now take place in an integrated upper secondary school (*gymnasieskola*), which has replaced the previously separate, academically oriented (*gymnasium*), vocationally oriented (*yrkesskola*) and 'continuation' (*fackskola*) schools. The gymnasieskola is open to everyone under the age of 20.

The gymnasieskola has 16 *national programmes*. Two of these (one in natural sciences, the other in social sciences) are primarily intended to prepare students for higher education, and the other 14 are primarily vocational. But the vocational programmes can also be used as qualifications for entry to higher education; there are to be no 'dead end' programmes in upper secondary education.

In the vocational programmes, at least 15% of the students' study time is to consist of training at a place of work. However, these programmes provide, not complete job training, but basic education in preparation for such training later, which will include study at university in some cases.

As well as the syllabus for each course, the government sets the minimum overall study time for the programmes, and the distribution of time within them between different types of study. All programmes must include eight *core subjects*, in addition to the *characteristic subjects* of the particular programme. The core subjects must be allocated 30% of study time over the three-year period, divided as shown in Figure 2.

The characteristic subjects of each programme occupy a further 55% of study time. The remaining 15% is divided between subjects chosen by the student, subjects chosen by the school and a student *project*.

Students normally attend a gymnasieskola in their own municipality, if there is one, though their parents may choose one in another municipality or a private school. At the end of their upper secondary schooling, students can

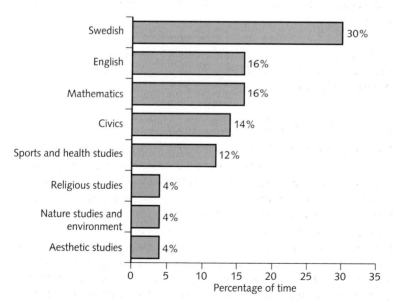

Sweden figure 2   Division of time among the core subjects of the gymnasieskola curriculum, from 1994

obtain a leaving certificate summarising their grades in all the courses they have completed. About 30% of those leaving gymnasieskola go on to higher education within five years (and substantial numbers also enter higher education later in life, see below).

Private schools

Traditionally, Sweden has had very few private schools, catering for fewer than 1% of pupils of compulsory school age (0.7% in 1985). But from 1992, each municipality has been required to fund private schools in its area at a rate per pupil of 85% of the average cost per child of education in the municipality's own schools. The schools are allowed to supplement this by charging 'reasonable' fees. New private schools are being established at a rapid rate (taking 1.5% of pupils of compulsory school age in 1993). They must be approved by Skolverket, and are required to follow the national curriculum. But they have considerable autonomy in teaching methods, and may be based, for example, on Montessori or Waldorf (Rudolf Steiner) principles – though they no longer need to be based on different educational principles from state schools to qualify for state support.

Apprenticeship

Apprenticeships combine vocational training as an employee in a company with study, mainly in the core subjects of upper secondary education, though an individual syllabus is drawn up for each apprentice. Apprenticeships last three years.

Special education

Pupils with serious physical disabilities may attend special schools, or be given a special curriculum in ordinary schools. Sweden has eight special schools, five regional and three national, which must match, as far as possible, the education provided by the grundskola and gymnasieskola. Pupils with less serious disabilities may be helped in their ordinary classes by a remedial teacher. In all cases, the aim is to enable the pupil, wherever possible, to remain in or return to ordinary lessons.

The special schools are run by the Swedish Agency for Special Education (SIH), which also supports the teaching of pupils with physical disabilities in the grundskola and gymnasieskola.

For adults with physical disabilities, grants are available to help overcome obstacles to participating in adult education, for example problems of physical access or unsuitable teaching materials.

In addition, there are compulsory basic schools, upper secondary schools and training schools for the intellectually handicapped (*särskolan*) – the first two for children who can learn to read and write, and the training schools for those who cannot. About 12,000 children (1% of the school population) attend a särskola.

During the years of compulsory schooling, pupils in the compulsory basic school for the intellectually handicapped study the same subjects as those in grundskola, though every pupil has an individual teaching plan adapting the curriculum to his or her abilities.

The upper secondary school for the intellectually handicapped offers vocational education in national, local and individual programmes, parallel to the programmes of the gymnasieskola. All programmes last four years, and students have a guaranteed minimum teaching time of 3,600 hours. Leaving certificates are available, with grades awarded on a two- or three-point scale according to criteria laid down in the särskola syllabuses.

The training school for the intellectually handicapped, for pupils with more severe difficulties, concentrates on five teaching areas: communication and social interaction; motor skills; perception of reality and knowledge of the outside world; everyday activities; and creative activities.

Adult education for the intellectually handicapped offers adults an education equivalent to that offered to younger people in the särskola. It takes the form of self-contained courses, and students may choose a single course or combine more than one. There are normally no time limits for the completion of courses, and grades are awarded on a three-point scale (Distinction, Pass and Fail).

All education for the intellectually handicapped is already run or being taken over by the municipalities.

Tertiary education

Almost all higher education (*högskola*) is the responsibility of the Ministry of Education and Science, through the VHS. (The major exception is the University of Agricultural Sciences, which is the responsibility of the Ministry of Agriculture.) Traditionally, higher education in Sweden was planned in detail and closely controlled by the national government. However, following the change of government in 1991, this policy has been replaced by one of deregulation, allowing more autonomy for the institutions and more individual choice for the students. Since 1993, the range of courses available and the way they are studied are decided by each university or college, and the student numbers and the financing of these courses are determined largely by student choice.

Higher education was extensively reformed in the late 1970s, to create a unified system including the universities and the professional colleges, which became university colleges. Under the auspices of the national government, there are now six universities, four specialised institutions of higher education and research (in technology, medicine, education and physical education/sport), and 22 small and medium-sized university colleges (seven in Stockholm alone). In addition, there are 26 colleges under the auspices of the county councils, offering training for the paramedical professions. And there are three major private institutions of higher education. (European Commission, 1995)

The number of students in higher education has increased substantially in recent years – by about 30% between 1991 and 1994. Just over 30% of Swedish young people go on to higher education within five years of completing their upper secondary schooling, and there are also many mature entrants. In all, around 50,000 people enter higher education each year. Total student numbers (full- and part-time) in higher education are about 240,000 undergraduates (55% women) and 16,000 postgraduates (36% women) (1992–3 figures). There is a high proportion of mature students. Of undergraduates, 55% are aged 25 or over, and 22% are 35 or over (1989–90 figures). (Statistics Sweden, 1994)

To allow people with jobs to participate in higher education, there are many single-subject courses, taught part-time, often in the evenings or by distance teaching. Distance teaching, traditionally by correspondence, has a long history in Sweden, and is now developing rapidly with the use of such new technologies as personal computers, fax, interactive video and picture telephone.

To gain admission to higher education, a would-be student has to satisfy *general admission requirements* – normally completion of three years in the gymnasieskola, an equivalent adult education institution (see below), or a comparable foreign school – and *special admission requirements* for the particular programme or course they wish to take – which are now set by the individual universities and university colleges. For students aged 25 or over, work experience can be an alternative way of meeting the general requirements. All applicants must have a good knowledge of both Swedish and English.

Universities and university colleges are now responsible for deciding the numbers of students to be admitted to their programmes and courses, and for the selection and admission of these students. Places are limited, and overall fewer than a third of applicants are admitted to the university or college programme of their first choice. For example, programmes in journalism are oversubscribed by 20 times, physical education and veterinary medicine by 13 times, architecture, medicine and social work by seven times, and gymnasieskola teaching by five times.

Traditionally, the curriculum of Swedish undergraduate education was specified in some detail by parliament, on the recommendation of the government, but since 1993, the individual universities and university colleges have much more autonomy here too. There are two kinds of first degree, *professional* and *general*. Professional degrees qualify for admission to specific professions (for example as doctors or teachers in the gymnasieskola). A general degree (*examen*) can be taken at three levels.

- diploma/certificate (*högskoleexamen*) (two years of full-time study, or the equivalent)
- bachelor's degree (*kandidatexamen*) (three years of full-time study, or the equivalent – of which 50% must be in the main subject, partly in the form of a thesis)
- master's degree (*magisterexamen*) (four years of full-time study, or the equivalent – of which 50% must be in the main subject, partly in the form of a thesis or two theses)

Teaching methods are decided by each institution, but lectures (to classes of up to 300) and seminars (with groups of about 30 students) are usual. The language of instruction is usually Swedish, but many of the textbooks and other literature used are in English.

Methods of assessment are also decided by each institution. For reporting results, a three-level scale (Distinction, Pass and Fail) is usual but not universal.

The numbers of undergraduate students in the main fields of study are shown in Figure 3.

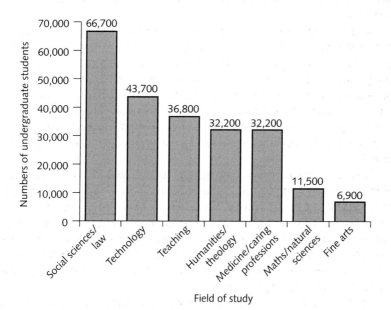

Sweden figure 3   Numbers of undergraduate students in the main fields of study, 1992–3

Note: These include full-time and part-time students, but not distance-learning students, who number about 10,000

Postgraduate education is confined to the universities, two of the university colleges and five specialist institutions. For admission to postgraduate education, as with undergraduate education, there are both general admission requirements – a minimum of 120 points altogether (i.e. three years' study) at undergraduate level – and special admission requirements – a minimum of 60 points (i.e. one-and-a-half years' study) in the subject to be studied. In addition, the department concerned must satisfy themselves about a candidate's suitability for postgraduate studies. The most important element in a postgraduate programme is the student's dissertation, but there are taught courses too. The dissertation has to be defended in public, and a Pass or Fail mark is awarded. A postgraduate degree can be taken at two levels.

- *licentiate* This is a traditional qualification (recently reintroduced in most faculties after abolition), which normally takes two to two-and-a-half years.
- *doctorate* This normally takes up to four years.

The government plans a massive expansion of postgraduate education, with the numbers at the beginning of the 1990s to double by the year 2000. Special postgraduate research posts and programmes in universities and colleges are to be established in co-operation with industry. In addition, the government has a programme designed to attract more women into postgraduate study and research. In 1992, there were 14,400 students in postgraduate education, 35% of whom were women.

The government also aims to encourage research at universities and university colleges, by a number of measures, including allowing them to operate research activities as research companies, operating under normal commercial conditions, with support provided in the form of share capital.

There are about 43,000 teaching and research staff in higher education institutions, of whom 55% are men. However, men dominate the senior positions, holding 94% of professorships and 80% of senior lectureships. (1992 figures)

The reforms of the 1970s established a uniform pattern of management for all universities and university colleges, which survives to a large extent. Each institution of higher education is run by a *governing board*, consisting of the *rector* of the institution and ten members. The rector and eight of the members are appointed by the government, the latter representing 'public interests' (in practice, the main political parties) and economic and cultural life. The other two members are student representatives.

Higher education is free for students. Undergraduate students under the age of 45 are eligible for means-tested financial assistance, 30% of which is a non-repayable grant, and the remaining 70% a loan. Postgraduate studies are financed by each university or college out of its research appropriation, or by an individual student combining research at a university or college with related employment, for example on an outside research project.

Adult education

About half of the adult population of Sweden engage in studies of some sort – some 100,000 of them as mature students in higher education (see above), but most in specifically adult education. Except in study circles (see below), no tuition fees are charged, and the fees in study circles are modest. However, there may be charges for study materials. All employees have a right to unpaid leave for any studies that must be pursued during working hours. Study grants are available – on an hourly or daily basis – to compensate for loss of income and for residential courses, to pay for board and lodging. About a fifth of government spending on education is on adult education, of which half is on grants to students on employment training. In addition, municipal governments, trade unions, private companies and voluntary organisations contribute to the funding of adult education.

Sweden has a wide variety of adult education institutions, including folk high schools, study circles, municipal adult education and employment training.

Folk high schools

Folk high schools provide free, mainly residential education for adults, in a wide range of topic areas. The schools offer both short courses (from as little as two days) and long courses (to as much as 80 weeks). In contrast with most of the Swedish education system, each folk high school decides its own curriculum, with a high degree of student participation.

There are about 130 folk high schools in Sweden, owned and run by county councils, trade unions, churches and voluntary organisations. They have about a quarter of a million students overall. No qualifications are required for admission, and some of the courses can qualify students for entry to university. Though there are no fees, there may be residential costs and charges for study materials. Participants are eligible for study grants for these costs, and to compensate for loss of earnings.

Study circles

A study circle is an informal group – usually with between five and 20 members – which meets regularly to pursue studies of some subject or problem area. An average study circle holds eight to ten meetings, lasting about 30 hours in all. Each group decides for itself how its work is to be conducted; although each has a 'circle leader', his or her duties are administrative, not teaching.

Study circles attract very large numbers of participants. In 1990–1, there were about 344,000 study circles, with a total of almost three million members – nearly 60% of the adult population of Sweden. Slightly more than half are women. The most popular subject areas, accounting between them for two-thirds of the total study time, are aesthetic subjects and civics.

The study circles are sponsored by voluntary educational organisations, but their costs are met by the national government (40%), by municipalities and from participants' fees (which are usually modest).

Municipal adult education

The main function of municipal adult education is to provide equivalent education, for adults, to the education available for children and young people (under 20) in the grundskola and gymnasieskola, with courses and qualifications comparable in standard. The main distinguishing feature of adult education is that it is modular in structure, enabling the students to decide on their own study programmes, workload and pace, according to their interests and needs, and their employment, family or other circumstances.

This type of adult education is mostly run by the municipalities. Though there are no fees, there may be charges for study materials. Employed students are entitled to unpaid leave, and eligible for study grants to compensate for loss of earnings.

At any one time, there are about 160,000 students in municipal adult education, over 60% of them women. About 45% take courses at the level of compulsory education, the remaining 55% at upper secondary level – 30% in general subjects, 25% in vocational subjects. In recent years, the government has been trying to increase the proportion of vocational study, and to tie it more closely to the immediate needs of the labour market.

The municipalities have a specific statutory duty to offer *basic adult education*, in which adults who lack the knowledge and skills that children acquire in compulsory education the opportunity to acquire them in adult education. About 25,000 people take part in basic adult education each year, of whom about two-thirds are immigrants and one-third Swedish.

Labour market training

Labour market training is intended mainly as basic vocational education or further training for unemployed people (or those facing imminent unemployment) over the age of 20.

Training courses last, on average, 25 to 30 weeks, and are meant to achieve relatively swift results in the form of employment. They are focused mainly on manufacturing industry, the caring services and office/administrative occupations. They are free for trainees, who also receive a training allowance. The courses are purchased for those trainees by county labour boards or employment offices, from a range of providers. One of these is the National Employment Training Authority (AMU), which organises employment training in about 100 training units throughout Sweden. But AMU now has to compete with other providers of training, including higher education establishments and private companies.

About 100,000 people receive labour market training each year, about half of them women. In 1992, 51% of these were employed six months after completing their training.

Minorities

Statutory provision is made for the education of minorities, both indigenous and immigrant.

For the Sami (Lapp) population – about 17,000 in number – there are *nomad schools*, which provide an ethnically adapted education corresponding to the junior and intermediate years of the grundskola.

There are large numbers of residents in Sweden of non-Swedish nationality: about 10% of pupils of compulsory school age are the sons or daughters of foreign parents. Some of these parents are immigrants, others refugees. In both cases, their children often need special support in school, usually because of language difficulties. Support mainly consists of (i) the teaching of Swedish, and (ii) the teaching of other subjects through the child's home language. Municipalities have an obligation to provide both forms of support – though they are not compulsory for the children – but they need not provide home language teaching if there are too few pupils (fewer than five per teaching group) or if no suitable teacher is available. About 25% of home language teachers in the grundskola and 18% of those in the gymnasieskola are unqualified – the highest proportions of any category of teacher. Over 90 home languages are taught in Swedish schools, the most common (in 1992) being Finnish, Spanish and Arabic.

Adult education can also be provided in home languages other than Swedish. In addition, newly arrived adult immigrants are entitled to basic courses in Swedish, provided by their municipality, as soon as possible after their arrival in Sweden. These courses are free, and last 700 hours on average.

Funding

Sweden spends 7.8% of its GDP on education, virtually all of it public expenditure. About 87% of this expenditure is directly on public institutions, and 13% subsidies to private institutions. (1994 figures)

Of this, 66% is spent by the national government, much of it in the form of grants to the municipalities, 30% by the municipalities themselves and 4% by the counties. (The government's grant to a municipality is based straightforwardly on the number of children of the relevant ages.) Just under half of this expenditure is on teachers, and just under a quarter on premises. The remainder is accounted for mainly by administration, school meals, teaching materials and social welfare. (1990–1 figures)

Annual expenditure per student in the gymnasieskola is 25% greater than in the grundskola. In schools for the intellectually handicapped, expenditure per pupil is over four times that in the grundskola. (1990–1 figures)

The funding of higher education is almost entirely by the national government, in the form of annual lump sums directly to each institution. The basic principle of allocation is remuneration for results achieved: 40% of the grant is related to the number of full-time equivalent students taught at the institution, and 60% to the number of credit points earned by these students. About 60% of the total is spent on undergraduate and 40% on postgraduate studies.

Teaching profession

Sweden has 157,800 school teachers in all: 44,400 in preschool establishments (plus 48,000 other instructors and attendants), 84,000 in the grundskola and 29,400 in the gymnasieskola. (1992–3 figures, European Commission, 1995)

Teachers' organisations have been very influential in Swedish education. They have legal rights of 'co-determination', that is rights to information and to opportunities of influencing decisions.

Initial teacher training is the responsibility of the national government, and teachers at all levels of schooling are trained in universities and university colleges. Teachers are employed by the municipalities, however, and the municipalities are responsible for inservice training. Responsibility for the management training of head teachers is shared between the national government and the municipalities.

Traditionally, teaching in the grundskola at the junior and intermediate levels was by class teachers, trained for teaching at one or other level (but not graduates), and at the senior level by graduate subject teachers. Since 1988, however, the distinction between class and subject teaching has been blurred; teachers trained since 1988 study and qualify to teach either Years 1–7 or Years 4–9 in a range of subjects as part of an integrated teaching team. Successful completion of either course confers graduate status; normally this will be at bachelor level for teachers of the younger age-range, but may be at either bachelor or master level for teachers of the older age-range.

Teachers in the gymnasieskola are trained for one year in the theory and practice of teaching, after at least three years at university studying two or three subjects. (Teachers qualified under the new system to teach Years 4–9 of the grundskola may be able to qualify to teach in the gymnasieskola by extending their subject studies.) In addition, the gymnasieskola has senior teachers, who have doctoral degrees or equivalent qualifications, and vocational teachers, who have had long experience of their trade plus teacher training. (See OECD 1995, pp. 64–5 and Part One Appendix 13.)

Education inspectorate

The implementation of national aims and policies in the municipalities and schools is monitored by the evaluation department of Skolverket through its field organisation (see above).

ACRONYMS AND ABBREVIATIONS
AME   National Employment Training Authority
SIH   Swedish Agency for Special Education
VHS   National Agency for Higher Education

ACKNOWLEDGEMENT
We are very grateful to the Swedish Embassy in London for supplying us with extensive information about education in Sweden.

REFERENCES
Archer, E. G. and Peck, B. T. (no date) *The Teaching Profession in Europe*, Glasgow: Jordanhill College of Education.

Department of Education and Science (1989) *Selected National Education Systems II: a description of six further countries as an aid to international comparisons*, London: Department of Education and Science Statistics Branch.

European Commission (1995) *Structures of the Education and Initial Training Systems in the European Union*, Luxembourg: Office for Official Publications of the European Commission.

Hunter, B. (ed.) (1995) *The Statesman's Year Book, 1995–1996*, London: Macmillan.

Larsson, S. (1989) 'Glossary', in Ball, S. J. and Larsson, S. (eds) (1989) *The Struggle for Democratic Education: equality and participation in Sweden*, Lewes: Falmer Press.

Ministry of Education and Science (1993) *Knowledge and Progress: a summary of the Swedish Government's Bills on higher education and research*, Stockholm: Ministry of Education and Science.

OECD (1995) *Reviews of National Policies for Education: Sweden*, Paris: Organisation for Economic Co-operation and Development.

Skolverket (1992) *Swedish National Agency for Education*, Stockholm: Skolverket.

Skolverket (no date) *Adult Education*, Stockholm: Skolverket.

Skolverket (no date) *Compulsory Basic School*, Stockholm: Skolverket.

Skolverket (no date) *Immigrant and Refugee Pupils*, Stockholm: Skolverket.

Skolverket (no date) *The New Upper Secondary School*, Stockholm: Skolverket.

Skolverket (no date) *Pupil Welfare*, Stockholm: Skolverket.

Skolverket (no date) *Schools and Adult Education for the Intellectually Handicapped*, Stockholm: Skolverket.

Skolverket (no date) *Schools and Teaching for Pupils with Impaired Hearing/Vision and Physical Disabilities*, Stockholm: Skolverket.

Skolverket (no date) *Upper Secondary School*, Stockholm: Skolverket.

Statistics Sweden (1992) *Statistisk Arsbok för Sverige 1993*, Stockholm: Statistics Sweden.

Statistics Sweden (1994) *Education in Sweden 1994*, Stockholm: Statistics Sweden.

Swedish Institute (1992) *Fact Sheets on Sweden: primary and secondary education*, Stockholm: Swedish Institute.

Swedish Institute (1992) *Fact Sheets on Sweden: adult education in Sweden*, Stockholm: Swedish Institute.

Swedish Institute (1994) *Fact Sheets on Sweden: higher education in Sweden*, Stockholm: Swedish Institute.

Weyler, K. (1993) *Current Sweden: big changes in Swedish education*, Stockholm: Swedish Institute.

BACKGROUND

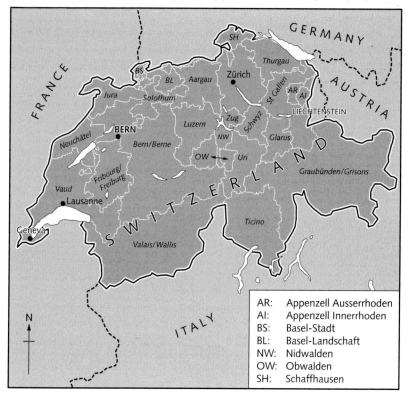

Switzerland and its cantons

A united Switzerland was first formed in the years 1798–1803 by Napoleon, who established it (albeit temporarily) as a federal republic, instead of the more loosely associated league of cantons that had developed since the 13th century. After his defeat in 1815, the Congress of Vienna recognised Switzerland's territorial integrity and permanent neutrality, and these have survived through the two World Wars and the 'Cold War' until the present.

Switzerland is a member of the Council of Europe, but not of the EU, NATO or the United Nations (UN) as such, though it does participate in or support many UN agencies, including UNESCO, the World Health Organisation and the UN High Commission for Refugees.

POPULATION
• • • • • • • • • • • • • •

Population	7.0 million in 1995 (up 0.7% per annum from 1985)
Land area	41,300 sq. km
Population density	166 per sq. km

Of the 7.0 million population, 1.2 million (17%) are resident foreigners. More than half of these come from three countries: over a third from Italy, and a tenth each from the former Yugoslavia and Spain. A slightly lower percentage of resident foreigners than of Swiss citizens continue their education after the compulsory years: some 14.5% of the population of upper secondary schools are resident foreigners, compared with 16% of the population as a whole.

The figures for land area and population density cannot be taken at face value, since about three-quarters of the land is mountainous and not regarded as habitable, and the population density varies greatly among the cantons – from 23 per sq. km in Graubünden to 5,441 in Basel-Stadt.

ECONOMY
• • • • • • • • • • •

GDP	$241 billion (1992)
GDP per capita	$35,000 (1992)
In employment	3.5 million (1992)

Switzerland has the highest GDP per capita of the major countries of Europe. However, the national figure masks wide variation between cantons. The GDP per capita in Zug, for example, is almost twice that in Appenzell Inner-Rhoden.

In the early 1990s, Switzerland suffered an economic recession, which took unemployment to levels unprecedented in its history, though modest by comparison with other European countries. Unemployment rose from 0.5% of the workforce in 1990 (a typical postwar Swiss figure) to 4.7% in 1994, a peak from which it is now declining. Unemployment is much higher in the French and Italian-speaking populations (7.1%) than the German-speaking (3.4%). It is higher among women (4.9%) than men (4.1%), and lower (3.8%) among young people aged 15–24 than in the population as a whole. (1994 figures)

RELIGION
• • • • • • • • • •

About 47% of the population identify themselves as Protestant, 46% as Roman Catholic and 7% as having no religion (1990 Census). There is no state religion, and religious freedom is guaranteed. State schools are non-denominational, but there are denominational private schools.

LANGUAGE
There is no Swiss language as such, and Switzerland has four national languages: German (spoken by 64% of the population), French (19%), Italian (8%) and Romansch (fewer than 1%). German is the majority language in 19 cantons, French in six and Italian in one (Ticino). The number of Romansch speakers is small and declining. They mostly live in one canton – Graubünden – but they are a minority of its population. All four languages are spoken in a variety of dialects; this is especially true of Swiss German, but even Romansch has five distinct dialects.

Each canton decides its own language policy in education – for example, the language or languages of instruction in its schools, and the first 'foreign' language to be taught (which is usually French in German-speaking cantons, and vice versa).

Four cantons (Bern/Berne, Fribourg/Freiburg, Valais/Wallis and Graubünden/Grisons) are officially bilingual, with a two-language school system. However, even officially monolingual cantons often have substantial linguistic minorities. Overall, 86% of the population in German cantons, 84% in the Italian canton and 73% in French cantons speak the official language as their mother tongue. Linguistic minorities are largest in large-city cantons, especially Geneva, where 39% of the population do not speak the official language (French) as their mother tongue.

GOVERNMENT
Switzerland is a federal republic, consisting of 26 cantons, each with its own government. (Strictly speaking, there are 20 cantons and six 'half-cantons', but we shall follow Swiss practice and usually refer to them all as cantons.) The powers of the federal government are limited to those functions explicitly assigned to it by the constitution (see below); apart from those, the cantons are unrestricted in their independence and authority to enact laws. All citizens over 18 have a vote – though women only since 1971. An unusual feature of Swiss government is the importance of the referendum. At federal level, this can be invoked by a petition of 50,000 voters (100,000 for an amendment to the constitution) or from eight cantons, and can overturn any decision of parliament. At cantonal level, referendums are often automatically held to ratify legislation or major executive decisions.

The responsibilities of the federal government are closely defined by the constitution, and severely limited in many areas, including education, for which the cantons are mainly responsible. There is no federal ministry or department of education, though the federal Department of the Interior is required by the constitution to ensure the provision by the cantons of free, compulsory education, open to members of all religious denominations, and the

Department of Economic Affairs oversees the provision of vocational training, in some but not all occupations.

The federal government may also establish and support higher educational institutions of its own, and there are currently two federal institutes of technology. Formally, the federal government has power to set entry requirements only for these two institutes and for medical education. In practice, however, the same standards are required and accepted for admission to the entire range of higher education. In effect, therefore, the federal government defines the structure of the senior secondary school leaving certificate – the *certificat de maturité* – and thus has a strong influence on the curriculum of the schools preparing students for higher education.

Federal government spending accounts for 12% of total public expenditure on education in Switzerland. Most of this (9% of total public spending) is on the universities.

The 26 cantons of Switzerland range in size from Zürich (with a population of 1.3 million) to Appenzell Inner-Rhoden (with 13,000). The cantons are mainly responsible for the provision and administration of education, from preprimary education to university. Each canton decides on the structure of its schools, their curricula and teaching materials, the training, conditions and salaries of their teachers, the length of the school day, week and year, and so on. There is wide variation among them. However, the cantons try to co-ordinate their policies and arrangements, mainly through the Swiss Conference of the Cantonal Directors of Public Education, which first met in 1897, but was established formally in 1970. In 1970, 21 of the 26 cantons agreed to make basic common arrangements, including the starting age (six) and duration (nine years) of compulsory schooling.

They also agreed to prepare recommendations for all cantons to help harmonise syllabuses, teaching materials, transfer of pupils from primary to secondary schools, transfer of pupils between cantons, intercantonal recognition of qualifications, nomenclature for types and stages of schooling, and teacher training.

Such harmonisation is important to allow pupils to move easily between cantons. This is necessary not only because families sometimes move their homes, but because few cantons are large enough to offer all the types of educational institution, and in particular universities and the schools that lead to university study. Despite these developments, however, much variation among cantons remains.

Cantonal spending accounts for 54% of total public expenditure on education in Switzerland. Of this, 22% of total spending is on compulsory schooling, 11% on postcompulsory intermediate schools, 10% on vocational training, and 9% on universities.

There are over 3,000 communes in Switzerland, mostly small; only about 100 have populations over 10,000. In many cantons, the communes are responsible for school buildings, and in some cantons, the communal governments share the duties, powers and costs of education – especially primary education – with the cantonal government. Overall, communal spending accounts for 34% of total public expenditure on education in Switzerland, most of it (30% of total spending) on compulsory schooling.

EDUCATION

Education in Switzerland is compulsory and free in all cantons for nine years between the ages of six and 15. Each canton has its own education system, and there are many differences among them, for example in the division between primary and secondary stages. However, there are basic similarities between most of the systems, in part because of the work of the Swiss Conference of the Cantonal Directors of Public Education (see above), and the diagram of the education system shows a typical arrangement.

INSTITUTIONS

Preprimary education

Preprimary education (*Kindergarten/école enfantine*) is available usually for two years, though in some cantons for only one and in others for three. It is not compulsory, but virtually all children (98%) attend for at least one year, and 75% for at least two years.

In 1992–3, there were some 144,500 children in preprimary education, about a fifth of them resident foreigners. About 95% overall were in state-run schools.

Primary education

In most (18) cantons, primary education (*Primarstufe/degré primaire*) lasts six years. In four cantons, it lasts four years, in three it lasts five, and in one (Ticino) the nine years of compulsory education are not differentiated into primary and secondary stages. Several cantons where primary education lasts four or five years plan to extend it to six years, so as to ease the movement of children between cantons, and to postpone selection, since primary education is comprehensive but lower secondary education is differentiated. Each class in primary schools normally has all subjects taught by the same teacher. The average primary class size in Switzerland is 19, but this varies between cantons – from 15.5 in Jura to 21.5 in Thurgau. (1988–9 figures)

In 1992–3, there were some 420,100 children in primary education, about a fifth of them resident foreigners. About 98% overall were in state-run schools.

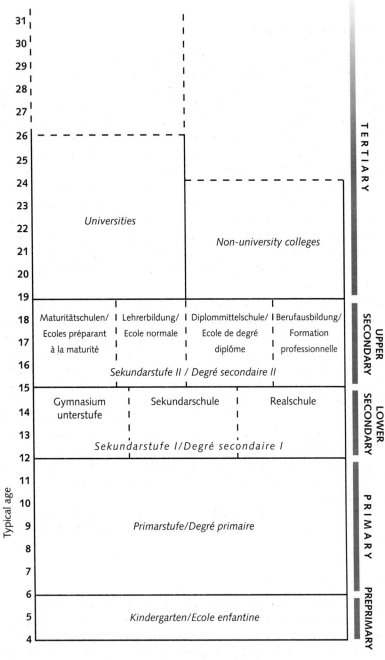

Note: This diagram is highly simplified; it shows a typical set of arrangements for Switzerland, and glosses over numerous important differences between cantons. It should be used in conjunction with the text

Switzerland's education system

Lower secondary education

The lower or 'first cycle' secondary school (*Sekundarstufe I/degré secondaire I*) completes the years of compulsory education. It varies in duration from canton to canton between three and five years, corresponding to the variations in the length of primary education described above. It is also differentiated according to entrance requirements and the educational routes that pupils are likely to follow. This differentiation also varies from canton to canton, with two, three or four distinct types of school of stream. A common arrangement is to have three types, as in the following example of Luzern.

- *Gymnasium (Unterstufe)* – a school with high entrance requirements, preparing pupils to go on ultimately to a university or institute of technology
- *Sekundarschule* – a school with average entrance requirements, preparing pupils to go on ultimately to vocational, non-university, tertiary education
- *Realschule* – a school with basic entrance requirements, preparing pupils to go into employment after vocational training or apprenticeship at senior secondary level

In practice, there is little movement between streams, and assignments to a non-university stream is already in effect irrevocable. However, about 60% of lower secondary pupils in Switzerland are still in schools or streams that leave open the possibility of going to university. (Girls are slightly more successful than boys in getting into these schools or streams.) Some cantons (notably Zürich and Geneva) have experimented with comprehensive lower secondary schools, but these remain experimental and small in scale.

Teaching is normally subject-based, with subject-specialist teachers. There is no final examination and no certificates or diplomas are awarded at the end of compulsory education.

The average lower secondary class size in Switzerland is 17.5, but this varies between cantons – from 14.5 in Glarus and Graubünden to 20.5 in Jura. (1988–9 figures)

In 1992–3, there were some 279,600 children in lower secondary education, about a fifth of them resident foreigners. About 95% overall were in state-run schools.

Upper secondary education

Upper secondary education is for students between the ages of 15 and 18 or 19. It is not compulsory, but about 88% of the population complete an upper secondary course – 93% of males, 82% of females (percentages of 20-year-olds in 1990). There is a clear division between general education and vocational education/training. In 1992–3, there were 281,800 students in upper secondary education – just over 70% of them in vocational and just under 30% in general education.

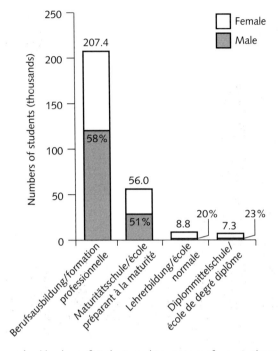

Switzerland figure I   Numbers of students, and percentage of men, in the main types of upper secondary education, 1991–2

With variations between cantons, there are five main kinds of school for this age-group. The first kind, available in some cantons, is in effect a tenth, non-compulsory year added on to the nine years of compulsory education. It is intended to help students who do not feel they have completed their schooling satisfactorily to do so, and to offer vocational guidance to those who have not yet chosen any vocational training. The other kinds are as follows; student numbers are shown in Figure I.

Berufsausbildung/Formation professionnelle
Students may either attend vocational schools full-time, or divide their time between a vocational school and apprenticeship with a company in a manner explicitly modelled on the German 'dual system'. In either case, the curriculum they follow is regulated for most occupations by the federal government, with over 30 different occupational categories. (See Figure 2 for numbers of students of the most popular occupations.)

Courses last from two to four years. At present, students are awarded federal certificates of aptitude on successful completion of their courses and examinations. About 13% of students drop out during the courses. Of those

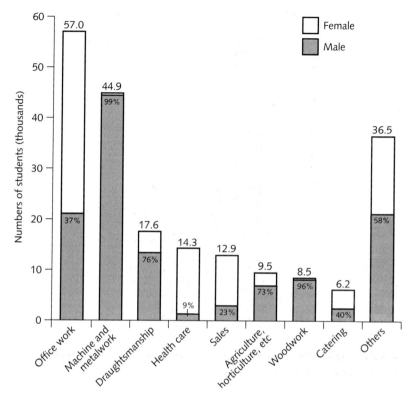

Switzerland figure 2   Numbers of students, and percentage of men, in the main areas of vocational upper secondary education, 1991–2

who take the final examinations 93% pass; of the 7% who fail, most (5%) retake the examinations (1990 figures). There are plans to replace these certificates with a vocational *Baccalauréat*, equivalent in status to the existing academic Baccalauréat, and qualifying for admission to appropriate courses in higher education without taking any entrance examination.

Under the dual system, apprentices attend a vocational school for a day or one-and-a-half days per week. Sixty per cent of this time is spent on theoretical training for their occupation, and the remaining 40% on general culture and sport. For their time with the company, apprentices may find themselves in traditional *craft apprenticeships*, each apprentice working alongside a single 'master craftsman' in the normal course of his work, and gradually acquiring the necessary skills; this is more characteristic of apprenticeships in small firms. In larger firms, *industrial apprenticeships* are more common, with apprentices working part of the time in training workshops with full-time instructors.

The actual provision of vocational schools and supervision of apprenticeships – even for those occupations federally regulated – is by the cantons. There is a larger private sector in vocational education than in other sectors, not just in providing apprenticeships but also in establishing and running vocational schools (with state subsidies) and defining the characteristics and qualifications for various occupations.

There is no attempt by either the federal or the cantonal governments to plan the numbers of trainees in different occupations, or to direct would-be students or apprentices to different courses. This is left to individual decisions and market forces. Vocational schools are, however, required to accept any student who has obtained an apprenticeship contract; thus, employers have a particularly strong influence.

In 1991–2, there were some 207,400 students in vocational schools, about 42% of them female and 17% resident foreigners. About 95% overall were in state-run schools.

About 73% of each age-group complete upper secondary vocational training courses – 78% of males, 67% of females (percentages of 20-year-olds in 1990). Vocational education and particularly the dual system are more popular in German-speaking cantons, where 81% of the age-group participate (68% in the dual system), than in French and Italian-speaking cantons, with 67% participation (50% in the dual system). Four-fifths of those completing upper secondary vocational training go straight into employment; one-fifth proceed to tertiary education.

Maturitätsschulen/Ecoles préparant à la maturité
These schools provide general education to prepare students for the leaving certificate (certificat de maturité). As noted above, the structure of the maturité is in practice defined for the whole of Switzerland by the federal government, and it qualifies students for entry to higher education throughout Switzerland. Five types of maturité are currently recognised, each with 11 subjects: any type qualifies for admission to any university course. There is a core of nine subjects common to them all, with two special subjects for each type. The common subjects are as follows.

- first national language (French, German or Italian)
- second national language (French, German or Italian)
- history
- geography
- mathematics
- physics
- chemistry
- natural sciences
- drawing or music

The special subjects for each type concentrate on classical languages, modern languages, mathematics or economics.

In 1991–2, there were some 56,000 students in schools preparing for the maturité, about 14% of them resident foreigners. About 90% overall were in state-run schools.

About 13% of each age-group are awarded a certificat de maturité – 14% for males, 12% for females (percentages of 20-year-olds in 1990). The percentage is higher in French- and Italian-speaking cantons (19%) than in German-speaking cantons (11%).

Lehrerbildung/Ecole normale
In some cantons, these teacher training schools provide a general education to train teachers for preprimary, primary and lower secondary schools. From 1995, their primary teaching qualifications will be recognised throughout Switzerland, not just in the canton where the qualification was obtained. The *Lehrerbildung/école normale* qualification also gives limited access to higher education.

In 1991–2, there were some 8,800 students in teacher training schools, about 79% of them female and 3% resident foreigners. About 98% overall were in state-run schools.

About 2% of each-age group qualify as teachers in this way – 1% of males, 3% of females (percentages of 20-year-olds in 1990).

Diplommittelschule/Ecole de degré diplôme
These 'diploma schools' provide general education, but as a preparation for vocational training, either at tertiary level or at upper secondary level itself.

In 1991–2, there were some 7,300 students in diploma schools, about 76% of them female and 17% resident foreigners. About 89% overall were in state-run schools.

Special education

At present, children who have difficulty in following the normal school syllabus are taught in specialised classes or schools, to which they are assigned by the local authorities after consultation with a psychologist or doctor, and with their parents' consent. However, there is growing interest in attempting to integrate children with learning difficulties into regular schools and classes – partly because of changes in educational ideas and partly because the numbers of pupils in primary schools are declining.

In 1991–2 there were 38,000 children in special schools – 5.2% of all the children in compulsory education. About 38% of them were female, and 40% resident foreigners.

Tertiary education

In tertiary education there is a clear distinction between institutions with and those without university status: only the former can award degrees. In 1992–3, there were 146,300 students in tertiary education – 62% of them in universities or the equivalent, the rest in various types of tertiary vocational education and training. In the tertiary vocational sector, private institutions are much more important than elsewhere in the Swiss educational systems.

Universities

Switzerland has 12 institutions of university status, with such titles as *université*, *haut école* and *Hochschule*. Ten are run by cantons, and the other two are federal institutes of technology (in Zürich and Lausanne). For admission, students must hold the certificat de maturité, or an equivalent qualification. (In theory, any type of maturité qualifies for admission to any university.) The universities award diplomas, first degrees and postgraduate degrees, including doctorates.

In 1991–2, there were some 89,200 students in the university sector, about 40% of them female. Nineteen per cent are citizens of foreign countries, not all of them normally resident in Switzerland. All institutions in this category are state-run.

Just over 10% of each age-group begin a course of university study, though there are wide variations between cantons, ranging from 6% to 27%. Overall, about 7% eventually obtain a first degree. The average length of a first-degree course is six years, but there are large differences between subjects, and between regions.

Although just under 40% of the students at Swiss universities are women, there are wide variations between regions, between institutions and between subjects. Overall, the percentage of women is higher in French-speaking (43%) than in German-speaking (37%) universities, and much higher in those with a wide range of subjects, including arts subjects, than in those that concentrate on science and engineering or on economics, business and administration. The highest percentage of women is in the University of Geneva, with 53%; it is the only Swiss university in which more than half of the students are women. The lowest percentages are in the two federal institutes of technology, with 16% in Lausanne and 19% in Zürich. (1991–2 figures)

Höhere Fachschule/Ecole professionnelle supérieure

The higher vocational school sector grew out of the traditional Swiss engineering colleges, but other colleges have been modelled on them. Most of them are still in various branches of engineering (with 72% of all students), but there are also higher schools of business and administration (13% of students), social work (12%), industrial design (2%) and home economics (1%). For admission, students must at present hold a federal certificate of aptitude and also sit a competitive examination, though the planned vocational Baccalauréat will qualify holders for direct admission. At present, the higher vocational schools award diplomas, not full degrees, but there are plans to give some of them equivalent status to universities.

In 1991–2, there were some 15,200 students in higher vocational schools, about 15% of them female and 10% resident foreigners. Virtually all (over 99%) attend state-run institutions.

Teknikerschule/Ecole technique

The technical schools train their students for technical and management functions at middle-management level.

In 1991–2, there were some 5,000 students in technical schools, about two-thirds of them studying full-time. Almost all (97%) were male. About 12% were resident foreigners. This is one of the sectors where private institutions are important, with about 21% of students.

Preparatory courses for higher professional examinations

These courses are organised by trade associations, for higher professional examinations regulated by the federal government. (It is not necessary to take any such courses in order to sit the examinations; candidates may prepare instead by correspondence or individual study.) They are intended for holders of upper secondary vocational qualifications with several years' work experience. Two levels of qualification are recognised, professional and higher professional: roughly speaking, the former certifies that the holder can hold a position of responsibility within a business or organisation, the latter that he or she can manage a business or organisation.

In 1991–2, some 16,600 students took these courses, 23% of them women and 12% resident foreigners. Most of them studied part-time. Usually, about 60% of courses are at the lower level, 40% at the higher, and about 70% of students at both levels pass their examinations. This is one of the sectors where private provision is important, with about a quarter of students taking private courses.

Teacher training

Teacher training for lower secondary schools normally takes place at tertiary institutions, sometimes attached to a university, but their certificates do not have equivalent status to university degrees.

Other types of training

In 1991–2, about 17,000 students participated in a wide variety of vocational courses outside the above categories, mainly for occupations that are not regulated by the federal government, including nursing and the creative arts.

Just over half (51%) were women, and 19% were resident foreigners. Overall, some 37% were taking private courses, and about 60% were studying part-time.

Funding

About 5% of Swiss GDP is spent on education each year. Education is the largest item of public expenditure – 18.6% of the total in 1989, compared with 15.6% on welfare, 12.1% on health and 7.5% on defence.

Educational expenditure is divided unequally between the federal government (12% of the total), the cantons (54%) and the communes (34%). Most of the federal government's expenditure is on universities, and most of the communes' on compulsory schooling. The cantons' expenditure is spread more evenly across the entire range of provision, but compulsory schooling is the largest single item. (1989 figures)

Just over half the total expenditure (54%) is on compulsory schooling, with 18% on universities, 15% on vocational training and 13% on academic upper secondary schooling. However, the expenditure per student in universities is more than three times that per pupil in compulsory schooling or vocational training, and almost twice that per student in academic upper secondary school. (1988 figures)

Teaching profession

The teaching profession comes under the jurisdiction of the cantons, not the federal government, and there is considerable variation among them in training and qualifications, as well as in status, salaries and conditions of work. However, some generalisations about training can be made. Training for primary school teachers normally takes place at upper secondary level (in the Lehrerbildung or école normale) and for secondary teachers at tertiary level. Lower secondary teachers are usually trained at a teacher training college or a university department of education.

For admission, they need a certificat de maturité (or a primary teaching qualification), and their courses typically last three years. Teachers in upper secondary schools preparing students for the maturité (professeurs de gymnase) must be university graduates in their teaching subjects, and take an additional course of teacher training lasting one or two years, depending on the canton. The training of teachers for upper secondary vocational schools is much more varied, differing among subjects as well as among cantons; courses can be full- or part-time, and have different balances of theoretical study and practical experience.

Swiss teachers have relatively little opportunity for promotion, compared with many other European countries, as few schools have a hierarchy of senior posts apart from the head teacher and deputy head teacher. However, the salaries and the prestige of 'ordinary' members of the teaching profession in Switzerland are relatively high.

The younger the age-group taught, the higher is the proportion of female teachers. In Switzerland as a whole, there are about 27,000 teachers in primary schools (59% women, 41% men), and 19,000 in lower secondary schools (32% female, 68% male). (1987–8 figures) At the extremes, virtually all (99%) preprimary teachers are women, but only 3% of university professors. (1989–90 figures)

Parent/school relationships

In most cantons, parents play no direct part in the running of schools. However, many decisions at cantonal or communal level about education (or anything else) are made or are subject to approval by referendum. In some communes, this extends to the appointment of teachers by plebiscite.

ACKNOWLEDGEMENT

We are grateful to the Federal Statistical Office, Bern, for supplying us with extensive information about education in Switzerland.

REFERENCES

Archer, E. G. and Peck, B. T. (no date) The Teaching Profession in Europe, Glasgow: Jordanhill College of Education.

Egger, E. (1984) Education in Switzerland, Bern: Swiss Conference of Cantonal Directors of Education.

Kummerley & Frey Geographical Publishers (1993) Switzerland: people, state, economy, culture, Bern: Kummerley & Frey.

Costa, C. et al. (1991) The Swiss Educational Mosaic: a study in diversity, Bern: Federal Statistical Office.

Federal Statistical Office (1993) Statistisches Jahrbuch der Schweiz 1993/Annuaire statistique de la Suisse 1993, Bern: Federal Statistical Office.

Hunter, B. (ed.) (1995) The Statesman's Year Book, 1995–1996, London: Macmillan.

Meier, H. (1990) Switzerland, twelfth edition, Bern: Co-ordinating Commission for the Presence of Switzerland Abroad.

OECD (1995) OECD Economic Surveys: Switzerland 1994–1995, Paris: Organisation for Economic Co-operation and Development.

SECTION 2

WESTERN EUROPE:
CROSS-NATIONAL COMPARISONS

This section presents various educational and background comparisons between all or some of the major countries of Western Europe. Comparing educational systems and processes across countries is not straightforward, partly because different countries often do things differently, and partly because some of the most basic categories are defined differently from country to country. To take just a few examples, education may be *public* or *private*; *preprimary, primary, secondary, further* or *higher; academic, technical* or *vocational*; and *full-time* or *part-time* – but these terms are often understood in different ways, and the boundaries between them drawn in different places from one country to another. The need to find equivalent words in different languages adds to the complications.

The comparisons below need to be treated with caution, therefore, and the notes to the individual tables read carefully. The tables may be useful for showing how much variation can be found in educational systems and processes across Western Europe. They are sometimes less suitable for making precise numerical comparisons between one country and another.

BACKGROUND

POPULATION

The 16 major Western European countries (those covered in Section One plus the UK) have a population of 382 million in total, less than a tenth of the population of the world. In the European Union (EU), a little less than a third of the population is under 25 years old – 117 million in all. The proportion of young people in the population is falling, especially rapidly in countries where it has been high.

The populations of the major Western European countries are shown in Figure 1.

About a fifth of the population of the EU are pupils or students in educational institutions – about 72 million in all, of whom 45 million are in compulsory education and 10 million in higher education. (European Commission, 1996)

ECONOMY

A measure of how rich or poor the different countries are is their *Gross Domestic Product (GDP) per head of population* (Figure 2). And an indication of their relative economic development of the countries is given by the percentages of their employees who work in the *agricultural sector* (Figure 3) – the lower the percentage in agriculture, the more advanced its economic

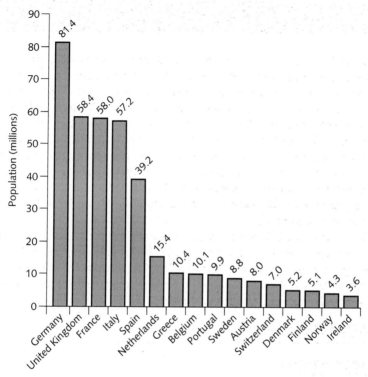

Europe figure 1   Populations of the major countries, 1994 (OECD)

development is generally taken to be. In all the countries of Western Europe, the majority of employed people now work in the service sector, and the percentage of the workforce employed in agriculture is falling from year to year.

In almost every country of the EU, the higher people's educational qualifications are, the lower is their level of *unemployment*. Exceptions are Italy, where unemployment is lower for those with upper secondary qualifications than for those with tertiary qualifications; and Greece, where unemployment is lower for those with only lower secondary education than for those with upper secondary or tertiary education. (European Commission, 1996, pp. 7 and A8)

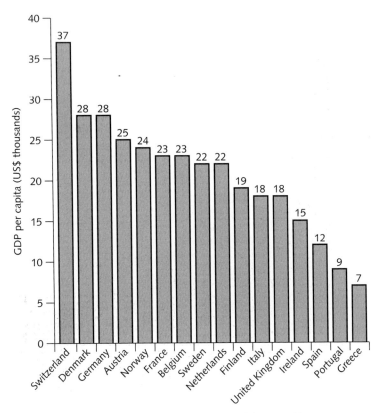

Europe figure 2   GDP per capita (in US$ thousands) of the major European countries, 1994 (OECD)
Note: The Greece and Norway figures are for 1993

EDUCATION

There have been extensive changes in recent years to the structure and operation of the education systems of many Western European countries. Though there are important differences from country to country, there are also trends common to several countries. (See European Commission, 1995, p. 5) These include:

- the expansion of preprimary provision;
- the extension of the period of compulsory schooling, both by lowering the starting-age and by raising the leaving-age;
- the introduction or extension of common/comprehensive education, especially during the years of compulsory schooling;
- the development of vocational education, especially at secondary level, with

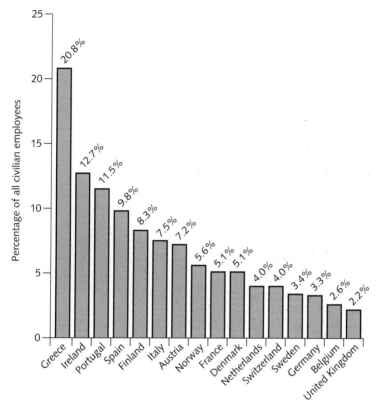

Europe figure 3   Percentage of all civilian employees working in agriculture, 1993–4 (OECD)
Note: The Belgium figures are for 1992

attempts to enhance its status compared with academic education and to increase opportunities of combining vocational and academic studies;
- the dramatic expansion of tertiary education;
- the devolution of administrative and financial responsibilities from national or local government to individual establishments.

Every country in the EU except Scotland now has a statutory curriculum, and most though not all countries have detailed statutory allocations of time to the different subjects. The exceptions are (at primary level) France, the Netherlands, Portugal and the UK, and (at secondary level) Finland, Ireland and the UK again, which allow more flexibility to schools and teachers.

No major Western European country now allows corporal punishment in schools, with the exception of the UK, where it is still permitted in private schools (though it has been prohibited in state schools since 1987).

ATTITUDES TO EDUCATION

Across Western Europe, according to the European Attitudes Survey, just over 60% of people express confidence in education; the only national or international institution in which more people have confidence is the police. But confidence in education varies from country to country, as is illustrated in Figure 4.

STATE AND PRIVATE EDUCATION

All the major countries of Western Europe have private schools as well as state schools, though the size of the private sector varies widely, as Figure 5 illustrates. Comparisons between countries are not straightforward, however, as some private schools in some countries receive state funding, and definitions vary from country to country. (For example, Church schools receiving state funding are defined as state schools in the UK, but as private schools in the Netherlands.)

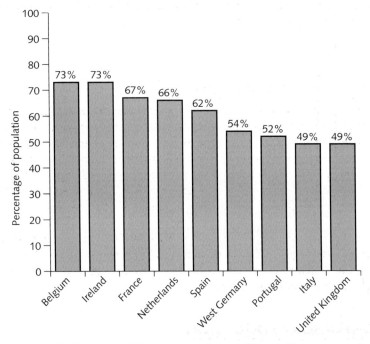

Europe figure 4 Percentage of the population of various Western European countries expressing 'a great deal' or 'quite a lot' of confidence in education, 1990 (Adapted from Ashford and Timms, 1992)

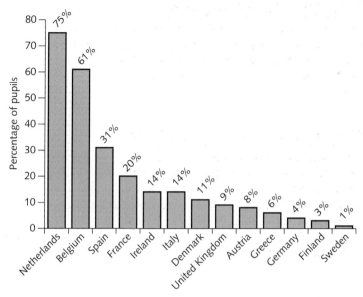

*Europe figure 5   Percentage of primary and secondary pupils in private schools, 1992–3
(European Commission, 1996, B2)*

PREPRIMARY EDUCATION

The percentage of children in preprimary education varies dramatically across Western Europe, as is illustrated in Figure 6. At the extremes, almost all three-year-olds in France and almost none in Ireland are in preprimary education. (Three-year-olds have been used in this table as their education is 'preprimary' everywhere in Europe. For four-, five- and even six-year-old children, there is considerable variation from country to country in the proportions of the population in preprimary and primary – sometimes compulsory primary – education.)

There is also variation from country to country in the percentages of mothers of three-year-old children who are in employment; this is illustrated in Figure 7. (Figures for fathers of three-year-old children who are in employment are not readily available.)

COMPULSORY EDUCATION

The years of compulsory education differ from country to country, as Figure 8 shows. In many countries, the compulsory period has been increased in recent years, by both the lowering of the starting-age and the raising of the leaving-

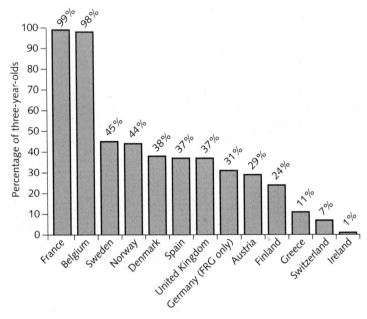

Europe figure 6   Percentage of three-year-olds in preprimary education (public or private, full- or part-time), 1992 (Adapted from CERI, 1995, P02 [A1])

age. In many countries too, large numbers of children start their schooling before and continue it after the compulsory years (as is illustrated in Figure 6 above and Figure 14 below).

PRIMARY EDUCATION

Primary education is now universal throughout Western Europe, but there are significant variations between countries in the amount of time children spend in school: these are illustrated in Figure 9.

Most primary schools in Western European countries have 'mixed-ability' classes, but children are sometimes grouped by ability within these classes. This is illustrated in Figure 10.

In most EU countries with a nationally prescribed timetable, primary pupils devote more time to their mother tongue and to mathematics than to any other subject. The study of a foreign language is compulsory in primary schools in Austria, Belgium (Brussels region only), Denmark, Finland, Greece, Italy, the Netherlands, Norway, Spain and Sweden. For 90% of children the language studied is English, and for most of the remaining 10%, French.

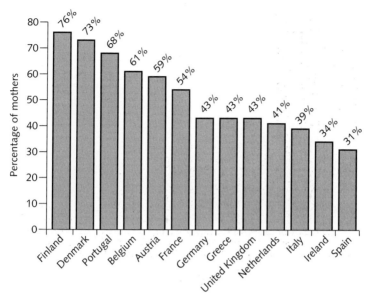

*Europe figure 7   Percentage of mothers of three-year-olds who are in employment,
1992–3 (European Commission, 1996, C5)*
Note: The figures for Sweden and the non-EU countries are not available

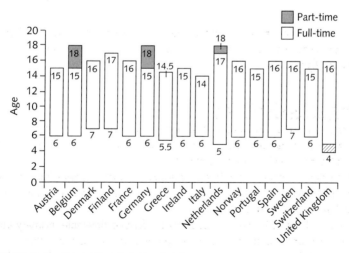

Europe figure 8   Years of compulsory education
Notes: (i) The ages shown are approximate, as different countries set different points
within the year in which children reach these ages as the starting- and leaving-dates; (ii) in
Northern Ireland, the starting-age is four; in the rest of the UK, it is five

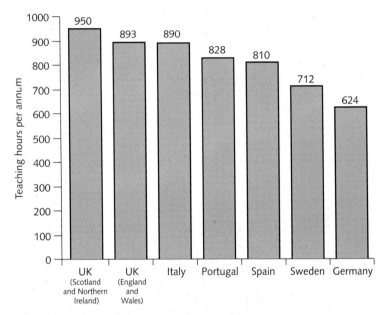

Europe figure 9   Minimum number of teaching hours per annum at age nine, 1994 (European Commission, 1996, D2)

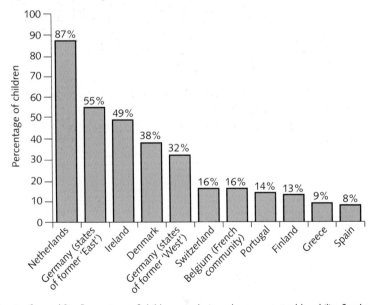

Europe figure 10   Percentage of children aged nine who are grouped by ability for the teaching of reading, 1990–1 (CERI, 1995, P21)

The pupil/teacher ratio in primary schools has fallen in recent years in almost every country, but it still varies widely across Europe, as Figure 11 illustrates.

Teachers in primary education are predominantly female everywhere (see Figure 12 overleaf), but this predominance is not reflected in headships of schools anywhere (see Figure 13 overleaf).

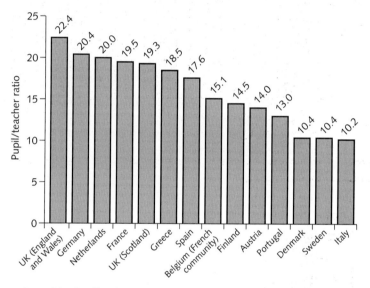

Europe figure 11   Pupil/teacher ratios in primary schools in the state sector, 1993 (European Commission, 1996, 12)
Notes: (i) The Portugal figure is for 1990; (ii) the Belgium figure is for preprimary and primary education combined

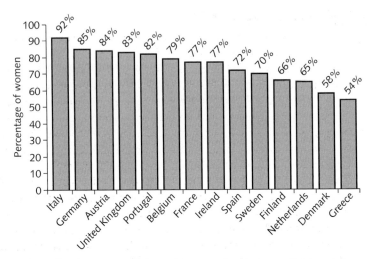

Europe figure 12   Percentage of women among teachers in state and private primary schools, 1993 (European Commission, 1996, 13/14)
Notes: (i) The Belgium and UK figures include preprimary teachers; (ii) the Portugal figures are for 1990; (iii) the Finland figures are for 1992

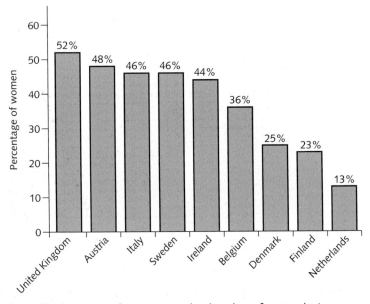

Europe figure 13   Percentage of women among head teachers of state and private primary schools, 1993 (European Commission, 1996, 15/16)

SECONDARY EDUCATION

The percentage of 16–18-year-olds in education and training varies from country to country, as is illustrated in Figure 14. As Figure 8 shows, education is compulsory during different portions of this age-range in different countries. (Some of the older students in Figure 14 are in tertiary rather than secondary education.)

Secondary education – especially upper secondary education – in many countries is formally divided between general education and vocational education, and even where it is not, a distinction can often be made between students following predominantly general and predominantly vocational educational courses. The division is illustrated in Figure 15 overleaf.

In most countries, there are more female than male upper secondary students in general education, and more male than female students in vocational education. The exceptions are Austria and the UK, which have marginally more males than females in general education; and Spain, Finland and the UK again, which have more females than males in vocational education. (1992–3 figures, European Commission, 1996, E7/8)

The pupil/teacher ratio in secondary schools has fallen in recent years in almost every country, but it still varies widely across Europe, as Figure 16 illustrates. Teachers in secondary education are predominantly female in most countries, as Figure 17 shows (though teachers in *vocational* secondary education are predominantly male). In all countries, however, secondary head teachers are predominantly male; this is illustrated in Figure 18.

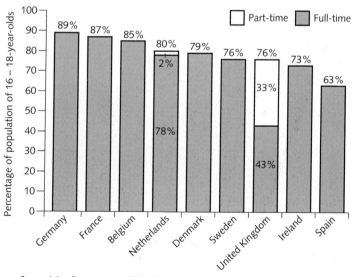

Europe figure 14   Percentage of 16–18-year-olds in education or training, around 1991
(Adapted from OECD, 1995, Table 14)

Note: The definitions of 'full-time' and 'part-time' vary from country to country

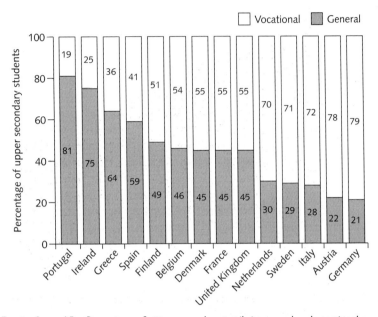

Europe figure 15   Percentage of upper secondary pupils in general and vocational education, 1992–3 (European Commission, 1996, E3)

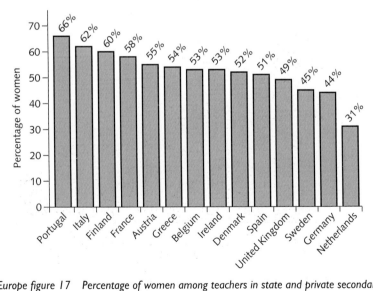

Europe figure 17   Percentage of women among teachers in state and private secondary schools, 1993 (European Commission, 1996, 13/14)
Notes: (i) The Portugal figures are for 1990; (ii) the Finland figures are for 1992

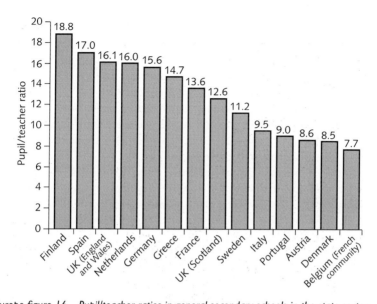

Europe figure 16   Pupil/teacher ratios in general secondary schools in the state sector, 1993 (European Commission, 1996, 12)
Notes: (i) The Portugal and Spain figures are for 1990; (ii) the Belgium figure includes technical and vocational education; (iii) the Germany figure is for lower secondary education only (the pupil/teacher ratio in upper secondary education in Germany is 11)

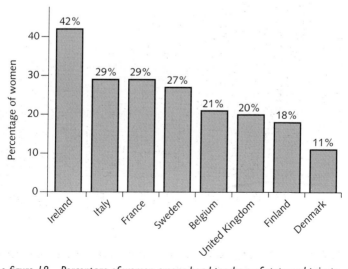

Europe figure 18   Percentage of women among head teachers of state and private secondary schools, 1993 (European Commission, 1996, 15/16)

TERTIARY EDUCATION

There are over 10 million students in higher education (i.e. first-degree and postgraduate level tertiary education) in the EU now, about twice as many as in 1975. The percentages of students in the main subject areas of higher education in the EU as a whole are shown in Figure 19.

The percentage of the population in university varies from country to country, as Figure 20 illustrates. (In most countries, there is also a non-university higher education sector, but this is in all cases smaller than the university sector, and often much smaller.)

Historically, more men than women have completed university education in every European country. Now, however, the total number of women in higher education in the EU as a whole is almost exactly equal to that of men, though there are variations from country to country (Figure 21) and from subject to subject (Figure 22).

Teachers in higher education are predominantly male in every country, but precise comparisons between the countries cannot be made because of differences in the kinds of data available.

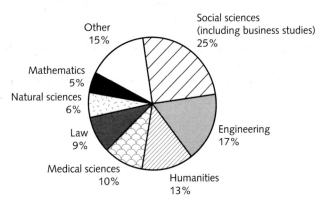

Europe figure 19   Percentage of higher education students in different fields of study, EU, 1992–3 (European Commission, 1996, F6)

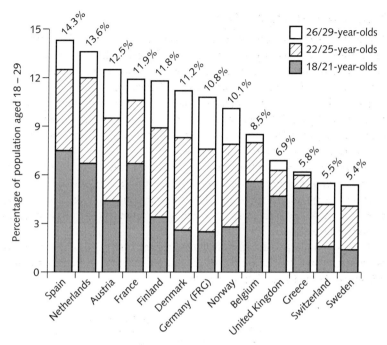

*Europe figure 20 Percentage of the population aged 18–29 in university, 1992
(Adapted from CERI, 1995, P06)*
Note: *The percentages have been calculated on the assumption (only approximately correct) that within each country the populations aged 18–21, 22–25 and 26–29 are equal*

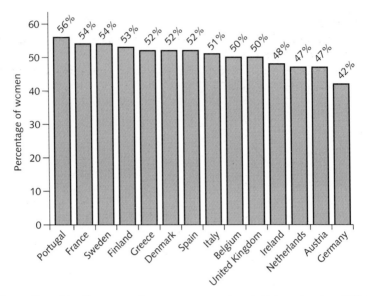

*Europe figure 21   Percentage of women among students in higher education, 1992–3
(European Commission, 1996, F4)*

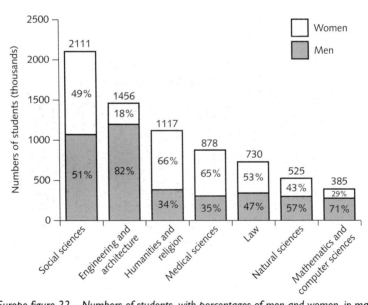

*Europe figure 22   Numbers of students, with percentages of men and women, in major
subject areas of higher education in the EU, 1992–3 (European Commission, 1996, F8)
Notes: (i) Comparable data on France, Belgium and Luxembourg are not available;
(ii) data on law for the UK are not available*

FUNDING

The percentage of GDP spent on education varies from country to country. This is illustrated in Figure 23.

Annual expenditure per pupil or student at each of the major stages of education is illustrated in Figure 24.

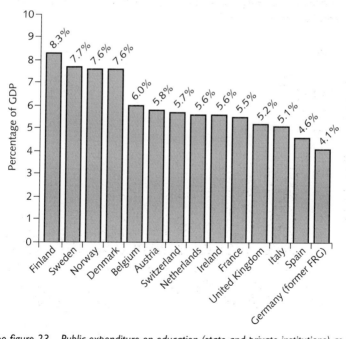

Europe figure 23   Public expenditure on education (state and private institutions) as a percentage of GDP, 1992 (CERI, 1995)
Notes: (i) The Germany figure is for the territory of the former Federal Republic (West Germany) only; (ii) the Norway figure includes expenditure on state institutions only

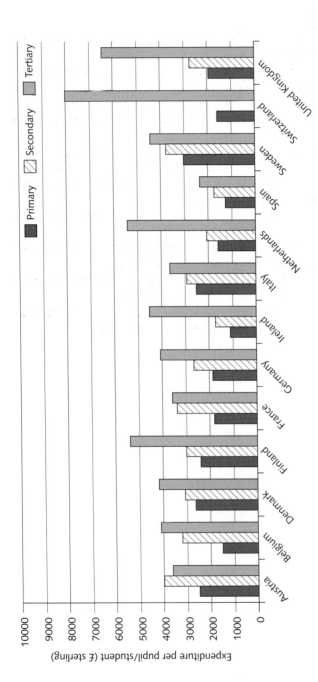

Europe figure 24   Expenditure per pupil/student (full-time equivalent) in publicly financed establishments, 1992 (UK Government Statistical Service, 1996, Table DD)

Notes: (i) Expenditure figures are in £ sterling calculated at equivalent purchasing power for 1992; (ii) the category 'secondary' includes 'further' education; (iii) the figures for Germany apply to the states of the former Federal Republic (West Germany) only; (iv) comparable figures for secondary education in Switzerland are not available

REFERENCES

Ashford, S. and Timms, N. (1992) *What Europe Thinks: a study of Western European values*, Aldershot: Dartmouth Publishing Company Ltd.

CERI (1995) *Education at a Glance: OECD indicators*, Paris: Organisation for Economic Co-operation and Development.

European Commission (1995) *Structures of the Education and Initial Training Systems in the European Union*, Luxembourg: Office for Official Publications of the European Commission.

European Commission (1996) *Key Data on Education in the European Union*, Luxembourg: Office for Official Publications of the European Commission.

Mackinnon, D. and Statham, J. with Hales, M. (1996) *Education in the UK: facts and figures*, revised edition, London: Hodder & Stoughton.

OECD (1995) *OECD Economic Surveys: Austria: 1994–1995*, Paris: Organisation for Economic Co-operation and Development.

OECD (1995) *OECD Economic Surveys: United Kingdom: 1994–1995*, Paris: Organisation for Economic Co-operation and Development.

OECD (1995–6) *OECD Economic Surveys* – country by country, all: Paris: Organisation for Economic Co-operation and Development.

(UK) Government Statistical Service (1996) *Education Statistics for the United Kingdom, 1995 Edition*, London: Her Majesty's Stationery Office.

INDEX